Shakespeare and Audience in Prac

Shakespeare in Practice

Series Editors:

Stuart Hampton-Reeves, Professor of Research-informed Teaching, University of Central Lancashire, UK, and Head of the British Shakespeare Association

Bridget Escolme, Reader in Drama, Queen Mary, University of London, UK

Published:

Stephen Purcell
SHAKESPEARE AND AUDIENCE IN PRACTICE

Andrew Hartley
SHAKESPEARE AND POLITICAL THEATRE IN PRACTICE

Forthcoming:

Don Weingust
SHAKESPEARE AND ORIGINAL PRACTICES

Darren Tunstall
SHAKESPEARE AND GESTURE IN PRACTICE

Bridget Escolme
SHAKESPEARE AND SITE-SPECIFIC PERFORMANCE IN PRACTICE

Kathryn Prince
SHAKESPEARE AND SPACE IN PRACTICE

Paul Prescott
SHAKESPEARE AND REVIEWING PERFORMANCE IN PRACTICE

Alexander Huang
SHAKESPEARE AND DIASPORA IN PRACTICE

Kevin Ewert
SHAKESPEARE AND DIRECTING IN PRACTICE

Shakespeare in Practice
Series standing order
ISBN 978–0–230–27637–6 hard cover
ISBN 978–0–230–27638–3 paperback
(*outside North America only*)

You can receive future titles in this series as they are published by placing a standing order. Please contact your bookseller or, in case of difficulty, write to us at the address below with your name and address, the title of the series and the ISBN quoted above.

Customer Services Department, Macmillan Distribution Ltd, Houndmills, Basingstoke, Hampshire RG21 6XS, England

Shakespeare and Audience in Practice

Stephen Purcell
University of Warwick, UK

First published 2013 by
PALGRAVE MACMILLAN

Palgrave Macmillan in the UK is an imprint of Macmillan Publishers Limited, registered in England, company number 785998, of Houndmills, Basingstoke, Hampshire RG21 6XS.

Palgrave Macmillan in the US is a division of St Martin's Press LLC, 175 Fifth Avenue, New York, NY 10010.

Palgrave Macmillan is the global academic imprint of the above companies and has companies and representatives throughout the world.

Palgrave® and Macmillan® are registered trademarks in the United States, the United Kingdom, Europe and other countries.

ISBN 978–0–230–36403–5 hardback
ISBN 978–0–230–36404–2 paperback

This book is printed on paper suitable for recycling and made from fully managed and sustained forest sources. Logging, pulping and manufacturing processes are expected to conform to the environmental regulations of the country of origin.

A catalogue record for this book is available from the British Library.

A catalog record for this book is available from the Library of Congress.

Printed in China

For Zoë

Contents

List of Illustrations   viii

Acknowledgements   ix

Series Editors' Preface   xi

Prologue   xiii

Part I Introduction

1 *I, Malvolio* and Its Audiences: A Case Study   3

Part II In Theory

2 Making Sense of the Stage   27

3 Agency, Community, and Modern Theatre Practice   43

Part III In Practice

4 Controlling the Audience?   65

5 Framing the Stage   74

6 Playing with the Audience   94

7 Immersion and Embodiment   128

8 Constructing the Audience   147

Part IV Debate and Provocation

9 *Pocket Henry V*: A Collaborative Debate   157

Notes   173

Reading List   177

Index   189

Illustrations

Figures

1.1 Malvolio (Tim Crouch) prepares to hang himself, with
the help of an audience member. Image from Latitude
Festival, 2011, copyright Bruce Atherton and Jana
Chiellino   8

5.1 Gower (Rawiri Paratene) speaks to the audience during
The Children of the Sea, 2005. Image courtesy of Royal
Botanic Garden Edinburgh   80

5.2 Kate (Simon Scardifield) and Petruccio (Dugald
Bruce-Lockhart) in Propeller's *The Taming of the Shrew*,
2006, copyright Philip Tull   86

6.1 Oliver Dimsdale (Sir Toby Belch) and Nicolas Tennant (Sir
Andrew Aguecheek) in Filter's *Twelfth Night*. Still: Ellie
Newbury, from *Twelfth Night*, a Filter Theatre production
in association with the Royal Shakespeare Company, as
featured in *What You Will*, a film by Filter/Guy de
Beaujeu/Simon Reade, 2012   122

7.1 Ophelia (Bethan Cullinane), Polonius (Richard Clews),
and Laertes (Ben Ingles) in dreamthinkspeak's *The Rest is
Silence*, 2012. Photograph by Jim Stephenson   131

7.2 Coriolanus (Richard Lynch), First Citizen (John Rowley),
and Second Citizen (Gerald Tyler) in *Coriolan/us*, 2012.
Mark Douet/National Theatre Wales   136

7.3 Mark Antony (Hans Kesting) speaks directly to the camera
during his funeral oration in *Roman Tragedies*, 2010.
Toneelgroep Amsterdam, copyright Jan Versweyveld   137

7.4 Audience members onstage during Ivo van Hove's *Roman
Tragedies*, 2010. Toneelgroep Amsterdam, copyright Jan
Versweyveld   138

Acknowledgements

The author and publisher wish to thank the following for permission to reproduce copyright material:

- Tim Crouch for the image from *I, Malvolio* (2011);
- Alan P. Bennell and the Royal Botanic Garden Edinburgh for the image from *The Children of the Sea* (2005);
- Caro MacKay and Propeller for the image from *The Taming of the Shrew* (2006);
- Simon Reade and Filter for the image from *Twelfth Night/What You Will* (2012);
- Lucy Godfrey and dreamthinkspeak for the image from *The Rest Is Silence* (2012);
- Julia Coles and National Theatre Wales for the image from *Coriolan/us* (2012);
- Marlene Kenens and Toneelgroep Amsterdam for the images from *Roman Tragedies* (2010).

Every effort has been made to trace rights holders, but if any have been inadvertently overlooked, the publishers would be pleased to make the necessary arrangements at the first opportunity.

I am particularly grateful to Tim Crouch, for his generosity in allowing me access to his production of *I, Malvolio* and its audiences, and to Propeller, for letting me case study their *Pocket Henry V*. Thanks are due also to the staff of The Egg and The Traverse theatres for accommodating this research and, of course, to the audiences themselves – especially the staff and students of The Ravensbourne School and Cowbridge Comprehensive School. I am, of course, immensely grateful to Penelope Woods for her co-authorship of Chapter 9, and her open-minded and invigorating approach to audience research.

I thank my colleagues and students, past and present, at both Southampton Solent University and the University of Warwick, many of whom have read or heard early drafts, or participated in practical workshops, and whose ideas have contributed to the book's development in numerous ways. I am very grateful to the series editors, Stuart Hampton-Reeves and Bridget Escolme, for their helpful and encouraging comments and criticisms. I am, as always, especially grateful to the producers and actors of The Pantaloons theatre company; our work together over the years has had a profound effect on my thinking about the role of the audience in modern Shakespearean performance. Finally, I'd like to thank Zoë and my family, without whose support this book would never have been completed.

Series Editors' Preface

The books in the *Shakespeare in Practice* series chart new directions for a performance approach to Shakespeare. They represent the diverse and exciting work being undertaken by a new generation of Shakespeareans who have either come to the field from practice or have developed a career that combines academic work with theatrical practice. Many of these authors are based in Drama departments and use practical workshops for both teaching and research. They are conversant with the fields of English Literature and Performance Studies, and they move freely between them. This series gives them an opportunity to explore the hinterland between both and to give a greater prominence to some of the key questions that occupy performance studies in the study of Shakespeare.

We intend this series to shape the way in which Shakespeare in performance is taught and researched. Our authors approach performance as a creative practice, which can be treated as a work of art in its own right. We want to create a new curriculum for Shakespeare in performance, which embraces the full complexity of the art of theatre and is underpinned by performance theory.

The first part of each book explores the theoretical issues at stake, often drawing on key works in performance studies as well as seminal writings by theatre practitioners. The second part of the book consists of a series of critical studies of performance in practice, drawing on theatre history but chiefly focusing on contemporary productions and practitioners. Finally, we have asked all of our authors to engage in a debate with another scholar or practitioner so that each book ends on a note of provisionality and unresolved debate.

All of our books draw on a wide range of plays so that teachers can choose which plays they want to focus on. There will be no volume on *Hamlet*, *A Midsummer Night's Dream* or *Romeo and Juliet* – every volume can be used as a model for every play in the canon. Similarly, none of the books exhaust the research possibilities that they open: there is more, much more, work to be done on every topic in this series.

Studies of Shakespeare in performance often leave aside the audience. Either the critic's own response is used to voice the audience, or the audience is effaced altogether. Questions about the role of the audience in constructing the theatrical event are often posed, but rarely answered, at conferences and seminars. Leaving the audience out of theatrical analysis is problematic, but including them is, if anything, even more problematic. How does one give voice to an audience? Is an audience exterior to the performance, or is it part of it – in which case, it is possible to 'read' the audience in a critical way? What research tools do we need to conduct such work? Or is the audience an illusion? Stephen Purcell's addresses how notions of audience, audience configuration, audience expectation and audiences as they figure in play texts all produce meaning in the theatre. His work is the ideal book with which to begin this series.

Stuart Hampton-Reeves
Bridget Escolme

Prologue

If this book were a dramatic performance, it might start with a prologue. An actor might step forward and address this introduction to you directly, looking you in the eye, smiling to welcome you. I, on the other hand, do not know who 'you' are. You may be browsing in a bookshop, reading in a library, scrolling down an e-book. You might have skipped forward and read other parts of the book already; you might have started here in order to make a judgement as to whether or not you wish to continue reading. You are a different kind of audience from the audiences considered in this book.

If this introduction were a dramatic prologue, it might ask you for 'audience'. In the earliest examples of the word recorded in the *Oxford English Dictionary*, 'audience' means simply 'the action of hearing' or 'attention to what is spoken'; slightly later, the word also signified a formal hearing or interview. Shakespeare uses the word 31 times in his dramatic works, and in most instances, it is employed in the sense of something that can be granted: in ten cases, it is used in conjunction with the verb *to give*, and in four, with *to have*; 'audience' is also something that can be 'craved', 'vouchsafed', and 'gained' in Shakespeare. For Shakespeare, then, 'audience' is something that one can give and receive, promise or withhold. It is active. It is processual. It is an item of exchange and part of a transaction. 'Give me audience, friends' (3.2.2), pleads Brutus to the plebeians in *Julius Caesar*; later in the same scene, Antony's famous line 'Friends, Romans, countrymen, lend me your ears' (3.2.74) is a similar request for audience, though it does not use the word itself. For Antony and the citizens of Rome, audience is the first act in a pact of complicity which, as the play goes on to show, will have far-reaching consequences.

Only twice in Shakespeare – in *Love's Labour's Lost* (5.1.131) and *A Midsummer Night's Dream* (1.2.22) – is the word used to signify a group of playgoers.[1] Even in the latter, though, it seems to be a comic misuse of the word: when Bottom suggests that 'the audience look to their eyes', it is a mistake of the kind that he makes again towards the end of the play, when he claims that 'The eye of man hath not heard, the ear of man hath not seen ... what my dream was' (4.1.208–11). Derived from the Latin *audire* (to hear), to give 'audience', or to *be* an 'audience', is to *listen*. As Andrew Gurr points out, though, from 1600 onwards, Shakespeare's preferred term for his customers changes (2004: 111). In *Hamlet* (3.2.41) and *The Winter's Tale* (4.1.20), we find theatregoers referred to as 'spectators'.

This problem of terminology indicates one of the key concerns of this book. How best to describe the group of people who gather to watch a play? Audience or spectators? Hearers or seers? A unified group or separate individuals? Implicated parties or detached observers? Where I have attempted to account for my own theatregoing experiences, the problem is compounded: do I describe an audience of which I was a member as 'us', or should I be wary of attempting to speak for my fellow playgoers? Should I describe that group as 'them', or does that disclaim my own implication in the formation of that group? What about 'me'? 'Her'? 'Him'? An audience is generally all of these things at once.

This book will move between a variety of perspectives in order to explore these questions. Part I, 'Introduction' pays close attention to a single Shakespearean production (Tim Crouch's *I, Malvolio*) as it was performed in four different contexts: it considers the roles played by the text, its performance, and its context in the formation of audience response, before attempting to document that response with reference to my own impressions, audience feedback, and other written accounts. Part II of the book, 'In Theory', surveys some of the most influential conceptualisations of the audience in performance studies: Chapter 2 explores what it is that we do when we make sense of the stage, while Chapter 3 considers the interventions of modern theatre practitioners who have challenged the role of the audience and concludes with an outline of some of the practical research currently being undertaken by scholars of theatrical reception.

Part III, 'In Practice', is by far the longest section of the book and is, in many ways, its main focus. Over five chapters, it applies many of the ideas explored in Part II to the analysis of modern Shakespearean performance practice. As John Russell Brown argues, the job of the Shakespearean critic ought to be to 'explore the dynamic relationship between actors and audience as the plays come to life between them both' (1999: 42). Part III is an attempt to do just that, examining both the Shakespearean text and numerous examples of the plays in performance to consider the various practices of modern Shakespearean spectatorship. Shakespeare does, of course, have a huge modern audience via the mass media, but that diffuse audience is a very different phenomenon from the group that gathers in time and space to experience something together. The focus of this part is therefore on live performance, and though I have attempted to draw from as wide a range of theatre practices as possible, the productions considered inevitably reflect my own theatregoing experience. Numerous examples are drawn from the reconstructed Shakespeare's Globe – not because practice there is necessarily more authentically Shakespearean, but because its shared light and standing playgoers frequently serve to foreground its audiences' reactions, and because those responses have been unusually well documented.

It seems fitting that a book that takes as its theme the two-way interaction between stage and audience should attempt some sort of dialogue with its readers. This is, of course, fairly difficult to put into practice, since books are by their nature fixed products, monologues rather than dialogues. I have attempted to counteract this by interspersing a series of suggestions for exploratory workshops throughout Part III: these are invitations for you to test the book's ideas, to use them as a springboard for your own thinking and theatre practice, and to answer some of the questions which this text leaves hanging. Part IV, meanwhile, is titled 'Debate and Provocation', and like Part I, it is a case study of the audience response to a modern Shakespearean production (in this case, Propeller's *Pocket Henry V*). It takes the form of a conversation between me and another academic, and though its title implies a formal argument, our dialogue turned out, in fact, to be an open-ended discussion in which both of us were led to renegotiate our initial impressions. It is hoped that you – whoever you are – will take this as a cue to debate some of the book's ideas yourself.

Part I
Introduction

1
I, Malvolio and Its Audiences: A Case Study

There is a potentially bewildering multiplicity of angles from which one can approach the subject of theatre audiences. Some studies focus on the cues for audience response in the dramatic text; some on the ways in which theatre practice itself might shape spectators' reactions. Others will record the impact of different audience responses upon the ways in which a production makes meaning. Those who are more interested in particular audiences might focus on the ways in which a sense of audience identity is formed, considering the social context of the event at which a given group of spectators has amassed. Some will analyse this group in depth, documenting their reactions, identifying discernible sub-groups, or tracing patterns of response. Others will direct their attention towards the ways in which such audiences are constructed in reviews or other retrospective characterisations. In the discussion of any given production, then, the word 'audience' might refer to a number of different identities.

This chapter will attempt to illustrate this phenomenon by making a detailed case study of one particular Shakespearean production and its audiences. *I, Malvolio* is a one-man play which has been touring both in the UK and internationally, on and off, since 2010. Written and performed by Tim Crouch, it retells *Twelfth Night* from the perspective of Shakespeare's puritanical steward. Over the course of it, Malvolio turns on the audience and charges them with complicity in his unhappy fate, before getting his long-promised revenge.

Crouch's play is highly alert to the role of its audiences in the production of its meaning. At its climax, Malvolio prepares to hang himself, and then decides against it. He stands onstage in stained long johns, washes the dirt from his face, and speaks directly to the audience:

> And while I sit in hideous darkness I start to think. I think about this. All this. I think about you. All of you. With your dead eyes and your slack jaws.
>
> (2011a: 28)

I, Malvolio is intensely preoccupied with the nature of its own audience, and its protagonist hectors his audience for their imagined attitudes throughout. But the dead-eyed and slack-jawed audience projected by Malvolio is presumably not the engaged and self-aware audience anticipated by Crouch's script; after all, the play seems to demand an audience who are willing to question the ethics of their own role in the theatrical exchange. Moreover, both of these imagined audiences are textual constructions – neither necessarily bears any resemblance to the actual audiences who attended the play over its substantial tour. I saw the production four times in four radically different contexts, and indeed, the various audiences of which I was part were remarkably different from one another, in some instances responding in ways that seemed to directly contradict the identities asked of them by the text. Upon closer analysis, it became clear that even within a single audience, multiple identities were being negotiated.

Crouch is very clear about his intended audience. Both the published script and much of the production's publicity material describe *I, Malvolio* as a play 'for young audiences', and it is the fourth in a series of five Shakespearean retellings aimed at upper-primary and lower-secondary schoolchildren; the series also includes *I, Caliban* (2003), *I, Peaseblossom* (2004), *I, Banquo* (2005), and *I, Cinna (The Poet)* (2012). In one of two interviews with me, Crouch described the piece as having been conceived especially for audiences of secondary-school age, 'because it seems to connect with those transitions around discipline and structure . . . a very potent area at the ages of 11 to 15'. He repeatedly portrayed the production as a 'young person's version' of his controversial play *The Author*, in that it was about 'the lengths an audience is prepared to go to to get its kicks' (interview).

Crouch's desire to ask the audience to turn their attention onto themselves is a key characteristic of his work for both adults and children. Most of his pieces begin with some kind of acknowledgement of the audience as a group, and are structured in such a way that he can be responsive to their input. In *My Arm*, for example, he collects objects from the audience for use as props in the play; *I, Banquo* starts with a request from its protagonist for the audience to 'just imagine' that they are friends; the character who begins *The Author* asks members of the audience what their names are, and whether they are 'all right'. Questions like 'How are you feeling?', 'Can you see all right?', and 'Is it okay if I carry on?' permeate his plays, and as they are repeated, it becomes clear that these are not only practical questions, but also philosophical ones. 'I want any production of mine', Crouch told me, 'to encourage an audience to understand themselves as a group, to understand themselves as an individual within that group – not just ethically, but on lots of different levels' (interview).

The fictional audience

Superficially, *I, Malvolio* positions its audience as unthinking hedonists with a cruel and vindictive streak. Crouch spends the first 20 minutes or so of his hour-long monologue building up a playful antipathy between Malvolio and the audience; Malvolio accuses them variously of dropping litter, of smoking cigarettes, of drinking alcohol, of groping one another, and of failing to go to church, punctuating his accusations with questions that invite affirmative vocal responses ('That what you'd do, is it?'). This tirade rapidly becomes so grossly over-exaggerated that a great deal of humour is derived from Malvolio's hysterical mischaracterisation of his audience's perceived liberal sensibilities; at one point, he rages that they

> wear baggy trousers and experiment with hallucinogenic drugs and go around in gangs and frighten old people and worship elephants and undermine society and vandalise this phone box and dance naked and sacrifice virgins.

> (2011a: 16)

Malvolio has, one would hope, misjudged his audience to a comical extent.

On the other hand, some of his accusations might stick. 'This is you', he says, doing an impression of an audience member as a cartoonish bourgeois liberal:

> Oh, what shall I do today? [...] I know! I'll go to the theatre. That's what I'll do! I'll see a play! Oh yes! A play! La la. Won't that be entertaining.

> (2011a: 17)

'Look at yourselves', he invites us later in the same sequence, as the play anticipates audience amusement. 'LOOK AT YOURSELVES. With a ghastly rictus of amorality frozen on your ugly faces' (2011a: 17). Imagining us to be taking pleasure in his victimisation at the hands of Sir Toby Belch, he accuses us, quoting *Twelfth Night*, of being 'idle, shallow things', and asserts that he is 'not of [our] element' (2011a: 19). As he contemplates suicide, he says:

> You bully me. Because you don't approve of the way I live my life. You don't approve of the way I look, the way I think.
>
> (2011a: 24–5)

'Look what you have done', he concludes, as he prepares to hang himself. 'Look what you have allowed. Here. In the theatre' (2011a: 26).

Of course, Malvolio does not go through with his suicide. Changing his mind, he recruits audience members to help him put on his clothes while he finishes his retelling of *Twelfth Night*. Finally, dressed in the clean black tail jacket and waistcoat one might expect of a modern-day butler, he concludes the play by telling the audience precisely how he will exact his 'revenge' upon them:

> I will leave you sitting here. Sitting here with nothing to do. Sitting there. With the lights on. With the blood in your backsides. Waiting for someone to show you out. Waiting for the dust to settle. Feeling a little foolish.
>
> (2011a: 34)

Promising that he is going 'to fetch something to show you', he vacates the stage, and leaves the audience – in silence, and without any other cue that the play has finished – to decide when and how to get up and leave the theatre. This is the ending that the script anticipates, in any case.

The audience in performance

While the play clearly scripts an identity of sorts for its audience, it also encourages them in subtle ways to resist it. Crouch has spoken at length about the kind of theatre 'that controls a space, and controls an audience's relation to that space', and affirms that he wants 'to challenge those things, so there is a genuine sense that power is disseminating' (interview). He allows what he calls 'faultlines' in the script, so that without altering the structure of the piece, he can be 'responsive to what's going on in the space'. Certain passages leave room for Crouch the performer to improvise: one stage direction dictates that Malvolio *'organises the audience'*, allowing Crouch to respond directly to any perceived signs of disorder or hedonism within that audience. Moments later, he leaves the stage briefly, with the order that when he comes back, he expects 'everyone and everything to be exactly where I left it' – but as the stage direction notes, *'[t]here is a hint that MALVOLIO has really encouraged the audience to swap places, change clothing, etc. while he is out'* (2011a: 20).

The most interesting faultlines are those in which the script allows the audience a choice between cruelty and compassion. At one point, Malvolio discovers a sign saying 'Kick me' on his back, and invites an audience member onstage to kick him, before asking if it is the 'kind of thing you find funny' (2011a: 19). They may either refuse or accept, and if they go through with it, as Crouch illustrates, they might perform the action in any number of different ways:

> Last year in the Battersea Arts Centre, at the 'kick me' moment, a kid came out of the audience and really kicked me hard – and the audience gasped, because one of their own had kind of broken a contract, in a way. All I could do was to hold my nerve, and turn to them, and go, 'This is the kind of thing you find funny.' And it suddenly became a really serious moment.

The question of the audience's complicity becomes even more urgent as Malvolio attempts to enlist members of the audience to help him hang himself (Figure 1.1); the stage direction stipulates that he is *'always checking if they are all right about it, if they find it funny'* (2011a: 26). At this moment, says Crouch, 'there is a lovely dialectic that takes place within the audience between those who are just relishing it, and those who really want to challenge it'. If an audience member refuses to be involved, Crouch will find somebody else – but, he says, 'I do need to get to that point where we are counting down to somebody's death, and I need to release them out of that' (interview).

As this suggests, Crouch's responsiveness to individual audiences and audience members can only go so far – at some moments, the structure of the play *requires* particular kinds of audience reaction. In this sense, the audience's identity is, to some extent, coerced: 'Find that funny, do you?' is one of the play's repeated refrains, and Crouch *has* to make the audience laugh in order that Malvolio can then be offended by

Figure 1.1 Malvolio (Tim Crouch) prepares to hang himself, with the help of an audience member. Image from Latitude Festival, 2011, copyright Bruce Atherton and Jana Chiellino

their laughter. When the sign on Malvolio's back is revealed, for example, Crouch has structured a set of visual gags which are designed to elicit audience laughter ('It kind of doesn't fail to happen, but I sometimes have to exaggerate it a little bit to make sure'). He gives a line in which Sir Toby Belch 'defacates on the lawn' (2011a: 23) as another example:

I put 'defecate' in as a place-holder – I need to get them to laugh. 'Laugh, why don't you?' is the line. 'Laugh, why don't you?' If the line doesn't get them to laugh, it's a problem. So something has to be said that will make them laugh.

(Interview)

Thus, Crouch will use the child-friendly (and childishly comical) word 'poop' at a young person's theatre, and the more adult 'shit' with an audience of grown-ups.

As a seasoned performer, Crouch is, of course, aware that audience response can never be entirely anticipated by the script. He uses the metaphor of 'graphic equalisation' to explain variations in his performance:

There is a bandwidth, and there are frequencies on that bandwidth, and sometimes a show, or an audience, requires you to play higher frequencies, sometimes it requires you to play lower frequencies, and it all depends on what's coming at me from the audience.

(Interview)

But even such variations in his delivery of text cannot compensate for all potential responses. Where, in performance, audiences have resisted Crouch's invitations to laugh at Malvolio, he sometimes adds a line that draws self-reflexive attention to the mechanics of the piece itself: 'Let me explain the strategy of the show', says Crouch/Malvolio. 'I make myself look ridiculous; you laugh; I then attack you for laughing.' In one performance, as he removed his long johns to reveal a leopard-print thong, he added: 'This is the apotheosis of the strategy I was expounding on earlier.' Interestingly, Crouch sees such ad-libs as betrayals of the text, and characterises them as 'breakages':

I'm excited about the game beginning at the beginning, and ending at the end. It was a similar thing with *An Oak Tree*: there were loads of notional breakages in the game of *An Oak Tree*, but actually there are no breakages in the overarching purpose of the play, and everything is scripted. Everything. Even those 'How are you doing?' lines. It's all scripted. I want to retain the integrity of the piece.

'I shouldn't have to ad lib', he concludes, 'but there are times, particularly with an older audience, where I do' (interview).

Context: The audience and the theatrical event

In recent years, theatre theorists have found it useful to think of the meanings generated by a play as issuing not only from the writing, direction, design, and performance, but also from the context of its production: the nature and layout of the space in which it takes place, the cultural status of the event, the price of tickets, the demographics of the audience, and so on. Susan Bennett argues in her book *Theatre Audiences* that 'theatre as a cultural commodity is probably best understood as the result of its conditions of production and reception' (1997: 106), and both she and other scholars have found it useful to use the term 'theatrical event' to describe these aspects of a performance (Bennett 1997; Sauter 2000; Tulloch 2005). I was a member of four different audiences of *I, Malvolio*, and in each case, the play constituted part of four remarkably different 'theatrical events'.

I saw the play for the first time at Latitude Festival in July 2011. Latitude is a festival of live music and arts which takes place annually in a huge rural park in Suffolk. Tickets in 2011 were either £170 for the full three days, or £70 for one day only, but children under 12 were eligible for £5 tickets, and children under five for free ones. Access to the festival site gives ticket-holders the choice between a large number of simultaneous attractions, and when I saw it at 6 p.m. on the Saturday, *I, Malvolio* was competing for its audience's attention with acts such as rock bands The Cribs, I Am Kloot, and Fight Like Apes; comedians Seann Walsh and Colin Hoult; theatre companies Fuel and CC41; the English National Ballet; performance poets Nikky Norton-Shafau and Michelle Madsen; and an interview with the author Esther Freud. The play attracted an audience of between 100 and 200 festival-goers, some of whom would have come to the performance on purpose, but many of whom would have chanced upon it by accident as they walked past.

The location for the performance was a raised open-air stage in a semi-secluded, wooded area. Some of the surrounding trees had been spray-painted white as part of Latitude's Narnia-themed 'Faraway Forest', and there was no specially demarcated audience space other than a clearing in front of the stage. Around 40 audience members sat in the clearing, while a growing number amassed around the periphery as the performance progressed. A few children were present (many of whom heckled Malvolio with increasing confidence), but most of the audience were adults. Being a festival audience, many of them were smoking and drinking, and the background chatter never completely subsided at any point – nor, of course, did the noise of the surrounding festival. This environment added much to Malvolio's attack on the audience's licentiousness; his question 'Are you all drunk?' (2011a: 19), for example, was met with an affirmative cheer. This was a space not limited by the codes of behaviour normally associated with theatre buildings, and its slightly unreal locale identified it as emphatically separate from everyday social space: festive, cocooned, and marked by ersatz 'magic'.

The second performance I attended was at the Edinburgh Festival Fringe in August 2011, in the Traverse Theatre. The Traverse is a highly regarded subsidised theatre devoted to developing and showcasing new writing, and each August it becomes an unofficial flagship of the Fringe. In 2011, *I, Malvolio* was in repertory with 17 other plays, many of them in the same studio. It was thus performed at different times each day, from 10.30 a.m. to 9 p.m., and ticket prices varied from £11 to £17 (with £6 concessions for those aged below 18, students, and other groups). Crouch is a leading figure at the Fringe, having won awards for all four of his previous plays at the Traverse (*My Arm*, *An Oak Tree*, *ENGLAND*, and *The Author*), and the advertising copy on the Traverse website and in their season brochure made much of this. These sources mentioned Crouch's intended audience only in their fifth paragraphs ('*I, Malvolio* is the fourth of his solo Shakespeare plays for family and younger audiences') and in their age recommendations (11+), and the comprehensive 2011 Fringe programme and accompanying website neglected to mention that the show was designed for young audiences at all. These factors meant that the audience for the play was overwhelmingly adult, while a capacity of just 111, combined with Crouch's reputation, ensured that most performances had sold out well before the festival had even opened. All audience members, therefore, had planned this theatre visit well in advance. The performance I saw was at 6 p.m. on a Friday, and many of the audience would presumably have been seeing other Fringe shows earlier or later the same day.

The physical set-up of the space was much more formal than its equivalent at Latitude. The location was the Traverse 2, the smaller of the Traverse's two theatre spaces: a square black box, with the audience arranged in straight rows on raked rostra around three sides of the space. Entering the auditorium through the acting space meant that the audience were very much on display to one another from the moment they arrived in the studio, and the houselights remained up throughout the show. The context seemed to foster an acute self-awareness. Crouch found it difficult to make the audience laugh at the appropriate moments: 'shits on the lawn', for example, was met with a stony silence, making the following line – 'Laugh, why don't you?' – rather problematic. There were only two children in the audience, so Malvolio's line 'Are there any adults here?' (2011a: 19) had to be delivered with an ironic roll of the eyes.

The context for my third experience of the play was different again. The Egg in Bath describes itself as a theatre 'especially for children, young people and their families', and the audience of the 1 p.m. Thursday matinee I saw was composed almost entirely of 11–14 year olds from a comprehensive school in Wales. Children's tickets were available at £5.50, but presumably the school had negotiated a lower price-per-head with the theatre. The students had been brought to The Egg for the day, and had spent the morning in an educational workshop run by the theatre. Crouch himself had attended part of the workshop and given the children a brief explanation of the play. Malvolio, he told them, 'hated' them, and did not want them there (Crouch himself was very friendly, of course, making a clear distinction between himself and the character). One child asked whether they would be allowed to heckle, to which Crouch replied that they were, but that they should be prepared for Malvolio to heckle back. The students were not familiar with the plot of *Twelfth Night*, but their teacher had given them a brief synopsis. The theatre itself, designed with young audiences in mind, is an intimate proscenium-arch space, with low, soft-backed seats and a raised, curving walkway around the edge of the auditorium; Crouch describes it as being 'like a womb'.

My last live experience of the play was in the Swan Room – an upstairs space in the Swan Theatre, Stratford-upon-Avon. I saw the show at the end of its run, on a Sunday evening. The room itself is dominated by a large archway which owes much to church architecture, and this, combined with its location at the heart of Stratford and the RSC, meant that we were in a distinctly 'holy' and rarefied kind of space. This was augmented by the use of straight pew-like rows, a reverberant acoustic, and the placement of Malvolio (and, by implication, the 'stage space') behind the arch, a site of spatial authority. This helped to separate Malvolio from the audience, but it did little to characterise us as riotous or debauched. As in Edinburgh, children were in short supply – the RSC Marketing Department informed me afterwards that over five performances, only 67 of the 296 tickets sold (23%) were bought at the £5 rate for under 26 year olds.

The live audience

Discussing the live responses of an audience is fraught with problems. In her book *Theatre & Audience*, Helen Freshwater challenges 'the common tendency to refer to an audience as "it" and, by extension, to think of this "it" as a single entity' (2009: 5). She is undoubtedly correct – any discussion of 'the audience' as a collective risks writing out the various different responses at play within that audience. But at the same time, every audience *does* have a collective identity of sorts: when a large number of people respond en masse by laughing, applauding, or even falling silent simultaneously, they temporarily enact a group identity, however tenuous and unstable it may be. At such moments, we participate in the act of telling ourselves stories about who 'we' are.

I transcribed the audible public responses of all four of the audiences cited above. There are, it must be admitted, some problems inherent in this strategy. First, my note-taking was necessarily determined by what I could hear from my position within each audience, and by what I thought significant enough to note down: it is likely, therefore, that I neglected to transcribe moments which would have had an impact upon the meaning of the experience for other members of the group. Second, communal responses are rarely an accurate gauge of the reaction of the whole group – a robust laugh, for example, might belie the fact that some audience members did not find anything funny at all. The received impression of audience response, therefore, might be skewed towards the reactions of the noisier members of the audience.

The audience at Latitude was by far the noisiest of the four. Malvolio's questions (especially those that invited yes–no responses) were generally answered loudly. Laughter was frequent, as was applause, and while the script's more literary jokes fell relatively flat, Crouch's ad-libs were welcomed. These responses allowed Crouch to cast us all the more easily as hedonistic and easily pleased idiots. A woman who was clearly inebriated engaged in a prolonged dialogue with Malvolio, heckling him as he turned back on her with some of his (scripted) questions:

> Who allowed you to leave home dressed like that? Looking like that? Have you no wit, manners nor honesty?...Is there no respect of place, person nor time in you? Are you drunk?
>
> (2011a: 19)

After acknowledging that the audience had got an accidental 'glimpse of testicle' during his onstage costume change, Crouch elicited the biggest laugh of the show by repeating what had by this point become Malvolio's catchphrase: 'Kind of thing you like, is it?' Later, as we applauded one of the volunteers for helping Malvolio with his shoes, Crouch ad-libbed mock outrage at our limited cultural expectations.

When a second volunteer left the stage after helping Malvolio with his jacket, the audience responded with loud, defiant applause and cheering.

Crouch used these vocal responses in order to emphasise the dialectic that was taking place among us. As he prepared to hang himself, he turned to us and asked, 'This is the kind of thing you like, is it?' This got a very loud response – several people shouted 'Yes', but a few called out 'No'. As Malvolio prepared his noose, a man at the back shouted 'Do it!', while moments later a woman from the same group called out *'Don't* do it!'. In an interview following this performance, Crouch worried that the high-maintenance audience interaction had caused him to lose 'all my subtlety, and any nuance; I shouted for an hour'. 'But', he added, 'I suppose I also felt totally energised' (interview).

The Edinburgh audience was in many respects the polar opposite of the Latitude audience. The line about not being properly dressed was delivered to a man in a T-shirt, and the line about being drunk to a quiet man with a plastic cup of beer. Both of them looked self-conscious, and rather than fostering a playful confrontation between Malvolio and the audience, the questions created a silent (and to my mind, uncomfortable) tension. Laughter was so sparse over the first 20 minutes of the play that Crouch ad-libbed a line about its absence, and there was certainly no applause for the audience volunteers. Once the play started to refer more explicitly to its Shakespearean source, however, the laughs became more frequent: Malvolio's observation that 'If this were play'd upon a stage now, I could condemn it as an improbable fiction' (2011a: 32) and his reference to the fool's 'stupid song' (2011a: 32) were met with particularly healthy laughs, and his incredulous description of Viola's 'lunatic' behaviour generated a small patter of applause (2011a: 30). There was a strong sense that this audience knew *Twelfth Night* very well, and that they enjoyed seeing it mocked. Crouch finally managed to elicit a spontaneous verbal response at the climax to his retelling of the plot of *Twelfth Night*; when he asked 'ARE ALL THE PEOPLE MAD?', multiple members of the audience replied 'Yes!' (2011a: 30).

The Egg provided Crouch with an audience much closer to that anticipated by his text. Lines such as 'Who organised this?' and 'Are there any adults here?' (2011a: 19) at last made perfect sense: many of the students pointed incriminatingly at their teacher. More importantly, the young teenage audience allowed Crouch to play with the ideas surrounding authority and discipline which he had hoped to explore. The students entered the auditorium in near silence (perhaps having been instructed by their teacher to be on their best behaviour), and seemed generally reluctant at first to vocalise any responses to Malvolio's questions. This 'good' behaviour, however, quickly gave way to a kind of licensed insubordination. Crouch started to provoke robust laughs around three minutes into the piece, and soon, his audience seemed to have realised the role-playing that was being asked of them. After Malvolio (mimicking the imagined voice of his tormentors) delivered the line 'Yes! I'll point! Let's all point and laugh at the funny funny man' (2011a: 18), most of the audience took up the cue and did precisely that; many of them repeated this defiance of Malvolio's authority a few minutes later, as he ordered, 'No laughing or I will report you' (2011a: 20). Nearly all of them visibly and deliberately slouched – many of them putting their feet up on the seats – when Malvolio told us to 'sit up straight'. In a fascinating collision of the conflicting codes of behaviour required by this particular theatrical event, this apparently 'bad' (but theatrically licensed) behaviour was then policed for real by an usher, who spent several minutes quietly asking the children to remove their feet from the seats. Their teacher also scolded them for this after the show had finished.

The ethical debate of the show was brought into stark relief by this audience. Having provoked a great deal of noisy and playfully antagonistic behaviour from his audience, Malvolio silenced them very suddenly with the line, 'You bullies. You big bullies' (2011a: 26). For these secondary-school students, this was evidently a highly charged word. Seconds later, as he prepared to hang himself, he invited a series of increasingly vocal answers to his questions: when he asked, 'Is everyone happy about this?', several of the children replied 'Yeah!'; 'Is everyone excited about this?' was met with not only an affirmative 'Yeah!', but also cheering; 'This is the kind of thing you want to see, is it?' was answered with both 'Yeah!' and 'No!', very loudly; and then finally, after a countdown, 'Is this the kind of thing you really, *really* want to see?' provoked a deafening response of not only 'YEAH!' and 'NO!', but also – in one particularly noisy case – 'DIE!'. Only moments after this combative, bear-pit atmosphere had reached the peak of its cruelty, however, Crouch engineered another reversal. As Malvolio lamented, quietly, that 'Nobody loves me' (2011a: 27), a large number of the audience vocalised a sympathetic 'Ahh!'. This was a palpable turning point. By the end of the show, Malvolio's final 'You find that funny?' was answered only by a single child. Crouch nodded sadly, and said, quietly, 'That's the kind of thing you find funny.'

The Stratford audience was probably the least responsive vocally, but this allowed other aspects of the show to come to the fore. Malvolio's departure from the stage halfway through the piece was endured with a well-behaved silence, and unlike every other audience I'd encountered so far, nobody took the opportunity to disobey his instruction for 'everyone and everything to be exactly where I left it' (2011a: 20). Crouch began to ad-lib reactions to individual audience members in order to generate laughs, and by the time he reached Malvolio's deconstruction of the plot of *Twelfth Night*, the laughter was more free-flowing. As in Edinburgh, the Stratford audience seemed more comfortable laughing at *Twelfth Night* than at Malvolio's character comedy.

Malvolio's revenge, though, worked more effectively here than at any other venue. At Latitude and in Edinburgh, audiences had realised that the show was over almost as soon as Crouch left the stage, and applauded with confidence. At The Egg, Malvolio's final exit was followed by an outburst of playful misbehaviour, as nearly all of the children in the audience swapped seats, before realising, in a moment of communal disappointment, that Malvolio had cheated them of their pay-off (their teacher eventually led the applause with the observation, 'I think Malvolio's had his revenge'). At Stratford, however, the audience behaved in precisely the way anticipated by the text: sitting in silence, with the lights on, waiting for someone to show us out. Crouch's exit was followed by an uncomfortable silence of over two minutes, in which we looked self-consciously around at one another, before two audience members at the front finally and very deliberately started to clap. Significantly, not everybody joined in (presumably because a large proportion of the audience were still anticipating closure of some sort), and after another uncomfortable silence, the same pair of audience members chose to get up and walk out. Everybody else then started to move, though in a rather subdued and suspicious manner, as if half expecting the performance to resume at any moment. In a way, of course, it had never stopped.

Audience feedback

An analysis of the observable responses of an audience can be useful, but as I have suggested, it has certain limitations. It gives an inevitably subjective and impressionistic account of the overall audience response, and may neglect resistant, nuanced, or minority reactions. For this reason, I issued two of my four audiences with questionnaires about their responses to *I, Malvolio*. Tim Crouch himself supported me in this research and was very generous in allowing me an unusual level of access to both his audiences and his production.

This experiment was necessarily limited by practicalities. I conducted it only at the Traverse and at The Egg, where the particularities of the events' organisation allowed me to meet most of the audience beforehand in order to distribute the questionnaires and explain the aims of my research. I felt that it was important for me to do this not only for ethical reasons, but also to maximise the response rate, since this study is concerned not just with individual audience members but also with the audience as a whole group. The forms were short, asking audience members to identify their age bracket and to provide answers in their own words to just two questions: 'What were your first impressions of Malvolio as a character?' and 'Did your feelings change by the end of the play? If so, how?'. While further questions would undoubtedly have provided useful data, I felt it was important not to ask so many questions that potential respondents would be put off.

There are numerous methodological problems here. First, the very fact that these audiences were aware beforehand that their responses would be under scrutiny at the end may have made them unusually self-conscious. I eschewed multiple-choice and quantitative questions (asking the audience to indicate their sympathy towards Malvolio on a scale of 1–5, for example, or to tick boxes corresponding most closely to their emotional responses), because I wished to allow space for audience members to register responses that I might not have anticipated. This does, of course, assume that what audiences write is an accurate gauge of what they actually felt, and while this may be a problematic assumption, it is clearly also a necessary one. I was also keen not to ask unnecessarily leading questions. The questions I posed are relatively open-ended, but they do anticipate a difference between the audience's affective responses at the beginning and at the end of the performance. While this may be a reasonable assumption of any narrative-based show, it might have steered what my respondents decided to write.

The timing of the questionnaire is also difficult. In order to maximise the response rate, I collected the forms shortly after the end of each performance, rather than relying on audience members to post or email them over the subsequent days. The responses collected were therefore raw and immediate, and not necessarily the products of careful reflection. One audience member at the Traverse commented on this herself, saying that she would much rather dwell on the performance for a few hours before documenting her response. This echoes much of the recent research on reception, which tends to stress the processual nature of audience response. In many ways, our reading of a theatrical event begins long before the start of a performance (we might book tickets and read reviews months in advance) and lasts until months or even years afterwards. Peter Eversmann's research into 'the theatrical experience' has suggested that the collection of such 'raw' audience feedback will be highly skewed towards emotional, rather than intellectual, responses; his research team's in-depth interviews with a number of theatre professionals apparently revealed that

> [i]n the process of watching a show the perceptual and the emotional dimensions clearly take precedence over cognition. And whatever cognitive activity there is, seems more concerned with following the storyline and with storing the performance in memory than with analysing the performance itself.

It is only in the reactions that follow, he concludes, that 'the cognitive, analytic approach becomes dominant' (2004: 161). Whether or not a more cognitive analysis might be invited in the moment of performance by particular theatrical strategies (Brechtian alienation, for example) is not a question that his research explores.

The response rates from both audiences were good. At the Traverse, 48 of 111 audience members returned forms (43%), while 45 of 54 audience members completed them at The Egg (83%). What was striking amongst the Traverse audience was the variety of responses: while 21 described some sort of increased sympathy for Malvolio (44%), 12 indicated that they were unsympathetic from start to finish (25%), 7 claimed to have been sympathetic from the very start (15%), and 5 described a *decrease* in sympathy (10%). Even within these sub-groupings, of course, the reasons given and the expressions used were very different. A significant minority (46%) used unsympathetic terms to describe their initial impressions of the character, focusing on Malvolio's external behaviours: 'mad', 'angry', and 'dirty', and variations upon these terms, were used with the most frequency. 'Mad' – by far the most commonly used term – is a repeated word throughout both *I, Malvolio* and *Twelfth Night*. A smaller minority (19%) claimed to have seen Malvolio as a figure worthy of sympathy from the start, using terms such as 'abused', 'wronged', and even 'wise'. Again, many of these words are embedded in both the play and its source. Seven audience members referred to interpretations of the character derived from previous encounters with *Twelfth Night* (15%), and a further three commented on the absurdity of Shakespeare's plot (6%). Two audience members identified Malvolio's politics as specifically 'right-wing' or 'Tory'. The survey results give the audience an estimated average age of 47, and, significantly, none of the respondents were aged 16 or under.

At The Egg, of course, the average age was much lower – 96% of respondents were aged between 11 and 16, giving an estimated average of 13. Superficially, the results were similar to those from the Traverse: 29 were initially unsympathetic to the character (64%), and again, terms such as 'mad', 'angry', and 'dirty' were most common ('mad' topped the list once again). The term 'mean' was used by five respondents (11%), whereas none in the adult audience at the Traverse had used the term, indicating a significant difference in the perceived power dynamic between the performer and the audience. Ten respondents were generally sympathetic to the character at the start of the play (22%), and the reasons for this tended to differ somewhat from the adult audience: whereas 'abused' and 'wronged' were the most frequently used sympathetic terms at the Traverse, 'lonely' and 'depressed' were the most common here. By the end of the play, a much higher proportion of respondents reported increased sympathy for Malvolio – 64% – though 22% remained hostile to the character. A striking 40% – 18 individual respondents – used the phrase 'felt sorry for him' in their feedback, indicating an unusual level of similarity in audience response by the end. Fourteen referred either to his unrequited love for Olivia or to his loneliness – at 31%, a much higher proportion than at the Traverse's 4% – which suggested to me that the communal 'Aah' upon the line 'Nobody loves me' (2011a: 27) had played an important role in shaping this particular audience's reactions. Indeed, some of the respondents referred to this moment fairly directly ('my feelings did change at the end because he said nobody loved him'; 'I pitied him more towards the end when he talked about his love'; 'sorry for him because he had no love').

There were some surprises. While four adult respondents at the Traverse (two of them aged over 65) identified Malvolio specifically as an 'old man', not a single one of the young audience at The Egg did the same. The reasons for this are unclear, but perhaps indicate an element of role-playing: Crouch himself told me that, in Edinburgh, he had 'got the sense that audience members were having to make an imaginative hypothesis around how the audience would operate for the age group at which it was aimed' (interview). Certainly at least one of the respondents at the Traverse was aware of the disjunction between the play's intended audience and the audience at that particular performance, writing 'Young audiences indeed!' on the form. Perhaps the most interesting surprise at The Egg, meanwhile, was the prevalence of what might be called misreadings of the play. Seven respondents identified Malvolio as a 'tramp' (initially, at least) while another student projected her own ending onto the play, in which Olivia secretly loved Malvolio in return. It may be unfair to call these 'misreadings', of course, since the performance text of *I, Malvolio* itself does not necessarily disallow either. Rather, it may be that these particular audience members embody Jacques Rancière's 'emancipated spectator': 'He makes his poem with the poem that is performed in front of him. She participates in the performance if she is able to tell her own story about the story that is in front of her' (2007: 277).

A key discovery in both surveys was the evident importance of post-show discussion among peer groups in articulating audience response. The forms were processed in the order in which they were returned to me, and it was striking that forms which had been handed in consecutively often used precisely the same terms as one another. At The Egg, I identified three pairs of consecutive forms that used the same wording as each another, indicating that at least three separate sub-groups had used post-show discussion with their peers in order to arrive at an articulation of their response. At the Traverse, the writers of forms 46 and 47 both used the terms 'funny', 'wry', 'angry', and 'dignity', and both reported being moved to tears. A further two forms were written in the first-person plural ('we felt sympathy' and 'we found him easy to laugh at'), suggesting either an identification with the imagined group response of the audience, or, perhaps more likely, that a pair of audience members had filled in a single form together and documented their agreed shared response.

The audience after the event

As these observations indicate, at the moment of articulation, audience response ceases to be material and embodied, and becomes a construction of language. In my case study, this process of articulation was shared between as many of the individual audience members as were willing and able to participate. More usually, however, the documentation of audience response is left to smaller groups: reviewers, bloggers, and academics.

I surveyed all of the published reviews of the production that I could find. Significantly, most of these reviewed the production during its Edinburgh run – predictably, since the Fringe is attended by a huge number of reviewers, but problematically too, because the Edinburgh audience was neither typical of the play's wider audience, nor characteristic of its target audience. This was identified by Philip Fisher of the online *British Theatre Guide*, who noted that 'nobody in the house was under 20' and that, as a result, 'the atmosphere of mischief that Crouch has striven so hard to achieve did not happen'. While some reviewers focused on the ways in which the show constructed its audience, others took that construction for granted. Thus, for example, whereas *The Independent's* Holly Williams observed that Malvolio 'talks to the audience, casting us as an immoral rabble along with Sir Toby Belch and his gang of trick-sters' (23 August 2011), *The Scotsman's* Joyce McMillan identified the audience itself as being composed 'of relentless good-time boys and girls, laughing at Malvolio's humiliation, mocking the brief hope of love he enjoys' (22 August 2011). The majority of reviewers spoke on behalf of the whole audience, writing in the first-person plural: Crouch was 'suc-cessfully manipulating our laughter and turning it into self-loathing' (*Broadway Baby*, 22 August 2011), making us 'consider our own tastes for cruel humour' (*The List*, 22 August 2011), or picking 'at the knot of what we find funny, who we respect and the values we cherish' (*Guardian*, 24 August 2011). 'We try not to snigger like cruel schoolchildren', wrote Dominic Cavendish in *The Telegraph*, 'but snigger we do. […] What we end up thinking about Malvolio – and about ourselves – may surprise and even shame us' (18 August 2011). This use of the first-person plural may well be a rhetorical construction, inviting the reader to imagine that he or she is part of that 'we', but it is important to remember that its implicit projection of the audience response as both unified and predetermined is potentially misleading.

Most published theatre reviews are available online these days – some exclusively so – and it is not uncommon to find space for user-submitted comments beneath each article. Certain websites also encourage user-submitted reviews – the official Edinburgh Fringe web page for *I, Malvolio* featured seven, for example. Whether or not these provide a useful gauge of audience response is an open question. Clearly only moti-vated audience members will take the opportunity to document their response in these forums, and in the case of *I, Malvolio*, this was usu-ally because they wished to recommend the production. Though most of the reviews on this site are very short, they do provide some use-ful data: most of them focus on the play's emotional impact, but two also discuss its politics (one describes Malvolio as a 'conservative', while another considers the play 'very relevant in the context of the recent riots').

In the digital age, the play gains a secondary audience, not only through the publication of reviews, but also through the electronic distribution of digital tie-ins. The British Council's official YouTube channel hosts a three-minute video called 'Tim Crouch – *I, Malvolio*', as part of its 2011 Edinburgh Showcase. The video interweaves short clips of the show with an interview with Tim Crouch, and there is a space beneath it for user-submitted comments. By July 2012, the video had attracted 1,757 views, and two comments (both from users who had seen the show live). Crouch himself has also been running a Twitter account as @MrMalvolio, where he 'tweets' in character. Many of these tweets are ironic plugs for his shows: one, for example, advises 'god-fearing youth' to 'keep away' from Bath, before it links to The Egg's website (9 September 2011). Elsewhere, Crouch subtly encourages a political reading of his piece by writing with mock approval of the Campaign for Rural England (16 August 2011), or of David Cameron's call for 'a clearer code of standards that we expect people to live by & stronger penalties if they cross the line' (15 August 2011). By July 2012, the page had 127 followers, but as a publicly accessible page which is regularly retweeted on Crouch's own (much more highly followed) Twitter page, this is almost certainly an underestimation of its readership.

Finally, of course, the play gains an audience of readers when it is published in printed form. The printed play (which was available at most of the tour venues in a collection with three of Crouch's other Shakespearean retellings) asks the reader to imagine the audience for which the play is being performed and even scripts their anticipated responses at various points (2011a: 14, 19, 26, 34). That this textual audience is a construction of language is emphasised in the 'Afterword' to Crouch's collection of plays for adults, by Crouch's co-director Andy Smith (a smith). 'You are the reason for these plays' existence', writes Smith:

> You are the most important person in the room. And even though I don't know who or where you are, I want you to know that you have been considered – at every step of the way. I am considering you now.
>
> (Crouch 2011b: 205–6)

Smith's nebulous 'you' brings us full circle: from the audience as an imagined and anticipated construction, to a number of living, breathing bodies in a number of real, physical spaces, responding in ways that resist accurate documentation, to an audience which is once again the product of text.

Multiple audiences

This book's title refers to 'audience', but perhaps it should refer to 'audiences' in the plural. Audiences are not merely a number of different groups of people, but also a number of different discursive identities, encompassing imagined audiences (including those projected by the fictional character, by the writer, and by the live performer), social identities (determined by space, context, and event, among other factors), performed behaviours (in groups, individually, and individually in relation to the group), and retrospective characterisations (in post-show discussions, in questionnaires, online, in print, and in memory). Both text and performance can certainly anticipate a response, as indicated by the ways in which *I, Malvolio*'s audiences have laughed on cue, or unconsciously quoted from the text in their written feedback. In a similar way, the material conditions of production and reception can sculpt or steer particular readings of the piece: the educational context and communal reactions of the audience at The Egg, for example, seemed to be reflected in their responses to the questionnaire. But what my research into *I, Malvolio*'s audiences has shown more than anything else is that the responses of these audiences are never fully controlled. These audiences were never passive, never fully interpellated. The various audience identities requested by the piece in its many theatrical contexts often contradicted one another in interesting ways, and in practice, they were frequently subverted or resisted. Crouch's work, like Shakespeare's own, seems to allow a multiplicity of meanings which are as broad and varied as the audiences themselves.

Part II
In Theory

2
Making Sense of the Stage

On 15 May 1611, the Elizabethan doctor Simon Forman went to a performance of *The Winter's Tale* at the Globe theatre. He described the performance in some detail in his diary, concentrating mostly on the events of the plot: Leontes' jealousy, the abandonment and discovery of the infant Perdita, and so forth. Forman's account concluded with a description of Autolycus' tricks and a moral: 'Beware of trusting feigned beggars or fawning fellows'. We should note, with Andrew Gurr, that descriptions like Forman's 'reflect the convention of describing plays much more exactly than they indicate the writer's complete response to the experience' (2004: 138). Clearly, Forman's experience of the performance must have exceeded the few details he chose to record. What is striking, though, is that in composing his aphorism about the perils of 'trusting feigned beggars or fawning fellows', Forman was making a conscious effort to derive an articulable *meaning* from the performance.

The question of how audiences make sense of what they see and hear in the theatre is a central one for performance studies. This chapter will outline some of the most influential theories. Taking semiotics as our starting point, we will explore some of the central concepts behind this approach, before considering a number of the methodologies which have been developed both in response and in opposition to it.

Semiotics and cultural studies

Semiotics is the study of sign systems. One of the foundational figures in this field was the Swiss linguist Ferdinand de Saussure, whose posthumously published *Course in General Linguistics* (1916) introduced some of semiotics' key terms: not least the concept of the 'signifier' (the outward form of the sign) and the 'signified' (the mental image or concept evoked by the signifier). Saussure famously pointed out that 'the bond between the signifier and the signified is arbitrary' (1959: 67) – that, in other words, only linguistic convention allows meanings of any sort to be made. Thus, for Saussure, language itself constitutes our experience of the world: 'There are no pre-existing ideas, and nothing is distinct before the appearance of language' (1959: 112). Texts are comprehensible only in relation to the structures that govern our expectations.

Saussure's ideas formed the basis of Roland Barthes' highly influential analysis of systems of signification. In *Mythologies* (1957), for example, Barthes used a theoretical model that had been founded in linguistics to analyse the ideas encoded in other forms of cultural 'text', from political posters and soap-powder advertisements to margarine and striptease. Though Barthes did not write extensively about theatre, his 1963 essay 'Literature and Signification' gives a good sense of the basic assumptions underlying semiotic theatre criticism. For Barthes, theatre was a particularly complex sort of text:

> [A]s soon as it is revealed, it begins emitting a certain number of messages . . . at a certain point in the performance, you receive at the same time six or seven items of information (proceeding from the set, the costumes, the lighting, the placing of the actors, their gestures, their speech), but some of these remain (the set, for example) while others change (speech, gesture); what we have, then, is a real informational polyphony, which is what theatricality is: a *density of signs*.
>
> (1972: 261–2)

The semiotician Tadeusz Kowzan published a fuller analysis of theatre's 'semiological richness' in his 1968 essay 'The Sign in the Theatre', in which he identified 13 theatrical sign-systems: words, tone of voice, facial mimicry, gesture, movement, make-up, hairstyle, costume, accessories, décor, lighting, music, and sound effects (1968: 61–72). Keir Elam notes that while Kowzan excluded from his list both 'architectural factors' and 'occasional technical options such as film and back projection', he could be said 'to have identified the principal systemic categories, at least with regard to traditional performances' (2002: 45).

Kowzan's essay, like most semiotic approaches, is predicated on a very simple idea: that in a theatrical performance, 'everything is a sign' (1968: 57). But not all signs on stage have the purely arbitrary connection between signifier and signified suggested by Saussure. Kowzan distinguishes between *natural* signs and *artificial* ones: natural signs are 'those whose relation with the thing signified results from the laws of nature alone' – smoke, for example, being a natural sign of fire – while artificial signs are 'those whose relation with the thing signified relies on a voluntary and more often collective decision' (1968: 59). In the theatre, though, argues Kowzan, *all* signs belong to the artificial category. A pale face, for example, may be a natural sign of illness in the real world, but on the stage it acquires a greater sense of semiotic purpose:

> The spectacle transforms natural signs into artificial ones (a flash of lightning), so it can 'artificialize' signs. Even if they are only reflexes in life, they become voluntary signs in the theatre. Even if they have no communicative function in life, they necessarily acquire it on stage.
>
> (1968: 60)

In a famous essay on the 'Semiotics of Theatrical Performance' (1977), Umberto Eco illustrates this phenomenon with reference to a fictional example in which a drunkard is 'exposed in a public place by the Salvation Army in order to advertise the advantages of temperance' (1977: 109). As soon as he is exhibited, argues Eco,

> the drunken man has lost his original nature of 'real' body among real bodies. He is no more a world object among world objects – he has become a semiotic device; he is now a *sign*.
>
> (1977: 110)

The drunk, continues Eco, refers not to '*the* drunk who he is, but to *a* drunk' (1977: 110). He has been chosen by the Salvation Army sergeant because of the colour of his nose, or the dishevelled nature of his hair and clothes, in line with 'a social code, a sort of iconographic convention'; the sergeant 'has been looking for the right man just as one looks for the right word' (1977: 111). The creator of the text – writer, designer, or, especially, director – has *encoded* the material reality of the stage, in the expectation that the audience will be familiar enough with the systems of signification employed in order to *decode* it.

This understanding of the theatre as a multi-layered sign-system has become highly influential: Anne Ubersfeld's *Reading Theatre* (1976), Keir Elam's *The Semiotics of Theatre and Drama* (1980), Elaine Aston and George Savona's *Theatre as Sign-System* (1991), and Marco De Marinis' *The Semiotics of Performance* (1993) are just four significant contributions to a crowded and illustrious field. As Marvin Carlson has observed, theatre semiotics has been especially preoccupied with the 'double operations' of theatrical signs, existing as they do both 'as present material objects and as signifiers of absent signifieds' (2007: 14). The spectator is aware of both the actor and the character whom the actor is portraying; of the material reality of the stage set, and of the fictional location which it represents. It was this recognition of the double functioning of theatrical signs which led Dan Rebellato, in a 2009 article, to argue that theatre is never 'illusionistic' in the truest sense of the word:

> In illusions we have *mistaken beliefs* about what we are seeing. No sane person watching a play believes that what is being represented before them is actually happening. We know we are watching people representing something else; we are aware of this, never forget it, and rarely get confused.
>
> (2009: 18)

Theatrical signs, argues Rebellato, do not function merely in order to call our attention to a fictional world; they are not straightforward signifiers, he suggests, but rather work along the lines of metaphor. In metaphor, he notes, 'we are invited to see (or think about) one thing in terms of another thing':

> There is no make-believe involved, no amassing of propositional information, no artful subtraction from one to create the image of the other. We know the two objects are quite separate, but we think of one in terms of the other.
>
> (2009: 25)

The notion that there is something more than signification going on in the practice of performance is one to which we will return shortly.

It may be helpful, though, before we explore these ideas any further, to give a brief practical illustration of semiotics as a method of performance analysis. I have chosen to analyse the version of Lady Macbeth's sleepwalking scene in Rupert Goold's adaptation of *Macbeth*, which was performed on stage in Chichester, London, and New York before being filmed for broadcast on BBC Four and a subsequent DVD release.[1] In many ways, the scene is especially suited to a semiotic reading: before Lady Macbeth arrives, the Gentlewoman describes her mistress's sleepwalking to the Doctor, implicitly inviting the audience to look for the same sorts of behaviours in the scene that follows; both characters then provide a commentary once Lady Macbeth has entered, drawing attention to key signifiers ('You see her eyes are open … Look how she rubs her hands'; 5.1.23–6). The Doctor even decodes the meaning of one of the signs himself: 'What a sigh is there! The heart is sorely charged' (5.1.51).

Goold's adaptation of the scene mixes apparently 'natural' theatrical signs (though, of course, these are 'artificialized') with more obviously metaphorical ones. The televised version takes place in a dimly lit vault, in the middle of which, under a harsh spotlight, stands a single sink. The setting clearly signifies that it is night-time, but bears connotations, too, of a shadowy, buried realm which might represent the darker recesses of the unconscious, or possibly even hell. The brightly lit sink, perhaps, is the scene's only symbol of possible salvation, in which sins might be 'washed' away. This metaphorical reading is further emphasised by Lady Macbeth's entrance: an old-fashioned elevator rumbles down from above, and a haggard Lady Macbeth (Kate Fleetwood) stumbles out of it wearing a modern nightgown and cardigan. Everything about her signifies torment: lit from above, her prominent cheekbones cast stark shadows down upon her face, which is very pale; her eyes have dark rings around them; she moves with a tottering motion and clasps her hands defensively. Her words 'Hell is murky' (5.1.34) once again seem to confirm the scene's central metaphor. She moves to the sink after crying out 'What, will these hands ne'er be clean?' (5.1.41), frantically opens a bottle of bleach (attempting at one point to prise it open with her teeth), and pours the contents onto her hands – the Gentlewoman (Polly Frame) screams as Lady Macbeth winces. Lady Macbeth sniffs her hands, and then sobs in despair as she recognises that 'All the perfumes of Arabia will not sweeten this little hand' (5.1.48–9). Absolution, it seems, remains unavailable to her: when she finally turns on the tap at the end of the scene, it runs red with blood. Her wide eyes in shadow under the harsh lighting, she realises, trembling, that 'What's done cannot be undone' (5.1.65). She returns to the lift, slamming the grille door shut behind her, and it resembles the bars of a prison. The key signifiers of the scene thus contribute to a reading that Lady Macbeth is trapped in a psychological hell of her own making.

Of course, not all spectators will read the scene as I have just done; I am not even sure that I read it in this way myself upon first viewing it. In his book *The Semiotics of Performance*, Marco De Marinis distinguishes between *analysis* of the kind I have outlined above ('the explanatory, descriptive approach of the scholar'), and *reading* – 'the audience member's reception during the course of theatrical communication' (1993: 93). One of the tasks of analysis, he explains, 'is to explain the rules and mechanisms underlying the processes of reading' (1993: 158). In a chapter titled 'The Spectator's Task', he draws upon Eco's notion of the 'Model Reader' to propose 'The Model Spectator': an imaginary audience member, constructed by the performance itself, who '*recognizes* all the codes of the performance text in question, reconstructing the entire structure of the performance text in the way that is textually proposed by the sender' (1993: 167). The Model Spectator, De Marinis observes, is not a *real* one, but 'a strategy of interpretive cooperation foreseen by, and variously inscribed in, the performance text' (1993: 166–7). The process of interpretation, then, is not an entirely subjective one, but rather, in the words of Hans Robert Jauss, 'the carrying out of specific instructions in a process of directed perception' (1982: 23).

According to this model, the spectator's role is pre-programmed into the performance by its producers. De Marinis characterises the creators of the performance text – writer, director, designer, actor – as 'senders'. The audience, meanwhile, are 'receivers'. This should not be taken to imply absolute passivity on the part of the spectator: De Marinis describes the spectator as 'co-producer of the performance, the active creator of its meanings' (1993: 158). He distinguishes between 'closed' performances, which 'predict [a] specific addressee', and 'open' ones, which are 'intended to reach a fairly nonspecific addressee' and 'do not foresee a rigidly predetermined interpretive process as a requirement for their success' (1993: 168–9). His theoretical model, however, seems to be based to a very great extent upon the former. In *The Semiotics of Theatre and Drama*, meanwhile, Keir Elam begins to move into a rather different understanding of spectatorship when he briefly considers the extent to which spectators can become 'senders': exerting an influence, via their expressions of attention, pleasure, or disapproval, both upon the performance itself and upon its reception by other members of the audience (2002: 86–7). Eco, too, notes the 'conversational' element to live theatre, suggesting that '[t]heatrical messages are shaped also by the feedback produced from their destination point' (1977: 117).

It is the *social* nature of theatrical meaning-making that forms the basis of what has become perhaps the dominant theoretical model of spectatorship in theatre studies. While Eco's essay on theatre semiotics retains the model of 'emitting' and 'receiving' information, it also stresses the importance of the 'contextual frame' in determining meaning: '[t]he fact that the drunk has been exposed under the standards of the Salvation Army obliges the audience to associate his presence to a whole system of values' (1977: 117). In his book *Is There a Text in This Class?*, Stanley Fish proposes that audiences derive cues for their readings of a text not merely from the text itself but from the shared values of the 'interpretive communities' to which they belong; this, he explains,

> is the explanation both for the stability of interpretation amongst readers (they belong to the same community) and for the regularity with which a single reader will employ different interpretive strategies and thus make different texts (he belongs to different communities).
>
> (1980: 171)

Texts do not signify in any 'pure' way, but rather in ways which are determined directly by their historical, geographical, and cultural contexts.

Susan Bennett's seminal book *Theatre Audiences* is built upon just such an understanding of spectatorship. 'It is at the nexus of production and reception,' she explains in the preface to her second edition, 'that the spectator exists' (1997: vii). Bennett discusses spectatorship in largely semiotic terms, characterising it as 'reading' or 'decoding', and her study focuses on the 'signs' and 'codes' of performance. Her model of the audience's reading of these codes proposes two 'frames' which condition that reading: on the one hand, an 'outer frame' which comprises the wider cultural constructions of the theatre event, and on the other, an 'inner frame' which 'contains the dramatic production in a particular playing space' (1997: 139). Thus, while the inner frame might facilitate a reading of performance of the kind explored above, that reading, for Bennett, will be heavily influenced by the norms and expectations generated by the outer frame: the cultural status of the event, its economic basis, its marketing, and so forth. Each spectator, furthermore, will respond differently depending on his or her gender, ethnicity, social class, sexuality, education level, sub-cultural affiliations, and so on. But the relationship between the frames, says Bennett, is interactive: 'Cultural assumptions affect performances, and performances rewrite cultural assumptions' (1997: 2). In Western theatre, she concludes,

> it is the tension between the inner frame of the fictional stage world, the audience's moment by moment perception of that in the experience of a social group, and the outer frame of community (cultural construction and horizons of expectations) which determine the nature and satisfaction of the interpretive process.
>
> (1997: 156)

Any act of spectatorship, therefore, is 'a politically implicated act' – something which Bennett identifies as a neglected factor both in 'theories of reading' and in 'theatre semiotics' (1997: 86).[2]

Modern practitioners of cultural studies, following Barthes, tend to emphasise what Sue-Ellen Case has described as 'the covert cultural beliefs embedded in communication' (1988: 117). This is particularly evident in studies of audiences of the mass media, as Nick Abercrombie and Brian Longhurst's book *Audiences* makes clear. Abercrombie and Longhurst note that in the earliest studies of media audiences, the essential model was one 'of the media as a narcotic where messages are injected into the mass audience as if from a hypodermic syringe' (1998: 5). As audience research developed, though, a new paradigm started to emerge, which Abercrombie and Longhurst define as one of 'Incorporation/Resistance'. They identify Stuart Hall's essay 'Encoding/Decoding' (1980) as a key juncture. Hall's essay argued that media texts are encoded with 'preferred' readings, usually corresponding with the values of the culture's dominant ideology, but that spectators do not always interpret the text along these lines: some will accept the 'dominant' reading; others will reject it entirely, resulting in an 'oppositional' reading; a third group, meanwhile, will combine dominant and oppositional elements to arrive at a 'negotiated' reading. In the 'Incorporation/Resistance' paradigm, argue Abercrombie and Longhurst, the problem of audience research is defined as 'whether audience members are incorporated in the dominant ideology by their participation in media activity or whether, to the contrary, they are resistant to that incorporation' (1998: 15). Other sorts of questions about the audience are, they suggest, 'almost un-askable or, at least, are not treated as serious or interesting contributions' (1998: 15).

We might now return to our example of Lady Macbeth's sleepwalking scene to see what these more sociologically oriented approaches might allow us to find in it. We might begin by attempting to identify some of the cultural beliefs which are encoded in the written text. I concluded my semiotic reading of the scene by suggesting that 'Lady Macbeth is trapped in a psychological hell of her own making'. A cultural critic might unpick the implications of this meaning: 'Lady Macbeth is trapped in a psychological hell of her own making' may be what is *signified* on what Barthes calls the 'first-order' of signification, but that meaning itself can be read on the 'second-order' of signification as the mere *signifier* for a cultural myth (2000: 114–15). Feminist critics, for example, reading Lady Macbeth in light of the deeply patriarchal social context in which her story was first dramatised, have often seen her as a misogynistic stereotype – Lisa Jardine analyses the character in relation to *Hic Mulier: Or, The Man-Woman* (1620), a Jacobean condemnation of 'masculine' women. Arguing that the 'drama of the early modern period is full of set-piece denunciations of the "not-woman" in her many forms', Jardine identifies Lady Macbeth as being part of a tradition 'which is careless of verisimilitude in the interests of the frisson of horror to be derived from such representations of threatening womanhood' (1983: 93, 97). Earlier in the play, Lady Macbeth took it upon herself to police her husband's masculinity: 'When you durst do it, then you were a man' (1.7.49); 'Are you a man?' (3.4.57); 'What, quite unmanned in folly?' (3.4.72). Prior to that, in a startling sequence of de-feminisation, she had called upon supernatural forces to 'unsex' her and to fill her 'from the crown to the toe top-full/Of direst cruelty' (1.5.40–2). Now, in the sleepwalking scene, the consequences of this behaviour become clear; as the Doctor puts it, 'Unnatural deeds/Do breed unnatural troubles' (5.1.68–9). Thus read, the scene becomes the culmination of a highly conservative morality tale about the dangers of women abandoning their 'natural' roles as subservient care-givers.

Goold's adaptation, of course, is aimed at a 21st-century audience, and its cultural context makes the reading outlined above less sustainable. Certainly, Goold borrows tropes from the modern horror film (not least the tap suddenly pouring blood), and in this respect one could identify a shared interest with the horror genre in the victimisation of 'aberrant' women. But Goold's adaptation also complicates the misogynistic reading. Earlier in the play, Fleetwood's Lady Macbeth had played the perfect hostess, helping her staff to prepare the evening meal as Duncan entered the kitchen to meet her (in a neat in-joke for spectators already familiar with the play, she went over to the sink to wash her hands before greeting him). As her husband instructed her to 'mock the time with fairest show' (1.7.81), she picked up a chocolate gateau before leaving the stage. The stereotype of the 'ideal housewife' was, it seems, being subverted: Lady Macbeth's crime was not an abandonment of her femininity, but rather a desire to be the perfect wife at any cost.

The production's 'Outer Frame', meanwhile, made certain implications about the production's claims to cultural authority. Audiences in London's West End, for example, would have paid fairly substantial ticket prices, and may well have read the production's glowing notices in the press, in which it was hailed as 'the *Macbeth* of a lifetime' (*Evening Standard*, 27 September 2007) or 'the greatest production of *Macbeth* I have ever seen' (*Telegraph*, 27 September 2007). By November, the production had won Best Actor and Best Director at the Evening Standard

Theatre Awards. Spectators were primed, therefore, to encounter a version of the play which was in some way definitive or revelatory, and they might have accepted what was by now a 'dominant' reading of the piece, or they may well have resisted it. Their readings of its gender politics would certainly have been inflected by their own genders, sexualities, and cultural backgrounds.

There is much to be said for this sort of cultural analysis of a performance's systems of signification, and indeed a vast amount of modern theatre scholarship takes this approach. The assumption seems to be that ideological exchange – incorporation and resistance – is the most interesting and important process going on at the level of audience reception. This may well be true in some cases, but I cannot help but wonder whether certain aspects of the spectator's experience are at risk of being neglected when the semiotic/cultural studies paradigm is adopted as a matter of routine. Indeed, in his discussion of Kowzan's thirteen theatrical sign-systems, Elam observes that it is 'doubtful...that each system is equally accessible to semiotic analysis' (2002: 45), while De Marinis admits that his model of 'The Spectator's Task' can account for the spectator's 'experiential activities...only to a very small degree' (1993: 158–9). I would like, then, to outline a very different approach to our example.

Phenomenology and embodiment

One of my reasons for choosing Kate Fleetwood's sleepwalking scene as a case study was that I remembered the powerful effect it had had upon me when I watched it in the theatre. With this in mind, I sat down with a notepad in order to document my 'live' experience of the scene as I re-watched it on DVD. Many of my resulting notes indicate that I did indeed 'read' the scene in a semiotic sense: I noted the symbolism, for example, of the lift, the light, and the sink. But most of my notes are more visceral. I found Fleetwood's contorted body and sickly facial features both engrossing and painful to watch: my notes emphasise her 'scratching, violent, tense, jerky movements' and her 'tense neck muscles', not for what they signified, but for the physical phenomena themselves. I was struck by the pathos of the moment at which Fleetwood sucked her thumb, just as a child might, upon the line 'Yet who would have thought the old man to have had so much blood in him?' (5.1.36–8). I found myself slightly alienated by the sequence in which she poured 'bleach' onto her hands, reminded that no professional actor would be asked to undertake such an act for real, and that the contents of the bottle were surely harmless in reality. But Fleetwood's action of sniffing her hand, and her subsequent line 'Here's the smell of blood still' (5.1.48), made me imagine the 'smell of bleach as [the] smell of blood', and I wrote 'SENSES' on my notepad in capital letters. Her 'sighs', I noted, were 'gut-wrenching sobs & then a shattering scream', and I was reminded at this point that Fleetwood's final scream was one of the moments which had had such a profound effect on me in the theatre. I concluded by noting her 'spitting delivery', and a moment in which she extended her hand, 'as if pleading', to the Doctor. As I look back over these impressions now, I am struck by the fact that my notes refer almost exclusively to 'Fleetwood' and not to 'Lady Macbeth'.

I do not wish to suggest that this impression of the scene is in any way a typical one: I come to it with my own cultural frame, as an academic, theatre director, second-time audience member, middle-class white male, and so forth. But what I hope it does indicate is that much more is going on in theatrical spectatorship than just the decoding of signifiers. Underpinning all of the theoretical models discussed above is the same basic understanding of spectatorship: that audiences 'read' the signifiers of the stage in a way that is fundamentally similar to the process of reading a written text. Implicit in some of them, though – for example, Dan Rebellato's concept of the stage-sign as metaphor – is the notion that in theatre, the medium itself often commands as much interest as the thing represented. We experience the behaviour of the stage not as computers might, receiving and processing data, but as embodied beings. Peter Eversmann's in-depth interviews with audience members have revealed that spectators frequently express their responses to performance 'in a physical way':

> These reactions range from being alert and sitting on the edge of one's chair (both in connection with interest) to such behaviour as: feeling it in one's stomach, shaking, being breathless, being immobilized, shock-experience, cold-sweat, laughing and crying.
>
> (2004: 156)

Willmar Sauter's audience surveys and interviews have revealed a similar emphasis on the sensory and embodied aspects of theatrical spectatorship: he describes the three key elements to 'the reactions of the spectator' as 'paying attention to the performer, enjoying the skills of the acting, [and] attributing meaning to what one experiences' (2010: 250). Sauter names these three levels of response the *sensory*, *artistic*, and *symbolic* and suggests that the dominant modes of performance analysis founded in semiotics tend to privilege the symbolic at the expense of the other two (2010: 249–50)

Perhaps the most influential theoretical approach to the study of the non-semiotic aspects of theatrical spectatorship has been phenomenology. Founded as a philosophical discipline by Edmund Husserl (1859–1938), phenomenology is the study of immediate subjective experience – with the world as it presents itself to consciousness. Bert O. States, the author of numerous important works on the phenomenological approach to theatre, describes it as a methodology that deals with 'what cosmological physics might call "the first four seconds" of the perceptual explosion' (though States is anxious to point out that 'four seconds' is not used here 'in a strict durational sense'):

> It is beside the point to claim that the first four seconds are always tainted by a lifetime of perceptual habit within a narrow cultural frame. It is only the moment of absorption that counts: what conditions the moment and what follows it are somebody else's business.
>
> (2007: 27)

Owing to the nature of the project, it is, he says, 'probably the most personal form of critical commentary and hence is a useful counterbalance to the increasingly impersonal methodology in so much of today's criticism' (2007: 27). One of the central concerns of States' most important work of theatre phenomenology, *Great Reckonings in Little Rooms*, is the presence of the *real* on the stage; States gives Launce's dog Crab in *The Two Gentlemen of Verona* as a straightforward example. In performance, he argues, the dog 'usually steals the show by simply being itself':

> Anything the dog does – ignoring Launce, yawning, wagging its tail, forgetting its 'lines' – becomes hilarious or cute because it is doglike.... We have an intersection of two independent and self-contained phenomenal chains – natural animal behaviour and culturally programmed human behaviour.
>
> (1985: 33)

The pleasure, for States, lies in 'the "flash" at the intersection', which he deems 'equivalent to the punch line of a joke' (1985: 33). He is interested in 'the upsurge of the real into the magic circle where the conventions of theatricality have assured us that the real has been subdued and transcended' (1985: 34). Theatre, he argues, 'brings us into phenomenal contact with *what exists*, or with what it is possible *to do*, theatrically, with what exists'; the theatrical object is 'perceived not as a signifier but as a signified' (1985: 37).

As his terminology suggests, States does not see phenomenology and semiotics as mutually exclusive forms of analysis. Responding to Keir Elam's claim that 'any semiotics worthy of the name…is eminently phenomenological' (1986: 250), States asserts that 'in principle, Elam is right', and that there is 'no reason that the phenomenological and the semiotic attitudes cannot compatibly blend into each other' (2007: 32). He has one caveat, however:

> It is my sense that as long as semiotics holds the notion that all things (on a stage, for example) can be fully treated as *signs* – that is, as transparent codes of socialized meaning – it cannot adopt the phenomenological attitude in any 'eminent' way.
>
> (2007: 31–2)

States recognises, of course, that in the theatre, 'we *are* confronted by images and signs'. But, he adds, 'in the theatre something is *also itself* as well…though the bird in the feeder may be a sign of spring, it is not the sign of a bird' (2007: 32). The approach which he advocates is one which accounts for both levels of perception.

Bruce R. Smith makes Shakespeare the focus of his combination of linguistic and phenomenological analysis in *Phenomenal Shakespeare* (2010). 'Theatrical phenomena versus social facts, appearance versus reality, imaginative joy versus rational analysis,' he says at the beginning of his book: '*must* we choose between these binaries? Why can't we embrace both?' (2010: 6). Towards the end, he calls for a linguistics 'that takes into account touch as well as speech, seeing as well as hearing, feeling as well as decoding' (2010: 166). Smith identifies his study as part of 'a counterturn to the "linguistic turn" of the 1960s and 1970s' (2010: 7), and much of his analysis focuses on the effects of language and performance on the human nervous system. He points out that the double meaning of 'humour' in Elizabethan discourse implies that Shakespeare's audience must have possessed a profoundly physiological, kinaesthetic understanding of the emotions: though medically inaccurate, the concept of the four humours is similar in many ways to the modern understanding of emotion-inducing hormones such as adrenalin, serotonin, and cortisol (2010: 34–5). Smith moves directly from phenomenology to cognitive science in order to explore the physiology of spectatorship. 'It is my sense of touch', he explains, that allows me to project what I can feel with my body here onto his body there and, reversing direction, to take what I see happening to his body there and feel it with my body here.

(2010: 151)

The process described here is based on the theory of 'mirror neurons', which Smith calls 'the physiological grounding for empathy' in both theatre and interpersonal relations (2010: 152–3).

Empathy, according to modern cognitive science, is an embodied process. The existence of mirror neurons was first proposed by the Italian neuroscientists Vittorio Gallese, Luciano Fadiga, Leonardo Fogassi, and Giacomo Rizzolatti in their 1996 paper 'Action Recognition in the Premotor Cortex'. Recording electrical activity in the brains of monkeys, the scientists noted that a particular set of neurons 'became active both when the monkey performed a given action and when it observed a similar action performed by the experimenter' (1996: 593). On a cognitive level, then, *observing* an action may not be entirely separate from *performing* it. This idea has become hugely influential in the study of human emotion and empathy (see, for example, Gallese 2001). In their 2005 essay 'Embodiment in the Acquisition and Use of Emotion Knowledge', cognitive psychologists Paula M. Niedenthal, Lawrence W. Barsalou, François Ric, and Silvia Krauth-Gruber summarise the evidence for four key claims of this body of work:

(1) Individuals embody other people's emotional behaviour; (2) embodied emotions produce corresponding subjective emotional states in the individual; (3) imagining other people and events also produces embodied emotions and corresponding feelings; and (4) embodied emotions mediate cognitive responses.

(2005: 22)

Pierre Jacob and Marc Jeannerod, meanwhile, distinguish between two different kind of visual perceptions: *visual percepts* and *visuomotor representations*. The former, they explain, 'serves as input to higher human cognitive processes, including memory, categorization, conceptual thought and reasoning', while the latter 'is at the service of human action'; they characterise them as ways of 'thinking about' and 'acting upon' the world respectively (2003: 45). Thus, for example, when I observed the underground vault in the clip from *Macbeth*, my brain might have generated a visual percept that enabled me to think about the image metaphorically; when I watched Lady Macbeth extend her hand towards the Doctor, however, I might have perceived it as a visuomotor representation, so that on some unconscious level my own body was imitating Kate Fleetwood's gesture of pleading and re-performing her own embodied emotion.

Theories of spectatorship derived from cognitive science are becoming increasingly prevalent in studies of performance. Scientist Richard Ralley and theatre scholar Roy Connolly argue in a joint 2010 article that 'exploring the theatre event via cognitive processes has a significant contribution to make to critical perspectives that locate the performance-audience relationship in social and cultural phenomena', and they summarise some of the research which might have direct relevance for performance analysts (2010: 51). Perhaps the most extensive study in this field to date, though, is Bruce McConachie's *Engaging Audiences* (2008), a book-length introduction to some of cognitive science's insights into the processes of theatrical spectatorship. McConachie's book is very wide ranging, but underpinning much of it is a dissatisfaction with the dominant theoretical approaches to spectatorship in performance studies; McConachie asserts that there are 'fundamental differences between readers making sense of signs on a printed page and the mostly nonsymbolic activity of spectator cognition', and he argues that certain kinds of response, rather than being culturally determined, are in fact hard-wired into us on a 'species level' (2008: 3, 18). McConachie is insistent that cognitive science undermines some of the fundamental assumptions behind both semiotic and phenomenological methodologies of performance analysis, and he asserts that 'the conclusions based on these theories – which would include many of the major books and articles in our field during the last 20 years – are potentially built upon sand' (2008: 13). At the same time, he argues that 'cognitive and cultural approaches to audiences need not be antithetical', and that 'our species-, cultural-, and individual-specific traits are interdependent and cannot really be separated' (2008: 5, 6). While he argues that 'social constructions of class, age, gender, and so on' are less important in the formation of response 'than we have generally supposed', he does not depart entirely from the cultural studies approach, and towards the end of his book he does read performances in light of the values of 'dominant culture' (2008: 20, 103).

This chapter, then, has explored a number of different ways of thinking about the activities undertaken by spectators as they make sense of a performance. Many of these approaches are not so much in opposition to one another as in negotiation: clearly most audience members are simultaneously reading, making cultural associations, forming group identities, encountering objects, and responding kinaesthetically, and it is up to the analyst to construct a narrative from these various activities. The theoretical approaches considered in this chapter have been concerned with the processes of spectatorship in general; many of the best-known theories concerning theatre audiences, however, are concerned not with what audiences *usually* do but with what they *ought* to do. In the next chapter, then, we will look at some of the ways in which major theatre practitioners have thought about spectatorship, constructing their practice in order to provoke certain kinds of audience behaviour, and conclude by considering the empirical research which has been undertaken by scholars interested in the responses of actual audience members.

3
Agency, Community, and Modern Theatre Practice

The key theorist–practitioners of the 20th century tended, as Jacques Rancière has pointed out, to see the kind of spectatorship associated with naturalism, cinema, or television as 'a bad thing', equating it with intellectual, political, or spiritual passivity. 'The most common conclusion', suggests Rancière, 'runs as follows':

> What must be pursued is a theatre without spectators, a theatre where spectators will no longer be spectators, where they will learn things instead of being captured by images and become active participants in a collective performance instead of being passive viewers.
>
> (2007: 272)

Rancière identifies Antonin Artaud's theatre of cruelty and Bertolt Brecht's epic theatre as the most definitive examples of the two ways, 'antagonistic in principle', in which this has been understood. On the one hand, in the Artaudian theatre, the spectator 'must be torn from his delusive mastery, drawn into the magical power of theatrical action, where he will exchange the privilege of playing the rational viewer for the experience of possessing theatre's true vital energies'; on the other hand, the Brechtian spectator 'must be confronted with the spectacle of something strange, which stands as an enigma and demands that he investigate the reason for that strangeness' (2007: 272). 'The project of reforming the theatre', says Rancière, 'ceaselessly wavered between these two poles of distant inquiry and vital embodiment' (2007: 272). It may be helpful to chart some of the most enduring ideas behind each of these paradigms before we return to Rancière's critique.

Artaud's ambitions for a re-energised form of theatrical spectatorship were articulated most forcefully in his 1938 book, *The Theatre and*

Its Double. For Artaud, the modern theatre had become too safe and sanitised, incapable of the direct and violent effect it ought to seek: a 'real stage play', he argued, 'upsets our sensual tranquillity, releases our repressed subconscious, drives us to a kind of potential rebellion' (1993: 19). Firmly of the belief that 'the masses think with their senses first and foremost', Artaud proposed a 'Theatre of Cruelty': 'a theatre where violent physical images pulverise, mesmerise the audience's sensibilities', that 'wakes us up heart and nerves' (1993: 65, 63, 64). This theatre would be made in order to 'appeal to the whole man, not social man' (1993: 82). Artaud suggested that audiences should be treated like 'charmed snakes' and brought 'to the subtlest ideas through their anatomies': some of his suggestions included the development of a 'physical language' rich in dream-like imagery, an incantational and non-literal use of verbal language, and the establishment of a theatre auditorium in which actors and audience shared a 'single, undivided locale without any partitions of any kind' (1993: 61, 74). Artaud's audience were to be seated in the centre of the action, encircled by it and immersed in it.

Artaud's ideas were profoundly influential. Peter Brook and Charles Marowitz staged a 'Theatre of Cruelty' season with the Royal Shakespeare Company in 1964, using Artaud's ideas as the starting point for their own experiments, and Artaud's thinking was clearly formative in the development of Brook's 'Holy Theatre' (see Brook 1990: 55–61). Brook's first production with his Centre International de Créations Théâtrales was *Orghast* (1971), an experiment 'to see whether there are elements in the theatrical vocabulary that pass directly, without going through the stage once removed of cultural or other references' (Smith 1972: 248). Staged at sunset and sunrise at an ancient burial site in Persepolis, *Orghast* was dominated by movement and visual imagery, chants, groans, and howls, and much of its spoken dialogue had been written in a new language ('Orghast') invented by the poet Ted Hughes in order to work on a universally human, physiological level. At around the same time, the Polish director Jerzy Grotowski was developing a 'poor theatre' centred upon 'the actor-spectator relationship of perceptual, direct, live communion' (1975: 19). In the holy theatre of ages past, argued Grotowski, the spectator had come to catharsis 'through fright and a sense of the sacred'; in modern times, though, it was 'much more difficult to elicit the sort of shock needed to get at those psychic layers behind the life-mask' (1975: 22, 23). Though he argued that Artaud's writings were 'based on different premises and took a different tack', Grotowski recognised them as 'an astounding prophecy'; he, too, recommended the 'violation of the living organism' as a means of providing 'the shock which rips off the mask' (1975: 23, 24, 22). One of his most important innovations was to advocate the design of a new performance space for each production: thus, for example, his audience sat on bunk beds to become patients at a psychiatric hospital in his production of *Kordian* (1962), while they became guests at a banquet in *Dr Faustus* (1963). As De Marinis notes, though, Grotowski ultimately rejected this 'somewhat constricting and basically authoritarian approach to audience participation', feeling that 'rather than deconditioning the audience, this approach risked blocking and further inhibiting them' (1987: 106).

While Grotowski's later work moved increasingly towards an introspective 'paratheatre', Brook's went the opposite way, aiming (in his own words) at 'a perception that is heightened because it is shared' (1987: 41). Brook's holy theatre was meant to serve a deeply social function, building 'a circle of unique intensity in which barriers can be broken and the invisible become real' (1987: 41). In the modern world, he argued, 'people who have long given up going to churches are still comforted by their secret prayers and private faith':

> We try to believe that family bonds are natural and close our eyes to the fact that they have to be nourished and sustained by spiritual energies. With the disappearance of living ceremony, with rituals empty or dead, no current flows from individual to individual and the sick social body cannot be healed.
>
> (1987: 136)

Brook's search for a health-giving, nourishing collectivity has informed much of his theatre work and that of numerous imitators. Susan Kattwinkel notes in the introduction to her 2003 collection *Audience Participation* that many of the practitioners covered in the volume share 'a desire for a Turnerian "communitas", in which the audience can feel like they are creating and expressing common sentiment along with the performers and each other' (2003: x).

Communitas is the anthropologist Victor Turner's term for the 'direct, immediate and total confrontation of human identities' experienced by a crowd at a moment of togetherness (1969: 132). Spontaneous *communitas*, he explains,

> has something 'magical' about it. Subjectively there is in it the feeling of endless power. . . . It is almost everywhere held to be sacred or 'holy,'

possibly because it transgresses or dissolves the norms that govern structured and institutionalized relationships and is accompanied by experiences of unprecedented potency.

(1969: 128–9)

For Turner, *communitas* is almost certainly a socially positive force: he explains that it 'preserves individual distinctiveness' and insists that it is 'neither regression to infancy, nor is it emotional, nor is it "merging" in fantasy' (1982: 45–6). It occurs, rather, in a moment of 'liminality' in which 'people "play" with the elements of the familiar and defamiliarize them' (1982: 27). Liminality, says Turner, 'presents, directly or by implication, a model of human society as a homogenous, unstructured communitas, whose boundaries are ideally coterminous with those of the human species' (1982: 47). In this sense, it might be usefully compared with the philosopher Mikhail Bakhtin's concept of *carnival*, in which the individual 'feels that he is an indissoluble part of the collectivity, a member of the people's mass body' (1984: 255). Carnival, suggests Bakhtin, 'affirms the people's immortal, indestructible character' (1984: 256).

This optimistic model of crowd collectivity is in some ways the opposite to the ideal of spectatorship proposed in the Brechtian paradigm. When Elias Canetti discussed the feeling of equality experienced during the 'discharge' of a crowd in his book *Crowds and Power*, he pointed out that this moment of oneness, 'so desired and so happy, contains its own danger':

It is based on an illusion; the people who suddenly feel equal have not really become equal; nor will they *feel* equal for ever. They return to their separate houses, they lie down on their own beds, they keep their possessions and their names.

(1962: 18)

Canetti goes on to point out that a crowd's awareness of its own transience can lead to a 'feeling of being persecuted' – 'a peculiar angry sensitiveness and irritability directed against those it has once and forever nominated as enemies' (1962: 22).[1] As Herbert Blau argues in *The Audience*, this sort of crowd is a 'dangerous illusion': 'we have seen the most ruthless discharge of history through the cancelled distance of the crowd, which remains alluring nonetheless' (1990: 5). For Blau, an alternative is to be found in Brecht's 'willingness to forgo the blessed moment of intimacy for the rigorous moment of perception, in the interests of which it becomes strategically necessary to restore the scrupulous distance' (1990: 5–6).

Brecht's aim, of course, was to find a style of theatre which would 'make the spectator adopt an attitude of inquiry and criticism' (1977: 136). Brecht felt that conventional theatre audiences were dangerously passive:

> They scarcely communicate with each other; their relations are those of a lot of sleepers. . . . True, their eyes are open, but they stare rather than see, just as they listen rather than hear. They look at the stage as if in a trance.
>
> (1977: 187)

Audiences of this sort were unlikely to leave the theatre and take meaningful political action. Brecht contrasted such spectators – those of the 'dramatic' theatre – with those of his own 'epic' theatre, which was designed to agitate and unsettle:

> The dramatic theatre's spectator says: Yes, I have felt like that too – Just like me – It's only natural – It'll never change – The sufferings of this man appal me, because they are inescapable – That's great art; it all seems the most obvious thing in the world – I weep when they weep, I laugh when they laugh.
>
> The epic theatre's spectator says: I'd never have thought it – That's not the way – That's extraordinary, hardly believable – It's got to stop – The sufferings of this man appal me, because they are unnecessary – That's great art: nothing obvious in it – I laugh when they weep, I weep when they laugh.
>
> (1977: 71)

Brecht had a strong antipathy towards theatre which, like Artaud's, had a viscerally hypnotic effect upon its audience; he insisted that in the epic theatre, the audience was not to be ' "worked up" by a display of temperament or "swept away" by acting with tautened muscles . . . no attempt was made to put it in a trance' (1977: 136). *Communitas* was something to be actively avoided, and the spectators were not to be treated as 'an undifferentiated mass'. The Brechtian actor was instructed not to 'address himself to everybody alike', but rather to allow 'the existing divisions within the audience to continue': 'He has friends and enemies in the audience; he is friendly to the one group and hostile to the other' (1977: 143).

Some of Brecht's followers have been more optimistic about the idea of a united audience. John McGrath, for example, founder of the Scottish political theatre troupe 7:84, argues in the introduction to his play *The Cheviot, the Stag, and the Black, Black Oil* (1973) that theatre 'can be the way people can find their voice, their solidarity and their collective determination' (1974: xxvii). *The Cheviot* took the form of a Scottish *ceilidh*, maintaining a Brechtian episodic structure while encouraging audience participation in its use of traditional Scottish music and song. Its content was overtly political: a history of the exploitation of the Scottish land and working classes, from the Highland Clearances to the modern-day boom in Scottish oil. McGrath's work is one of the case studies in Baz Kershaw's book *The Politics of Performance* (1992) in which Kershaw argues that 'the immediate and local effects of particular performances' – laughter, tears, applause, and so forth – might contribute to progressive political change by altering 'the structure of the audience's community and the nature of the audience's culture' (1992: 1). Collective responses, argues Kershaw, 'are the very foundation of performance efficacy': 'They are the first link in a chain that connects the individual experience of each audience member to the wider historical development of his or her society' (1992: 35).

It is possible to identify some parallels between these two paradigms and the competing models of spectatorship explored in Chapter 2. In many ways, the Artaudian paradigm, with its emphasis on the pre-semiotic and physiological aspects of spectatorship, shares a theoretical underpinning with the phenomenological and embodied approaches. For Artaud, theatre was 'not aimed at solving social or psychological conflicts...but to express objectively secret truths' (1993: 51). While social change was urgent and necessary, argued Artaud, theatre was unable to ask social questions 'in as effective and incendiary a manner as is needed', and even if it did, 'it would still be far from its intended purpose which is higher and even more mysterious' (1993: 31). The Brechtian paradigm, meanwhile, shares a great deal with semiotics and cultural studies – not least their mutual assumption that, as Susan Bennett puts it, the audience is 'already-always interpellated by ideology' (1997: 33).[2] Brecht's ideas have had what Bennett describes as 'a widespread and profound effect not only on theatre practice, but also on critical responses to plays and performance' (1997: 21), and Bennett's own *Theatre Audiences* is an important example of the latter.

Though they are, as Rancière puts it, 'antagonistic in principle', the Artaudian and Brechtian paradigms sometimes meet in the approach of a single theatre practitioner. The Brazilian director Augusto Boal, for

example, shared Brecht's commitment to left-wing social transformation, but felt that Brecht had not gone far enough in his quest to liberate
the spectator. As he explains in his 1979 book *Theatre of the Oppressed*,

> Brecht's poetics is that of the enlightened vanguard: the world is
> revealed as subject to change, and the change starts in the theatre
> itself, for the spectator does not delegate power to the characters to
> think in his place, although he continues to delegate power to them
> to act in his place.
>
> (2000: 155)

Boal's disclaimer here reveals his key departure from Brecht. For Boal,
'spectators' are by definition 'passive beings'; in order to be provoked
into political activity, they must be changed 'into subjects, into actors,
transformers of the dramatic action' (2000: 122). In Boal's 'theatre of the
oppressed',

> the spectator delegates no power to the character (or actor) either
> to act or to think in his place; on the contrary, he himself assumes
> the protagonic role, changes the dramatic action, tries out solu-
> tions, discusses plans for change – in short, trains himself for real
> action.
>
> (2000: 122)

Some of the techniques that Boal proposes in order to achieve this
include 'invisible theatre' – in which spectators witness a scene in a
public place, unaware that it is fictional – and 'forum theatre', in which
the spectator is invited to intervene directly in the dramatic action and
make changes to the scene. All of his various experiments, says Boal,
have the same objective: 'the liberation of the spectator, on whom the
theatre has imposed finished visions of the world' (2000: 155). The
theatre of the oppressed, he concludes, is 'a rehearsal of revolution'
(2000: 155).

A company whose work has been widely associated with Artaud's
'theatre of cruelty' but which nonetheless maintains a steadfast commitment to political activism is The Living Theatre, founded in the
late 1940s by Julian Beck and Judith Malina. One of their most infa-
mous pieces was *Paradise Now*, first performed at the Avignon Festival
in 1968. *Paradise Now* invited its audiences to participate in a series of
taboo-defying acts, including – in a sequence titled 'The Rite of Universal
Intercourse' – public nudity and sexual contact. The purpose, as Shomit

Mitter explains, was 'to ensure that the audience would experience rather than merely bear witness to the evolution of emancipation' (2005: 96). Audiences were invited to discover the oppressive nature of social, political, and cultural norms by flouting them, and the piece concluded with a procession into the street 'in a celebration of the death of authority' (Mitter 2005: 97). Malina has more recently described her aesthetic as an attempt 'to find some key to the horrible alienation of people sitting there listening', and to create for her audiences 'a true role in which choices must be made that will reveal to them their own decision making processes' (Callaghan 2003: 24–5).

The Performance Group's *Dionysus in '69*, which was first performed in the same year as *Paradise Now*, was very similar in many respects, though ultimately rather more sceptical in its politics. Directed by Richard Schechner, *Dionysus in '69* was staged in the flexible space of the Performing Garage on New York's Wooster Street. Spectators were seated upon wooden towers around the edge of the garage, and the action took place both in the centre of the space and among the audience. The narrative was based upon Euripides' *The Bacchae*, a tale of the controlling but repressed young king Pentheus and his destruction by the forces of Dionysus, the god of wine, fertility, and ecstasy. William Finley, the actor playing Dionysus, encouraged spectators to give themselves over to their impulses:

> Now for those of you who agree with what I've just told you – that I am the God – you're going to have a wonderful time tonight. (*audience laughter*) As for the rest of you... you're going to be in for an hour and a half of being up against the wall. (*audience laughter*) If you did agree, and believe what I just said, you can join us in what we do next, which is called an ecstasy. It's a dance for joy, in honour of me, the God... You only have to promise me one thing: if you feel the impulse to dance, or to anything you want – like wiggling your fingers, or clapping your hands, anything you want – just do it.[3]

In the communal dance that followed, both actors and spectators removed their clothing, many of them dancing with wild abandon – though others, of course, maintained their reserve. This tension between self-restraint and Dionysian hedonism was sustained throughout the performance: at one point, Pentheus would attempt to seduce a female audience member; at another, spectators were encouraged to join in with a ritual of mutual caressing similar to *Paradise*

Now's 'Rite of Universal Intercourse'. At the end of the performance, Dionysus/William Finley returned, wearing a suit and carrying a microphone, to announce his candidacy 'for President of the United States':

> Now, what I'm prepared to offer to you is absolute freedom.... You do what you feel like! And if you do what you feel like, you feel good! And if you cause pain, you feel good pain! But the most important thing to remember is: a vote for Finley in '68 brings Dionysus in '69! God bless you all!

Like *Paradise Now*, the sequence culminated in a procession out onto the street; cast and spectators sang and carried Finley aloft as he shouted political slogans.

Dionysus in '69's key departure from *Paradise Now*, however, was in its political implications. Its victory of the Dionysian was charged with ambiguity. Those spectators who had given themselves over to Dionysus had become complicit in his cruel destruction of Pentheus and his family; Schechner himself has described Dionysus as 'a capricious god enjoying jealous vengeance' (1990: 445). The crowd who followed Finley out onto Wooster Street at the end were performing the role of a politically powerful but unquestioning mob. Numerous productions since have adopted the same basic strategy of coercing their audiences into questionable moments of crowd behaviour in order to subsequently shock them at their own loss of self-control: Pip Utton's one-man play *Adolf* (1997) and Ontroerend Goed's *Audience* (2011) are notable examples. The effect is essentially Brechtian, alienating audiences from their own enactment of a powerful group identity. In each case, spectators find themselves forced into either direct involvement, active resistance, or passive complicity.

As this suggests, the audience is never *really* unified. Even those moments that are marked by the most powerful feelings of togetherness for some audience members are likely to generate feelings of alienation, exclusion, or resistance in others. Blau is sceptical about the widely held desire 'for the audience as community, similarly enlightened, unified in belief, all the disparities in some way healed by the experience of theatre'; for him, such desire 'could never be satisfied in the theatre as anything but a fiction' (1990: 10, 11). Blau argues that the audience is 'not so much a mere congregation of people as a body of thought and desire'; it is 'what *happens* when, performing the signs and passwords of a play, something postulates itself and unfolds in response' (1990: 25).

The idea of 'the audience' as a fictional construction that may never be fully lived by actual spectators has been explored in numerous post-dramatic theatre pieces. The most famous of these is perhaps Peter Handke's 1966 play *Offending the Audience*, a text in which an unspecific number of speakers address the audience directly, meditating on the processes and conventions of theatrical spectatorship. 'You are the subject matter,' a speaker informs the audience: 'You are the centre of interest. No actions are performed here, you are being acted upon' (1997: 15). An opening stage direction, however, makes it clear that '*Under no circumstance should the audience get the impression that the words are directed at them*' (1997: 5). A later line appears to confirm this: 'You need not feel that we mean you. You cannot feel that we mean you. No mirror is being held up to you. We don't mean you' (1997: 8). There is a sense that the piece both is and is not about the people who are watching it, because it describes an audience which it might reasonably second-guess but which it could not hope to fully anticipate. 'You have recognized the dialectical structure of the piece', it tells its audience at one point (who might, of course, have recognised no such thing). 'You have recognized a certain spirit of contrariness' (1997: 13).

Later pieces such as Forced Entertainment's *Showtime* (1996), Tim Crouch's *The Author* (2009), and Chris Goode's *Who You Are* (2010) owe an obvious debt to Handke's playful ambivalence. *Showtime* opens with a nervous solo performer telling his audience that there is 'a word for people like you' – insinuating an unhealthy voyeurism – before informing them that that word is 'audience'. *Who You Are*, meanwhile, characterises its audience in a way that makes the impossibility of such characterisations clear:

> There we are, in our rehearsal room, trying to figure out whatever theatre piece we're making.... And then somebody mentions you.... You, the audience, are not yet the audience. You're out there in the world, dispersed across your fifty or a hundred or five hundred lives. You, the audience, are watching the telly or making a sandwich or conducting extramarital affairs or looking up Popocatépetl on Wikipedia.
>
> (Goode 2011: 469)

Such impossibility is addressed even more directly in *The Author*, in which the fictional audience member Adrian sits among his (real) fellow spectators and observes that sometimes the most fantastical – the most made up thing in the theatre is us! . . . I saw a play last year. And I remember thinking, 'that writer has imagined me'. I've been imagined! Poorly imagined! The audience has been badly written.

(Crouch 2011b: 167)

Significantly, Crouch specifies that his play 'is set in the Jerwood Theatre Upstairs at the Royal Court Theatre – even when it's performed elsewhere' (2011b: 164). *The Author* provides a blistering attack on the complacency of a certain kind of spectatorship – Adrian boasts at one point, 'I've seen a dead baby get eaten! That was great!' – but the play stops short of accusing its own audience directly (2011b: 192).

As we have seen, much of the theory underpinning the most influential theatre practice of the 20th century is based on the idea that the usual, automatic processes of spectatorship are somehow unsatisfactory. In both the Brechtian and Artaudian paradigms, the spectator needs to be released from his or her passivity – into greater political awareness on the one hand, and into a more intense involvement on the other. In turning the audience's attention towards the practices of spectatorship, even pieces such as *Offending the Audience* might be seen as operating within the Brechtian paradigm; noting the play's self-description as 'the prologue to your future visits to the theatre', Tom Kuhn argues that Handke wanted his audience 'to watch *all* plays with greater irritation, mistrust and awareness', and deplored 'the dim-witted passivity and consumerism of the public' (1997: 27, xiii). The idea is prevalent in academic studies, too, from Bennett's contrast between the 'productive and emancipated spectator' and the passive one (1997: 4) to Graham Holderness's argument in *Cultural Shakespeare* that as the audience becomes 'further removed from the action', it becomes 'a passive consumer of a fixed ideology rather than an active constituency' (2001: 46).

Rancière, however, understands spectatorship rather differently. In his 2007 essay 'The Emancipated Spectator' (which forms the basis of his 2009 book of the same name), he argues that 'we must question the very footing on which those ideas are based' and queries the equivalence 'of seeing and passivity' (2007: 274). 'The spectator is active', he insists, 'just like the student or the scientist: He observes, he selects, he compares, he interprets' (2007: 277). Spectatorship, for Rancière, 'is not a passivity that must be turned into activity' but rather 'our normal situation': 'We learn and teach, we act and know, as spectators who link what they have seen and told, done and dreamed' (2007:

279). Theatre, he argues, need not attempt to 'liberate' its spectators, but should rather trust that they are free to make meaning in a way that is already active and empowered; it should 'call for spectators who are active interpreters, who render their own translation, who appropriate the story for themselves, and who ultimately make their own story out of it' (2007: 280).

Audience research

Like some of the theorists considered above, Rancière contests 'the presupposition that the essence of theatre is the essence of the community' and that there is 'something more interactive' and 'more communal' about theatre audiences than there is about audiences of the mass media (2007: 278). He argues that 'this "something" is nothing more than the presupposition that the theatre is communitarian in and of itself', and suggests that this assumption 'always runs ahead of the performance and pre-dates its actual effects' (2007: 278). In the opening chapter of his book *Liveness*, Philip Auslander likewise describes himself as having become 'impatient' with

> traditional, unreflective assumptions that fail to get much further in their attempts to explicate the value of 'liveness' than invoking clichés and mystifications like 'the magic of live theatre,' the 'energy' that supposedly exists between performers and spectators in a live event, and the 'community' that live performance is often said to create among performers and spectators.
>
> (2008: 2)

Catherine Silverstone finds these three 'clichés and mystifications' especially prevalent in actors' accounts of performing at the reconstructed Shakespeare's Globe, and describes them as 'fictions' (2005: 46).

The contributions of cognitive science, however, would seem to suggest that, in fact, a communal energy and a sense of community among theatre audiences are far from 'fictions'. McConachie surveys recent research which shows that 'emotions are catching' and notes that emotional 'contagion' in the theatre is 'automatic and usually very quick' (2008: 95, 97). He endorses Jill Dolan's book *Utopia in Performance* in which Dolan objects to Auslander's scepticism and affirms her commitment to a politically engaged humanism (Dolan 2005: 40, 141; McConachie 2008: 97). McConachie concludes a 2007 article by suggesting that experimental procedures 'from post-performance interviews to brain scanning' might 'resolve some of the ongoing disputes in our discipline' (2007: 577); Ralley and Connolly, meanwhile, suggest the employment of portable electronic data collection devices in order to research spectators' individual and communal responses (2010: 61–2). This method, they argue, would address 'multiple concerns' in theatre studies: 'the capture of concurrent responses, the unfolding of experience through time...and the fundamental question of the extent to which audience reactions diverge and converge' (2010: 62).

Empirical research into the actual responses of theatre audiences is unusual in theatre studies, but the field is growing. As De Marinis notes, while debate about what performance *should* do to a spectator is vigorous,

> [w]hat the spectator *actually* does while attending a performance and what action, or kind of action, the performance *really* carries out on the theatregoer are issues that have been neglected and continue to be neglected.
>
> (1993: 159)

In research on actual audiences, says De Marinis, 'we are dealing mostly with empirical inquiries of a rather traditional kind': demographic data about theatre attendance, the social composition of audiences, and so forth (1993: 160). Freshwater points out that theatre scholars who survey audiences for their responses 'remain in a small minority among theatre studies scholars' (2009: 33), and she speculates that

> perhaps a residual distrust of the mass and a lack of respect for the intellectual and interpretive capacities of 'ordinary' theatre-goers might explain why scholars continue to cite the opinions and reactions of published reviewers rather than asking audience members what they think.
>
> (2009: 37)

Certainly media studies is well ahead of theatre studies in this respect; a glance through the contents of the audience research journal *Participations*, for example, reveals that the vast majority of work in this area has been done on the reception of film, television, and popular music. Having said this, a great deal of valuable work has been done on theatre audiences too, and, as we shall see, it has both supported and challenged some of the discipline's major claims about the nature of theatrical spectatorship.

In fact, theatre studies has a long, if undervalued, history of empirical audience research. Sauter (2002) provides a very useful survey, and he begins his history in 1924 with the Russian director Vsevolod Meyerhold's attempts to document audience activity. Meyerhold's assistant director, Vasily Fyodorov, came up with a list of 20 possible responses:

> a silence; b noise; c loud noise; d collective reading; e singing; f coughing; g knocks or bangs; h scuffling; i exclamation; j weeping; k laughter; l sighs; m action and animation; n applause; o whistling; p catcalls, hisses; q people leaving; r people getting out of their seats; s throwing of objects; t people getting onto stage.
>
> (Stourac and McCreery 1986: 20)

Fyodorov recorded every instance of each of these at five performances during Meyerhold's 1924–1925 season, and the publication of the results apparently caused 'vigorous debate' (Sauter 2002: 116). Scientific advances have since made it possible for researchers to observe audience response in much greater detail: Heribert Schälzky, for example, was able to measure patterns in theatre spectators' heartbeats, breathing and sweating (1980), while Tim Fitzpatrick's research has involved the use of an 'eye-mark' camera that tracks spectators' visual activity against a video recording of a performance (1990, Fitzpatrick and Batten 1991). As Matthew Reason points out, research of this kind has also made use of push-button technology, recording 'likes' and 'dislikes'; neurophysiological scanning techniques; and the observation of physical or audible audience behaviour (2010: 18).

Such research tends to focus on what Henri Schoenmakers calls *reception processes* – the moment-by-moment experience of the spectator during a performance (1990). Schoenmakers identifies a second type of audience research as being concerned with *reception results* – spectators' responses *after* the event. This kind of research is much more prevalent in media studies, and tends to take the form of audience surveys and interviews. Bennett summarises two important studies of theatre audiences from the late 1970s and early 1980s: Frank Coppieters' audience interviews (1981), and Anne-Marie Gourdon's use of audience questionnaires (1982; Bennett 1997: 90–2). Coppieters' research into the responses of a university audience to two performances of *The People Show* in 1976 reached four main conclusions:

(i) One's attitude toward/perception of/relationship with the rest of the public is an important factor in one's theatrical experience.

(ii) Perceptual processes in the theatre are, among other things, a form of social interaction.

(iii) Inanimate objects can become personified and/or receive such strongly symbolic loadings that any anxiety about their fate becomes a crux in people's emotional experience.

(iv) 'Environmental' theatre goes against people experiencing homogeneous group reactions.

(1981: 47)

Coppieters' first two conclusions were echoed in Gourdon's study (1982), which stressed the social nature of theatregoing and the impact of context and expectation upon the formation of response. Both projects, says Bennett, encourage us 'to see complex connections between actual theatre audiences and social systems, between the notion of a theatre-going public and contemporary culture' (1997: 92).

A key figure in the development of the notion of dramatic performance as a sociocultural 'theatrical event' is Willmar Sauter. Sauter – now a leading member of the International Federation for Theatre Research's 'Theatrical Event' working group – provides a detailed retrospective of his audience research in a 2010 article in *About Performance*. He explains that he started carrying out audience interviews in 1980, collecting over 500 in one theatre season. Frustrated that 'there was no way of continuing the interviews after the performance', however, he began to develop more sophisticated methodologies (2010: 242). Sauter's next phase was to analyse the essays of his students, noting that although a 'real', socially diverse audience would be unlikely to write short essays for theatre researchers, the exercise showed that 'a free expression of opinions was preferable to interviews of any kind' (2010: 244). Sauter thus developed the methodology of 'Theatre Talks,' in which a small group of playgoers who have attended a performance together sit down afterwards and talk about it, and their externally chaired conversation is recorded for analysis. 'One of the basic principles of Theatre Talks', explains Sauter, 'is that no questions are actually asked':

The group leader accompanying each talk does not ask questions, but invites the participants to speak to each other. What they do not talk about is as interesting as the ideas and observations brought up during the conversation.

(2002: 124)

Sauter analysed the conversations of 25 groups, comprising 180 participants, each of whom had seen six shows in Stockholm over a period of seven weeks in 1983. He returned to the methodology in numerous subsequent projects.

Sauter's more recent use of 'semantic differentials' has allowed him to analyse audience reception in statistical form. Respondents are given a list of adjectives or statements, which they grade (on a scale of 1–10, for example) as being more or less reflective of their own feelings and opinions. The resulting data has provided some evidence for the influence of sociopolitical context on audience response, but some challenges too: groups of students from Holland, Sweden, and Germany responded to a production of *Carmen* in ways which were very different from each other group, for example, but there were 'almost no differences between male and female students' (2010: 253). An investigation into the alleged anti-Semitism of a controversial *The Merchant of Venice* at the Royal Dramatic Theatre in Stockholm, meanwhile, compared spectators' opinions before and after the performance, in order to determine whether or not it had changed their ideas about Jews. Sauter's team asked spectators to identify, on a five-point scale, the extent to which they either agreed or disagreed with particular statements about the reasons for anti-Semitism. The results, says Sauter, were 'shocking':

> One out of four spectators believed that the statement 'The reason for anti-Semitism is the behaviour of the Jews in history' was more correct after the performance than they had thought before. Moreover, 4% changed their opinion completely: before the performance they thought it was not correct, but after the performance they confirmed the same statement as being correct.
>
> (2010: 257)

Sauter's team then surveyed two other productions of the play, one in Berlin and one in a small town in Sweden; they found that the Berlin production, which 'consciously counteracted' anti-Semitic attitudes, prompted hardly any change in spectators' opinions on this matter, while audiences of the Swedish production showed 'a slight increase of anti-Semitism' (2010: 258). The project, concludes Sauter, indicates a possible 'new direction' for reception research: 'Instead of speculating about the effects of theatrical performances on their audiences, we have been able to show the actual outcome' (2010: 259).

John Tulloch's analysis of *Shakespeare and Chekhov in Production and Reception* (2005) builds upon many of Sauter's ideas. Tulloch describes his book as a collection of 'local case studies, most of them based on detailed ethnographic and qualitative research at theatres and among audiences in different countries' (2005: ix). Like Sauter, Tulloch employs the methodologies of Theatre Talks and semantic differential questionnaires in addition to more traditional interviews and surveys; he too notes the differences in patterns of response between different social groups, contrasting the responses of Russian literature students with those of Theatre students, for example, or comparing British and American students' readings of a particular production (2005: 98–112, 128–53). Much of his data is derived from responses to open-ended interview or survey questions, which are then post-coded by his research team into observable categories. Tulloch's analysis in Chapter 2 focuses on the 'sensory', 'artistic', and 'symbolic' aspects of spectatorship (described above), while Chapter 9 explores 'the liveness factor': 'a particular sensory pleasure in live physical proximity, even a sense of personal invitation, between actor and audience member' (2005: 73–4, 280). Tulloch's findings seem to support some of McConachie's assertions about spectatorship and embodiment, stressing the importance of sensory pleasures, intimacy, and community (2010: 285–6).

A great deal of empirical audience research seems to demand a reconsideration of 'liveness'. As we saw in Chapter 2, Peter Eversmann's interviews with Dutch spectators revealed an emphasis upon physical reactions; they also 'frequently stressed that the live presence of the actor is the essential formative element of theatre' (2004: 157). Matthew Reason criticises Auslander's *Liveness* on the basis that 'serious consideration of the perceptions of actual audiences is neglected', and describes the results of an 'exploratory exercise' into the question of 'how live performance is constituted for those that experience it' with students from the University of Edinburgh (2004). The National Endowment for Science, Technology and the Arts (NESTA), meanwhile, has investigated the phenomenon of liveness in relation to the National Theatre's recent practice of broadcasting theatrical performances live to cinemas around the world. Their research into the two NT Live pilots, *Phèdre* and *All's Well That Ends Well* (both 2009), 'confirms the centrality of "live" for the audience experience – both in the theatre and in cinemas' (Bakhshi et al. 2010: 2). NESTA's analysis of the responses of 1,316 cinema-goers and 1,216 theatregoers to a questionnaire shows that 84.3% of cinema audiences either agreed or strongly agreed with the statement, 'I felt real excitement because I knew that the performance was live' (2010: 9). Interestingly, the cinema audiences showed 'higher levels of emotional engagement with the production than those who had experienced the play at the National Theatre' (2010: 5) – NESTA found that 63.2% of cinema audiences claimed to have been 'transported to another world and lost track of time' (compared with 47.8% of theatre audiences), and that 88.2% felt themselves emotionally moved (compared with 72.7% in the theatre). One must question, of course, whether emotional engagement and imaginative escapism are the only measures of audience impact (the question is, perhaps, already biased towards a more cinematic understanding of spectatorship), but the findings are significant nonetheless. It may be that results like this indicate that not only are the theatrical performances broadcast by NT Live suitable for cinematic adaptation – some may actually be more suited to the medium than they are to the theatre. Laurie E. Osborne's work on DVD recordings of Shakespearean theatre productions has identified 'an increasing awareness of "to-be-filmedness" in live theatre' (2006: 54), and, indeed, NT Live's painstaking attention to visual detail and frequently filmic acting styles bear this out.

Audience research continues to play an increasingly important role in theatre studies. The tenth edition of *About Performance* (2010) was devoted to the theme of 'The Work of the Spectator in Live Performance', and many of its essays testify to a renewed drive in the discipline to investigate the responses of actual audiences rather than speculate on their behalf. Noting that academic writing 'inevitably privileges the readings of a select interpretive community', Fiona Fearon argues that 'the social production of meaning remains the preserve of experts unless we engage with some kind of ethnographic research of the "real" audience' (2010: 119). She, Reason, Sauter, and others provide examples of this kind of research in the volume.

Such practical research remains on the periphery of Shakespeare studies, but projects such as Penelope Woods' *Globe Audiences: Spectatorship and Reconstruction at Shakespeare's Globe* (2012) suggest that it is unlikely to remain so for much longer. Woods was embedded at Shakespeare's Globe for three years from 2007, undertaking research into the theatre's audiences. Woods and her research team held 40 open-ended conversations with 75 audience members during the 2009 season; she also noted the live responses of spectators in the theatre itself, as well as employing the more experimental methodologies of the 'Long Table' (a lengthy and informal discussion conducted by a group over food and wine, developed originally by the performance artist and academic Lois Weaver) and a more dispersed interview format in which spectators interviewed one another and reported back (2012: 351–2, 40). Woods decided that she was 'not interested in using written surveys to investigate audience response at the Globe', preferring the sociability of verbal conversation and reflection (2012: 48). Her study does, however, make use of the theatre's own market research data regarding audience demographics, and she frequently cites Front of House and Stage Management reports. Some of her conclusions are detailed in Chapter 7.

Theories of audience reception are, of course, implicit in almost any discussion of theatre, and this section of the book has merely surveyed some of the most influential. While its discussion has turned intermittently to Shakespearean performance, this has tended to be merely in order to illustrate particular methodologies or theories; Part III will take modern Shakespearean theatre practice as its focus. Ideas about what it is that a spectator does while watching a performance are clearly formative in any given theatre company's practice, as well as in its reception by reviewers. So, too, are assumptions about what it is that a spectator *should* do; indeed, many of the productions explored in Part III have had very specific designs upon their audiences. But audiences' actual responses are rarely circumscribed entirely by a production, and accordingly, the case studies in Part III will try to draw a sense, wherever possible, of spectators' actual reactions to performances. Much of this is drawn simply from my own observations of performances, live or on video, or from actors' and reviewers' accounts. The body of research on modern Shakespearean audiences, however, allows for a much more robust analysis, and studies such as those by Tulloch and Woods have, as the reader will see, proved extremely valuable. It is to be hoped that this body of work will continue to grow.

Part III
In Practice

4
Controlling the Audience?

This section of the book is about the practice of being a Shakespearean audience. It is easy to forget that being an audience is every bit as much a practice as, for example, acting, directing, or set design. We might think of the audience's role in the theatrical exchange as being merely to watch quietly and make sense of what happens in front of us. But as we saw in Part II, even this is not an entirely passive activity. Indeed, there is a strong case to be made that it is in the space between stage and audience that the 'play' actually happens. 'Play', as Jacques Lecoq recognised, is a verb as well as a noun. Plays *play* with their audiences, and audiences generally play in return. Without an audience to make sense of it, a play is much like Macbeth's 'tale/Told by an idiot': 'full of sound and fury,/Signifying nothing' (5.5.25–7).

The practice of being an audience is not fixed or unchanging. Practices are, by their very nature, processual; they are responsive to changes in their social contexts. For this reason, the chapters that follow will on the whole avoid discussion of the historical audiences for whom Shakespeare wrote his plays. This is not to deny the undoubted value in exploring the practices of playgoing in Shakespeare's own time: studies such as those by Harbage (1941), Cook (1981), Gurr (2004), and Dawson and Yachnin (2001) have provided immensely useful insights in this field, examining the social, institutional, material, and ideological frames of reference within which Shakespeare's spectators might have made sense of their theatrical experiences. It is merely that the focus of this section of the book lies elsewhere. The next few chapters are part of a growing body of work that explores the practice of being a *modern* Shakespearean audience: one might thus read it as a contribution to the conversation in theatre studies between such writers as Worthen (1997, 2003), Brown (1999), Escolme (2005), Tulloch (2005), and Kennedy (2009), all of whom examine particular examples of modern Shakespearean spectatorship. Such writing is, of course, subject to some very practical limitations: the author's theatregoing experience will inevitably be restricted to particular companies and their productions, and this book is no exception. As a result, the discussion here is mostly limited to productions that were performed in Britain during the late 20th and early 21st centuries.

There is a third body of writing on Shakespearean spectatorship that is concerned neither with specific historical practices nor with particular modern ones. This tradition, which has a long and illustrious pedigree, argues that certain kinds of audience practice are encoded within the written Shakespearean text itself. An early example might be found in Arthur Colby Sprague's *Shakespeare and the Audience: A Study of the Technique of Exposition* (1935), which suggests that Shakespeare's use of formal features such as soliloquies and asides steers the audience's affective response in particular ways. Such studies proliferated especially in the 1970s and 1980s, influenced perhaps by the reader-response criticism of figures such as Norman H. Holland, Wolfgang Iser, and Stanley Fish. Their titles frequently emphasise Shakespeare as a god-like (or, at least, director-like) controller of his audience's experiences: examples include Peter Bilton's *Commentary and Control in Shakespeare's Plays* (1974), E. A. J. Honigmann's *Seven Tragedies: The Dramatist's Manipulation of Response* (1976), Ann Pasternak Slater's *Shakespeare the Director* (1982), and Jean E. Howard's *Shakespeare's Art of Orchestration: Stage Technique and Audience Response* (1984). The idea of the author as a governing force is even clearer in essay titles that refer to 'Shakespeare's Control of Audience Perception and Response' (Howard 1980) or 'The Playwright's Reflections and Control of Audience Response' (Kernan 1982).

Though this chapter will take a very different view of the author's role in the production of audience response, it may be helpful to spend a few moments surveying some of the key ideas that emerge from this school of thought. Howard perhaps speaks for many when she states at the beginning of *Shakespeare's Art of Orchestration*:

> I assume that in writing plays for performance Shakespeare was partly writing with an eye to the potential responses of the audience; that is, as he orchestrated the play, he was indirectly orchestrating the theatrical experience of the viewer.

(1984: 6)

Howard argues that particular 'aural, visual, and kinaesthetic effects' are implied in the Shakespearean text (1984: 2), and she concludes that the audience's involvement in a play's 'rhythms of restraint and release' must become 'integral to our understanding of what the play is about and to an understanding, finally, of its moral vision' (1984: 202). This argument is echoed in Kent Cartwright's *Shakespearean Tragedy and its Double: The Rhythms of Audience Response* (1991), which asserts 'an Artaudian concern for the effect of performance upon an audience' and examines the ways in which Shakespeare's tragedies 'invite a rhythm of "engaged" and "detached" responses from the audience', producing a particular kind of 'conflict or tension' between these responses (1991: ix). The idea that particular rhythms are implied in the texts is widespread in modern Shakespearean theatre practice, too: Peter Hall's *Shakespeare's Advice to the Players* (2003) and John Barton's enormously influential *Playing Shakespeare* (1984), for example, provide sustained practical guides. For Hall, rhythm is encoded in the smallest details of the text, through which 'Shakespeare tells the actor when to go fast and when to go slow' (2003: 13), while Barton attempts to unearth 'the *hidden direction* Shakespeare himself provided in his verse and his prose' (1984: 6–7; emphasis original).

The level of control that is supposed to be exerted by Shakespeare on his audience's responses varies from study to study. Howard's title posits an author who 'orchestrates' his audience's responses; Cartwright also uses this verb, alongside the domineering 'marshal' and the more laissez-faire 'invite'. The latter is the preferred term in Robert Hapgood's study *Shakespeare the Theatre-Poet* (1988), in which Hapgood also speaks of Shakespeare's 'guidance' of his audiences. This choice of language implies a relatively permissive and gentle author who allows his audience scope for a variety of responses; indeed, Hapgood argues that Shakespeare's texts 'provide broad outlines within which a range of options are left open' (1988: 217). In a chapter titled 'Audience-Response: *Macbeth*', he examines Shakespeare's subject-positioning in *Macbeth* – the level of access, for example, which the play allows its audience to Macbeth's thoughts and feelings – and acknowledges that spectators will differ in their levels of identification with the character. He notes, however, that

[e]ven those most inclined to identify with him will not – if they are responsive to Shakespeare's pointers – be able to do so altogether. Shakespeare's method of showing us Macbeth's public as well

as his private self and of observing him from a variety of external perspectives tends to discourage our total immersion in Macbeth's point of view.

(1988: 228)

Hapgood's anxiety here that some spectators will not be sufficiently 'responsive to Shakespeare's pointers' is telling, and betrays the notion of the author-in-control which in fact underpins his book. Indeed, Hapgood describes his study as having been 'prompted by my neo-conservative desire ... to reassert the primacy of the writer's creative presence' (1988: vii). Elsewhere, it is clear that Hapgood's Shakespeare is very much the god-like director, seeking 'a single audience-response', for example, to Gratiano's mocking of Shylock in the trial scene of *The Merchant of Venice*. At first, argues Hapgood, the audience are 'in unison' with Gratiano and they 'join in the jubilation'; when the character's jeering continues, however, 'the unanimity begins to dissolve and audience-responses contrary to Gratiano's begin to set in'. 'There is little or no laughter', Hapgood assures us, 'at Gratiano's three final speeches in this episode' (1988: 218–19).

A flexible-but-masterful Shakespeare is evoked, too, in E. A. J. Honigmann's *Seven Tragedies* (1976). Where Hapgood posits an author who 'often drives with loose reins ... with a firm yet supple hand' (1988: 260), Honigmann notes that 'when the dramatist pulls us in this direction or that, we may observe the fact that he pulls, and the means employed, without always thinking ourselves obliged to define exactly what we feel' (1976: 3). In both cases, audiences are recognised as being free to respond in multiple ways, but the scope of those responses is imagined as having been anticipated and delimited by the playwright. Honigmann's Shakespeare 'adjusts his plotting, and much else besides, to ensure that the audience will respond as he wants', but 'in his best work the response may pull simultaneously in different directions' (1976: 1, 136). Thus, for example, an audience's response to Brutus must be 'divided', though 'we respond more and more unsympathetically' as the play develops (1976: 39). Honigmann's 'we', though, is a precarious construction. Occasionally, as in his discussion of *Macbeth*, he slips from the first-person plural into the first-person singular, asserting that 'we' do or do not respond to the play in particular ways, before concluding that '*I* see Macbeth, when he reappears after the murder, not as a devil, a fiend, but as a man who has done himself a terrible injury' (1976: 128; my emphasis). That his 'we' is really a mask for 'I' becomes even clearer when he argues that certain critics, such as Wayne Booth or

D. H. Lawrence, get 'our' responses wrong: 'we should beware' of taking Lawrence's position that Hamlet is a 'repulsive' character, for example, and 'we might wish to argue, against Booth, that we respond to Macbeth with diminishing rather than "mounting" sympathy' (1976: 60, 136). In this last example, 'we' is even more nebulous, since it seems to assert a universal (or at least 'correct') response to the character while demonstrating simultaneously that even major critics cannot agree what that response might be.

A surprising addition to the branch of audience studies that posits an author-in-control is Bruce McConachie's *Engaging Audiences* (2008). I say 'surprising', because elsewhere in his book, McConachie strongly advocates the use of empirical data in writing about audience response (see Chapter 2). When he writes about particular plays, though, he examines the audience responses implied by the texts, rather than actual responses to specific performances; thus, for example, he discusses the imagined, anticipated reactions of 'most spectators' and 'most auditors' (2008: 68–9). In a case study of *Twelfth Night*, he asserts that though historical context 'matters', 'the basic operations of moral understanding have not changed all that much since the initial performance of *Twelfth Night*' (2008: 151); he then goes on to apply cognitive linguists George Lakoff and Mark Johnson's 'metaphorical systems for morality' to a detailed reading of the play (2008: 153–63). Malvolio emerges from this analysis as a figure who 'deserves' his suffering, and though McConachie recognises that the 'ethics of specific cultures, historical periods, and subcultures within those larger frameworks' will encourage spectators to judge Malvolio in different ways, he insists that a condemnation of the character is the 'normative' response (2008: 162–3).

One of the problems with the sorts of audience studies cited above is that they are easily contradicted with reference to specific examples of the plays in performance. While I have certainly seen Malvolios who deserved their comeuppances, I have also seen their opposites: Stephen Fry's Malvolio at Shakespeare's Globe (2012), for example, was a quiet, dignified figure who was bullied and humiliated by his social superiors simply for doing his job. When I saw the production, his delivery of 'I thank my stars, I am happy' (2.5.164) elicited audible expressions of sympathy from the audience, and his hurt bewilderment in the final scene as the plot was exposed was met not with laughter but with a heartbreaking silence; though I cannot speak for the rest of the audience, I certainly did not feel that my sympathy for this figure was in any way aberrant, and the production's reviews tended to document responses similar to my own.[1] Hapgood's analysis of *The Merchant of Venice* is just as readily refuted with reference to recent theatre practice: at the Globe in 1998, Andrew French's Gratiano elicited laughs and cheers from the spectators well into the trial scene, as both the Globe's archive video recording and Michael Billington's *Guardian* review attest (*Guardian*, 1 June 1998). Some years later at the Royal Shakespeare Theatre, Rupert Goold's production of the play (2011) featured a Gratiano played by Howard Charles who was so viciously thuggish and overtly anti-Semitic that even his first mockeries in the trial scene provoked little laughter from the audience. If, as Hapgood proposes, 'Shakespeare seems to expect that at Gratiano's first sally, everyone in the audience will be with him and that at his last, no one will be', Shakespeare was apparently wrong on both counts (1988: 219).

It might, of course, be objected that productions such as these are simply failing to pay adequate attention to the 'hidden directions' encoded in Shakespeare's texts. This certainly seems to be Honigmann's understanding when, in his additional chapter on 'The Study of the Audience and the Study of Response' in *Seven Tragedies Revisited*, he laments productions which 'consciously and unconsciously...get between the author and the audience' (2002: 244). Discussing *King Lear*, Honigmann notes with some dismay that 'a modern audience sometimes laughs in the wrong places' (1976: 102); historian David Starkey used the same phrase to describe the modern Globe audience's responses in an interview during the live broadcast of the theatre's *Measure for Measure* on BBC Four in 2004. For these commentators, there is a 'correct' response to particular moments in the Shakespearean text, and any failure to achieve it must lie in the inadequacies of either production or audience: presumably it is unthinkable that Shakespeare himself sought a response which his plays are unable to achieve consistently.

I certainly do not wish to argue that it is impossible for a theatrical text to anticipate certain kinds of responses. Clearly, any dramatist writing successfully for a working theatre must have a good sense of the tastes and likely reactions of the theatre's target audience. Chapters 5 and 6 will explore some of the ways in which Shakespeare employed theatrical traditions which would have been familiar to his audiences, presumably because these devices could be relied upon to produce a reasonably predictable response. But such predictions are made in a particular time and place, in a specific cultural context; surely no 'mechanisms of controlling audience-response' can be expected, as Honigmann seems to believe, 'to work, more or less, in any period, not merely on this or that occasion' (2002: 243). While McConachie's disapproval of Malvolio may well have been the 'normative' response in Elizabethan London (though we could never know this for certain), the social and cultural conventions that conditioned that antipathy have changed since – Maria's charge that the character is a 'kind of puritan' (2.3.135), for example, no longer carries the weight that it must have done in an early 17th-century playhouse. In the same way, it is hard to believe that the horrific events of the mid-20th century, or the ongoing Israel–Palestine conflict, have had no substantial effect upon the ways in which modern audiences respond to Gratiano's anti-Semitism. Changes in language, dramatic conventions, theatregoing habits, living conditions, national and global politics, and much more are surely influential in shaping the ways in which audiences form their responses to Shakespeare's drama.

It is true that Shakespeare's plays sometimes make particular demands of their audiences. Chapter 5 will examine the literal requests made by Shakespeare's liminal chorus figures, while Chapter 6 will analyse some of the ways in which direct addresses from the plays' fictional characters can work to position audiences in relation to the performance. There are certainly passages in Shakespeare which seem to be structured in order to provoke particular responses at the most mechanical level: when Paulina draws the curtain upon Hermione's statue with the words 'see' and 'behold' (*The Winter's Tale*, 5.3.19, 20), for example, or when Hamlet instructs his mother to 'Look here upon this picture, and on this' (3.4.52), there is a clear invitation for spectators to direct their attention towards the objects indicated. Several passages seem to be written primarily to provoke audience laughter: examples might include Lance's 'itemisation' of the milkmaid in *The Two Gentlemen of Verona* (3.1.291–369), or Dromio's description of Nell's body as if it were the 'globe' in *The Comedy of Errors* (3.2.116–44). In both of these cases, the dialogue is structured as a series of one-liners, each with a quick set-up (Speed's 'items' in *The Two Gentlemen of Verona*, Antipholus's questions in *The Comedy of Errors*), and an equally speedy pay-off (Lance and Dromio's responses), in much the same way that a modern stand-up comedian might structure a sequence of jokes.[2] Jeremy Lopez argues that the frequency of punning routines in Elizabethan drama is an indicator of their popularity and notes that audiences 'know how to respond to puns: by acknowledging that they get the joke' (2003: 38). Whether such sequences provoke the invited laughter *today* is largely dependent on the ability of their performers to breathe life into dead puns: the most successful actors tend to employ mime and physical exaggeration in order to spell out the joke, or to point up the puns that have become lost to time with a shrug or an ad lib.

We can recognise a design in the texts, then, which is predicated upon the likely responses of Elizabethan and Jacobean audiences. But although such designs might be made to do similar work with modern audiences, they might also achieve very different effects. Shakespeare has become 'an enduring institution', argues Michael D. Bristol, because his plays are 'richly dialogized and thus answerable to unforeseen social and cultural circumstances' (1996: 11); they invite audiences to converse and to play with them, rather than interpellating spectators into predetermined subject positions. In a similar vein, John Russell Brown suggests that we should consider Shakespeare's plays 'as a site for collusion and remaking', rather than for 'the development and exposure of particular feelings', and notes that playtexts 'do not exist entirely in their own right' (1999: 15).

After all, it is audiences, not texts, who make meaning. This activity is undertaken in dialogue with the text, of course, but as Jennifer A. Low and Nova Myhill observe, 'many accounts of various sorts of spectatorship demonstrate that what a spectacle was intended to show and what its spectators ultimately made of it do not coincide with any great regularity' (2011: 5). Indeed, John Tulloch's research on audience responses to Trevor Griffiths and Richard Eyre's film version of *The Cherry Orchard* (1987) showed conclusively that only a small minority of respondents read the film 'from the spectator positions that the producers tried to design', with one scene being interpreted in line with Griffiths' stated intentions by only 7% of viewers (2005: 139, 152). To see audience response as prescribed by the text is, to borrow a famous phrase from Roland Barthes, 'to impose a limit on that text, to furnish it with a final signified, to close the writing' (1977: 147). For Barthes,

> a text is not a line of words releasing a single 'theological' meaning (the 'message' of the Author-God) but a multi-dimensional space in which a variety of writings, none of them original, blend and clash.
>
> (1977: 146)

It is the audience, or reader, upon whom 'all the quotations that make up a writing are inscribed without any of them being lost' (1977: 148). Barthes describes the act of reading in terms very similar to this book's understanding of spectatorship: 'as play, activity, production, practice' (1977: 162). It is this notion of audience practice to which W. B. Worthen subscribes when he argues that 'to think of performance as conveying authorized meanings of any kind, especially meanings authenticated in and by the text, is, finally, to tame the unruly ways of the stage' (1997: 3). The analyses that follow, then, should not be read as attempts to uncover something permanent about the effects of Shakespeare's plays in performance, but rather as an exploration of some of the meanings that audiences and theatre productions have produced in dialogue with those texts in particular circumstances.

5
Framing the Stage

Ushering the audience

There are several passages in Shakespeare's plays in which an audience is addressed, outside of the fictional world of the play, by a speaker who directly acknowledges their existence as a theatre audience. These take the form of prologues, epilogues, and chorus speeches. Six plays feature both a prologue and an epilogue (*2 Henry IV*, *Henry V*, *Troilus and Cressida*, *Pericles*, *All Is True*, and *Two Noble Kinsmen*), while four have epilogues only (*A Midsummer Night's Dream*, *As You Like It*, *All's Well That Ends Well*, and *The Tempest* – though this number rises to five if one counts *Twelfth Night*'s epilogue-like song). Four plays, moreover, feature a chorus or chorus-like figure who provides narration during the play itself (*Romeo and Juliet*, *Henry V*, *Pericles*, and *The Winter's Tale*). Such passages script both direct and indirect requests of the audience.

Douglas Bruster and Robert Weimann refer to these speeches as 'liminal'. Their book *Prologues to Shakespeare's Theatre* is, as its title suggests, specifically about prologues, but the theoretical model they propose is highly pertinent to a discussion of both epilogues and chorus speeches too. 'In ushering between stage and audience', they argue, 'the prologue inhabited and defined a threshold, a liminal space between the actual and the potential' (2004: 37). The concept of the 'liminal' derives from the anthropologist Arnold van Gennep's *The Rites of Passage* (1909), the focus of which was the 'symbolic and spatial area of transition' a subject must pass through during any social rite of passage (1960: 18). In liminality, he argued, a subject no longer remains within their former social status, but has not yet graduated to their new one: for a moment, for example, one is neither married nor unmarried, neither a member of the group nor an outsider. Van Gennep's understanding of the ritual process as a sequence of separation from everyday life, liminal transition, and subsequent re-incorporation was applied to a theory of theatrical performance by Victor Turner in *From Ritual to Theatre* (1982). In theatre as in ritual, Turner suggested, participants pass from normal social structure to 'antistructure', a space of liminality and play: they enter 'a period and area of ambiguity' where their roles are 'temporarily undefined' (1982: 24, 27). During this period, argues Turner, 'the past is momentarily negated, suspended, or abrogated, and the future has not yet begun' (1982: 44).

Van Gennep's phases of separation, transition, and incorporation clearly correspond with the performance-framing offered by prologues and epilogues. A prologue typically invites its playgoers to step outside of their everyday lives and enter a different mode of behaviour. The very act of speaking it is an implicit request for attention; indeed, some Elizabethan prologues quite overtly request silence from their audiences, while *2 Henry IV*'s prologue begins with the bold demand, 'Open your ears' (1). Sometimes a prologue makes a promise, as *Pericles*'s Gower does, 'To glad your ear, and please your eyes' (4), or asserts that paying due attention will be in the spectators' interests, and that the performance will be 'Worth two hours' travail' (*Two Noble Kinsmen*, 29). Prologues might beseech the audience's forbearance, requesting them to 'Piece out our imperfections with your thoughts' (*Henry V*, 23), or 'with patient ears attend' (*Romeo and Juliet*, 13). Sometimes they stress the need for the audience's imaginative investment, with an invitation to 'Think, when we talk of horses, that you see them' (*Henry V*, 26), or to 'Think ye see/The very persons of our noble story/As they were living' (*All Is True*, 25–7). Others, such as *Troilus and Cressida*'s, are more nonchalant: 'Like or find fault; do as your pleasures are' (30). Shakespeare's epilogues, meanwhile, are almost always an appeal for applause: an invitation for the audience to incorporate the nearly completed performance into ongoing life with a unanimous public gesture of approval. But while prologues and epilogues might well be thought of as 'separation' and 'incorporation' rites respectively, there is something ambiguous and transitional about them in themselves. A prologue announces the start of the play while simultaneously marking itself out as before-the-start; an epilogue not only comes after a play's conclusion, but also *constitutes* the conclusion. Mid-play chorus speeches seem similarly both to belong to the play and to stand outside of it: *Pericles*' Gower, for example, describes himself as standing 'i'th' gaps' (18.8).

Just as these figures' textual status is ambiguous, so is their relationship with the audience. Shakespeare's liminal speakers tend to be both

authoritative and deferential, commanding the audience with impera-
tives to 'Work, work your thoughts' (*Henry V*, 3.0.25) or to 'Be attent'
(*Pericles*, 10.11), while begging simultaneously for 'patience' and even
'pardon', flattering their hearers as 'gentle'.[1] Yu Jin Ko notes that
these appeals 'confer significant authority onto the audience, thus par-
tially releasing the meaning of the play from authorized interpretation'
(1999: 112). The stage may set the terms of the theatrical exchange and
may request particular kinds of response, but that exchange is entirely
reliant upon the audience's acceptance of those terms, which they may
do either completely, in part, or not at all. The liminal speech is indeed
a 'threshold', in Gérard Genette's sense of the term: 'a zone between
text and off-text, a zone not only of transition but also of *transaction*'
(1997: 2; emphasis original).

The speeches are liminal in an editorial sense, too. Tiffany Stern argues
that Shakespeare's prologues, epilogues, and chorus speeches – what she
calls 'stage-orations' – were probably temporary and 'the preserve of
early performances only' (2009: 82). They were generally written, she
suggests, in order to plead on the play's behalf during the first few performances, when the audience's performance of approval or disapproval
could make or break a play's (and its playwright's) fortunes. Companies are known to have composed prologues and epilogues for special
occasions, such as a boy player's graduation to his first adult role, or a
performance at court. Stage-orations, argues Stern, were seen as detach-
able, not an intrinsic part of the play text, and were 'regularly changed,
lost, found, and printed elsewhere' (2009: 82). Stern notes that *Romeo
and Juliet* has no prologue in the Folio, that *Henry V* has no Chorus
in its 'bad' quarto, and that the prologue to *Troilus and Cressida* sur-
vived only by chance. She suggests that several of Shakespeare's plays
(including *Merry Wives*, *2 Henry VI*, *The Tempest*, *Hamlet*, and *Othello*)
probably once had prologues which did not survive into print, and
that a line of Time's in *The Winter's Tale* ('remember well/I mentioned
a son o'th' King's', 4.1.21–2) seems to allude to an earlier prologue
which has also been lost (2009: 102, 107). Even the Chorus speeches
in *Henry V* – seemingly so central to the play's form and meaning –
may well have been regarded as temporary and provisional, since the
reference to the Earl of Essex's campaign in Ireland in the Act 5
prologue would have made sense only while the campaign was still
ongoing in the first half of 1599. Stern concludes that 'critics writing
about Shakespeare, and assuming prologues and epilogues were per-
manently part of the text, might profitably reconsider their position'
(2009: 118).

Given the evident detachability of Shakespeare's liminal texts, it is no surprise that they have frequently been cut in theatrical performance. This tradition was especially dominant during the era of 19th-century pictorial realism: James Loehlin notes that it had been customary to leave out *Romeo and Juliet*'s prologue until Henry Irving restored it at the Lyceum in 1882 (2002: 87), and Emma Smith reports that while *Henry V*'s Chorus was sometimes performed in the 18th and 19th centuries, it was just as frequently omitted or edited, presumably in order to avoid the scripted apologies for the 'unworthiness' of the play's presentation (2002: 83–4). Herbert Beerbohm Tree, a great advocate of pictorial realism, felt that any direct address to the audience would shatter illusion, so in his 1904 production of *The Tempest*, he replaced the epilogue with Prospero's 'Ye elves' speech (5.1.33–57) (Dymkowski 2000: 330). David Lindley reports that *The Tempest*'s epilogue was cut throughout most of the 19th century, but notes that it has been performed consistently in Stratford productions since the 1930s (2003: 84).

The 20th-century theatre's widespread challenges to realism evidently sparked a renewed interest in performing Shakespeare's liminal texts, and many modern productions have taken up the opportunities they offer for 'ushering' between audience and stage. It is in this liminal space that a production can define the kind of 'transaction' (to use Genette's term) that it wishes to make with its audience. Peter Brook's *A Midsummer Night's Dream* (1970), for example, famously concluded with the entire company departing through the auditorium, taking Puck's appeal to 'Give me your hands, if we be friends' (15) as a cue for the actors to shake the hands of audience members. By contrast, in Edward Hall's production for Propeller (2003), Simon Scardifield's Puck sat on the edge of the stage and spoke the epilogue very simply and sadly. Both productions had foregrounded the concrete reality of the stage – Brook's by creating the play's magical forest with stilts, trapezes, and circus tricks, Hall's with a small, all-male cast and a highly stylised design scheme – and in both cases, the stage's self-conscious presentation could quite evidently become the fictional world of the play only through the imaginative complicity and goodwill of the audience. But where Brook's production celebrated the unifying power of imaginative collaboration between actors and audience, Hall's seemed to mourn its passing.

There can be a particular kind of pleasurable charge when the moment of liminality is extended; Turner describes it as 'an instant of pure potentiality when everything, as it were, trembles in the balance' (1982: 44). In the epilogue to *As You Like It*, the actor playing Rosalind prolongs the audience's transition from the imaginative world to that of their

everyday lives by occupying a liminal space in which he or she is neither fully in nor fully out of character. In the text, the speaker is still
to some extent the female Rosalind during the first line ('It is not the
fashion to see the lady the epilogue', 1–2), but has morphed into a male
performer by the end ('If I were a woman...', 16–17). This ambiguity,
of course, presents an obstacle for the majority of modern productions
which feature a female actor as Rosalind: some have cut or altered the
line 'If I were a woman' (at the RSC in 1973 and 1992, for example,
and at Shakespeare's Globe in 1998), while others have cut the epilogue
altogether, or replaced it, as in Michael Boyd's 2009 production, with a
song. Juliet Stevenson saw the epilogue's ambiguity as a problem when
she performed it at Stratford in 1985, since the audience 'did not know
whether the characters were staying in Arden or not, or *who*, exactly,
was talking to them'; Stevenson preferred a reworked version in the
production's London transfer in which the epilogue 'clearly became a
separate event' (Shaw and Stevenson 1988: 71). Other Rosalinds have
embraced the epilogue's liminality: Sabrina Le Beauf performed it in
a 'Shakespeare Free For All' tank top at the festival of the same name
in 1992, for example, while at the Wyndham's Theatre in 2005, Helen
McCrory pulled out a copy of the Arden playtext to read the foot-
note to 'If it be true that good wine needs no bush' (3–4). At the
Globe in 2009, Naomi Frederick's Rosalind interrupted the audience's
applause to deliver her epilogue, hitching up her skirt upon the line
'If I were a woman' to reveal Ganymede's leather boots and breeches.
A male Rosalind, of course, will inevitably emphasise the speech's gender ambiguities: at the end of Cheek by Jowl's all-male *As You Like It*
(1991), Adrian Lester stepped forward, removed the headband which
he had worn in his female persona, and, as a figure who was somehow both male and female, flirted with some of the male members of
the audience (13–19). Alisa Solomon recounts her feeling upon witnessing this moment that it 'felt exhilarating, even liberating', reminding
her of contemporary performance works that 'take same-sex desire as a
given, not something to be explained, apologized for, or agonized over'
(1997: 26).

A playful sense of in-betweenness can be just as powerful, of course,
as the audience are ushered *into* a play, and the Cheek by Jowl *As You
Like It* is one of a number of modern Shakespearean productions to
have invented its own prologue (in this case, dividing the all-male cast
into 'men' and 'women' with the lines 'All the world's a stage,/And
all the men and women merely players'). The reason for this strategy
often seems to be to impose a sense of symmetry on a play where it is

missing in the text: *As You Like It* in particular seems to have attracted a number of 'invented prologues' which in some way anticipate its epilogue (some examples are given in Marshall 2004: 97). Productions of *The Winter's Tale*, too, frequently begin with some sort of sequence designed to foreshadow Time's speech in Act 4: Ronald Eyre's production (RSC, 1981), for example, opened with a masque in which the figure of Time was central, while at the start of Nicholas Hytner's production (National Theatre, 2001), the boy playing Mamillius delivered Shakespeare's Sonnet 12 as a Time-themed prologue, before returning halfway through the play as Time himself.

Other productions usher audiences into their fictional worlds in a more literal way. Iqbal Khan's production of *Much Ado About Nothing* (RSC, 2012) set the play in contemporary Delhi, and transformed the foyer of the Courtyard Theatre into as full a realisation of a modern Indian city centre as space and resources allowed. From the moment they set foot in the building, audiences were thus immersed in a visual cacophony of barrels, bicycles, fairy lights, parasols, and posters, against an incessant soundtrack of car horns and bicycle bells. Actors wandered the space in character as tourists, salesmen, police officers, and passers-by, interacting with each other and with the audience. This was modern India as commodity: sketched-in with easily portable signifiers and presented to the audience, who were positioned as tourists, as an exotic holiday destination. Spectators were invited to buy into this construction in a quite literal sense, too, since many of the products on offer – beads, scarves, garlands – were genuinely available to purchase from the theatre shop. Ian Rickson's *Hamlet* (Young Vic, 2011), meanwhile, provided what was perhaps a more nuanced process of separation and transition. This production invited its audiences to enter the Young Vic through its backstage space, which had been dressed to resemble the secure wing of a modern psychiatric institution. Playgoers were checked at the door by a surly orderly, before being allowed to continue, unsupervised, along a winding corridor which led past noticeboards, a bookcase, a small chapel, a drug cabinet, and an exercise room. Certain features of the decor seemed calculated to draw attention to themselves as symbols: a CCTV screen, a platter of 'funeral baked meats', the eclectic array of books on the bookshelf, a row of mysterious closed doors. When the play itself started, the audience had not only been introduced to its setting – the psychiatric hospital – but also been primed to read it metaphorically, and, perhaps, to 'find their own way' through it.

The most sustained sense of audience-ushering tends to come in productions of those plays which are most dominated by chorus figures:

Figure 5.1 Gower (Rawiri Paratene) speaks to the audience during *The Children of the Sea*, 2005. Image courtesy of Royal Botanic Garden Edinburgh

namely *Pericles* and *Henry V*. In Toby Gough's adaptation of *Pericles*, *The Children of the Sea* (Edinburgh Fringe, 2005), Rawiri Paratene's Gower literally ushered the audience around a series of locations in Edinburgh's Royal Botanic Garden (Figure 5.1). *The Children of the Sea* was performed by a combination of professional actors and survivors of the 2004 Indian Ocean tsunami, and its framing narrative depicted Gower telling the story of *Pericles* to a group of Sri Lankan orphans as the beginning of a healing process: 'lords and ladies in their lives', he assured us, 'Have read it for restoratives' (7–8). Paratene's Gower delivered fragments of Shakespeare's text alongside newly scripted narration for sequences where the dialogue had been replaced with mime or dance; he also drew attention to contemporary resonances, likening Marina's treatment in Mytilene, for example, to the modern-day trafficking of child prostitutes (Dachel 2006: 497). This Gower belonged both to the Sri Lankan setting of the frame, and to the here-and-now of performance; stopping at a location in the Garden with a clear view across the city, he announced, 'Here we are at Simonides' palace . . . ' – before adding, with a wry look, ' . . . in Edinburgh, Scotland'.

Another 2005 *Pericles* – Kathryn Hunter's production for Shakespeare's Globe – featured a frame-narrative in which Patrice Naiambana's Gower led Corin Redgrave's bereaved and elderly Pericles through a retelling of his own life story (the younger Pericles was played by a different actor), and once again, the idea was that the tale would bring about psychological healing for its hearer. Naiambana explained in the production's programme that his Gower was drawn from the West African tradition of the *griot* – an 'oral historian, story-teller and musician' (2005: 31). He often departed from the Shakespearean text, referring to and interacting with the audience, and like Paratene, he made several specific contemporary references (in this case, to subjects such as the Make Poverty History campaign, and President Bush's response to Hurricane Katrina). Dominic Cooke's RSC production of 2006 presented another *griot*-Gower in the form of Joseph Mydell. Like *The Children of the Sea*, Cooke's production was performed in promenade, though in this case the location was the converted Swan Theatre in Stratford. Mydell's Gower frequently took a position in the middle of the standing spectators, calmly narrating the ongoing tale to those around him, before summoning the world of the play by, for example, bringing his staff to the floor and swaying it slightly to create the sense of a ship at sea. In this performance, Gower's line 'Please you sit and hark' (20.24) was a direct invitation to the audience to sit down on the floor and witness the play's climax.

As these examples indicate, the tendency in the recent theatre history of *Pericles* is towards a presentation of the play as an example of collaborative, therapeutic, culture-transcending storytelling, which belongs at once both to the past and the present, combining Shakespearean myth with extra-textual contemporary references. Similar interpretations of the play could be found in, for example, James Roose-Evans' 2000 production for Ludlow Festival, Adrian Jackson's for Cardboard Citizens in 2003, and the National Theatre of Greece production by Giannis Houvardas which played at the Globe to Globe festival in 2012. In *Pericles*, the narrator's 'ushering' is presented almost without exception as both benevolent and trustworthy.

The story is not quite so straightforward when we come to the Chorus of *Henry V*. On the one hand, like the *Pericles* productions cited above, many productions of *Henry V* emphasise the Chorus's repeated requests for active audience engagement. In his appeals to the audience to 'let us.../On your imaginary forces work' (1.0.17–18), or to 'eke out our performance with your mind' (3.0.35), the Chorus co-opts the audience into a collaborative imaginative project, and productions such as the one which opened the newly reconstructed Shakespeare's Globe in 1997 unabashedly celebrate this complicity. In this example, Mark Rylance (who was the Globe's artistic director and also played Henry) delivered the opening prologue with what Emma Smith describes as an 'excited, exhortatory tone' (2002: 86), before eliciting a number of 'yeses' from the audience in answer to the question, 'Can this cockpit hold/The vasty fields of France?' (11–12); Pauline Kiernan reports that audiences 'invariably' responded in this way throughout the production's run (1999: 27). A series of different actors returned to deliver each subsequent Chorus speech, and the audience apparently remained vocal throughout, booing the conspirators as they were introduced during the Act 2 prologue, for example, and greeting Catherine in Act 3 with laughter, cheering and even wolf-whistles (Kiernan 1999: 30, 111; Smith 2002: 108, 137). Yu Jin Ko suggests that what the 'vocal members of the audience were affirming' at such moments was 'their intention of overcoming the various strains involved in the imaginative labour demanded of them by the play itself and the particular circumstances of its current performance' (1999: 107).

Other productions put deliberate strain upon the Chorus's relationship with the audience. In reviews of Nicholas Hytner's 2003 production for the National Theatre, Penny Downie's Chorus was interpreted variously as a 'history teacher' (*International Herald Tribune*, 28 May 2003), 'a hero-worshipping PA' (*Independent*, 14 May 2003), and a 'spin doctor who urges us to use our imaginations and then, without a trace of irony, tells us exactly what to think' (*Mail on Sunday*, 18 May 2003). Carrying a pile of books and wearing a long skirt and cardigan, this Chorus was, in Downie's own words, a woman who was 'steeped in history' and had 'fallen in love with her subject unquestioningly' (Downie 2003). The play itself, however, subverted her pro-Henry perspective, bringing up the lights on a Corporal Nym who was idly surfing TV channels in a pub just as the Chorus was trying to convince her audience that 'all the youth of England are on fire' (2.0.1). Adrian Lester's Henry was both calculating and callous, far from the heroic figure depicted in the Chorus's speeches, and as the play progressed, she slowly lost faith in her idealised image of him; by the epilogue, even her own official account of history had to admit the ultimate futility of his actions. In Michael Boyd's 2007 RSC production, Forbes Masson's Chorus was himself an anti-war figure, ironising his words as he spoke them. His prologue was delivered self-mockingly, replacing Shakespeare's reference to 'this wooden O' (13) with a disparaging description of the RSC's Courtyard Theatre as 'this rusty shed'. When he delivered the Chorus's promise to turn 'the accomplishment of many years/Into an hour-glass' (30–1), he corrected himself: 'Well, three-and-a-half hour glasses'. Later, as Geoffrey Streatfeild's Henry tried to claim that 'God fought for us' (4.8.120), Masson shook his head in disbelief. Perhaps most importantly, as Amanda Penlington observes, Masson's Chorus was able to distance himself from his own evocations of glorious English patriotism by the simple fact that he spoke them with a Scottish accent (2010: 177).

Estranging the audience

Gordon Parsons' review of Boyd's production described it as 'Brechtian', noting that the Chorus's commentary on the action of the play 'not only spurs our imaginations but inevitably encourages the audience to observe the action critically' (*Morning Star*, 14 November 2007). Parsons is echoing a strain of Shakespearean criticism here which considers Shakespeare's use of the Chorus a proto-Brechtian alienation device; Graham Holderness, for example, argues that '[t]he Choruses are there to foreground the *artificiality* of the dramatic event, placing a barrier between action and audience' (1985: 137).

Shakespeare's plays have frequently been interpreted as working to instil a critical distance between stage and audience. Brecht himself described Shakespeare's drama as 'a theatre full of A-effects' (1965: 58), though he also disapproved of what he perceived as Shakespeare's upper-class sympathies. Brecht was a 'fundamental inspiration' for Robert Weimann's analysis of Shakespearean dramaturgy in the latter's highly influential book *Shakespeare and the Popular Tradition in the Theatre* (1978), the English version of which was dedicated to Brecht's Berliner Ensemble colleagues Benno Besson and Manfred Wekwerth (Guntner et al. 1989: 231). For Weimann, Shakespeare's theatre was characterised by a 'dual perspective, which encompasses conflicting views of experience' (1987: 243): the authoritative fictional *locus* of Shakespeare's play-world would be regularly undercut, Weimann argued, by the *platea* dimension of the stage – those figures who belonged to the here-and-now of the audience. Weimann explains in a later article that 'the *locus* tended to privilege the authority of what and who was represented', while the *platea* dimension 'privileged the authority not of what was represented...but of what was representing and who was performing' (1992: 503). Thus the *locus* 'was usually defined in accordance with a certain amount of verisimilitude, decorum, aloofness from the audience, and representational closure', while the clowning, wordplay and direct address of the *platea* 'helped potentially to undermine whatever respect the represented *loci* of authority invoked for the Elizabethan audience' (1992: 503–4).

A brief analysis of *Romeo and Juliet* might provide an illustration of this theory. Certain characters in the play belong almost entirely to the fictional world of Verona: Romeo and Juliet themselves come from a story that predates Shakespeare's retelling by several decades. They speak in verse, frequently in rhyme, and present an idealised and elevated image of poetic love (the elevation is, of course, literal in the two famous balcony scenes, 2.1 and 3.5). But they share the stage with comic, prose-speaking characters who belong not to the historical world of Verona but to an Elizabethan present. The servants in 1.5 are clearly English, with names such as Peter, Anthony, Susan Grindstone, and Nell (1.5.9), while the musicians of 4.4 are called Matthew Minikin, Hugh Rebec and Simon Soundpost (4.4.156–62); the latter group, along with the clown Peter, interrupt 4.4's scene of mourning with a sequence of music and wordplay which is often cut in modern performance. Characters such as Juliet's Nurse, meanwhile, span both *locus* and *platea*, interacting regularly with both the *platea*-like characters and the characters of the main plot.

For Weimann, *platea*-like characters 'help point out that the ideas and values held by the main characters are relative to their particular position in the play' (1987: 228). Thus, for example, Mercutio – who, like the Nurse, combines elements of both *locus* and *platea* – subverts the stylised discourse of poetic love by mocking those who cry 'Ay me' or rhyme 'love' with 'dove' (2.1.10), just moments before we witness Juliet do both (the former at 2.1.67, the latter at 2.4.7). Likewise, the Nurse consistently undercuts Juliet's poetry with sexual innuendo; Weimann argues that 'Juliet's grace and the elevated nature of her love are delicately balanced by the robust tenor of the nurse's bawdy wit' (1987: 243). In light of this, suggests David Wiles, Elizabethan spectators must have perceived 'that their own identities and moral codes existed in relation to opposites and alternatives' (1987: 93). In *Romeo and Juliet*, he argues, 'the self-sacrificial, the reproductive, the lecherous and the institutionalized aspects of love all compete against the romantic' (1987: 94). It is a fundamentally Brechtian understanding of the play's workings: hegemonic and unconsciously adopted ideals are 'made strange' by the self-conscious and dialogic presentations of the stage.

One of the most striking passages in which Shakespeare juxtaposes a faraway fictional space with the world of his audience is the frame narrative to *The Taming of the Shrew*. The play's induction sequence frames *The Taming of the Shrew* itself as a play-within-a-play, part of an elaborate hoax designed to convince the drunken tinker Christopher Sly that he is a lord. For the Elizabethan audience, this framework would have provided a distinctly English counterpoint to the play-world of Padua – Sly speaks, for the most part, in colloquial prose, and makes specific references to inhabitants of, and locations around, 16th-century Warwickshire. It is impossible to say for certain how Shakespeare's company would have staged the play, but had Sly remained an onstage spectator for its entire duration, his presence may have worked, as Holderness suggests, 'in the self-reflexive, metadramatic and ironic manner of Brecht's epic theatre' (1989: 25). If this were indeed the case, argues Holderness, then Katherine's final speech of submission in the play

> might well have been delivered on the Elizabethan stage with appropriate detachment, distancing and irony to an audience highly sceptical of such propagandist rhetoric; offered as a challenge and provocation to debate rather than as an attempt at ideological incorporation.
>
> (1989: 25)

The Brechtian potential of the Sly framework has certainly been explored in a number of modern stagings of the play, where it has allowed varying degrees of disjunction from the main 'taming' plot. Since Sly no longer belongs directly to the world of the audience, several productions have re-cast him as a modern spectator: Michael Bogdanov's *Shrew* (1978), for example, opened with a drunken Sly harassing a female usherette, complaining that 'no bloody woman's going to tell me what to do', before invading the stage and tearing apart the set; the Globe's 2012 production had a modern-dress, lager-swilling Sly climb up onto the stage from the yard, to gasps of shock from surrounding playgoers.

Edward Hall made extensive use of the Sly framework in his production for Propeller (2006) (Figure 5.2). When I saw the production at London's Old Vic in 2007, the framing was evident as the audience entered the building: actors in character as modern-day wedding ushers were milling around in the aisles of the auditorium, and were gradually joined by more of the cast as the beginning of the play approached. Dugald Bruce-Lockhart's Sly was sitting onstage, fully lit, interacting with (or, rather, making gestures at) various spectators in both the stalls and the galleries. It soon became clear that we had been cast as guests at Sly's wedding, and that he was extremely drunk; as the play began, Sly staggered into the ceremony and collapsed at the altar, causing his veiled bride to run away sobbing. The father-of-the-bride, condemning

Figure 5.2   Kate (Simon Scardifield) and Petruccio (Dugald Bruce-Lockhart) in Propeller's *The Taming of the Shrew*, 2006, copyright Philip Tull

his prospective son-in-law as a 'whoreson drunken knave', sent him packing.[2] The suggestion for Sly's gulling then became not the invention of a single 'Lord', but an idea which was shared and developed by all the characters present on stage. As the plan began to take shape, actor Simon Scardifield, instructed to 'dress you in all suits like a lady/And call him husband', left the stage through a mirrored wardrobe.[3]

As Sly's gulling began, the register of performance changed quite radically. The first scene had already shifted from one mode of theatricality to another: the pre-show audience interaction had established the induction's wedding as a role-play event from whose reality the audience were not excluded, but as soon as the actors began to speak the words of the adapted script, the play entered a more conventional register in which characters spoke in scripted Elizabethan English, and as if they were unaware, or at least only intermittently aware, of the audience's presence. The entrance of the players was then exploited for a further layer of theatricality. The first two entered in commedia masks, rattling tambourines, and announced the title of their play-within-a-play as *The Taming of the Shrew*. Katherine, now in costume, stepped out of a wardrobe and approached Petruccio. Carnivalesque tango music struck up, and the whole company, now changed into brighter, more exuberant costumes, emerged from the wardrobes behind her. Tony Bell's Tranio delivered the final lines of the Induction with his arm around Sly, before Tam Williams's Lucentio entered, bowed to Sly in the manner of an Elizabethan performer acknowledging the presence of an aristocratic patron, and began the first scene of the 'inner' play. Lucentio and Tranio themselves then became an onstage audience as they opened a wardrobe to discover most of the company 'inside' it, and interpreted the first appearance of Katherine, Baptista, Bianca, Gremio, and Hortensio as yet another layer of performance:

LUCENTIO. But stay a while, what company is this?

TRANIO. Master, some show to welcome us to town.

(1.1.46–7)

As this second group of characters entered the scene, the audience at the Old Vic were confronted with the spectacle of an onstage audience watching an onstage audience: Sly on his pink beanbag at the side, observing Lucentio and Tranio as they hid either side of a wardrobe, themselves observing and commenting upon Baptista's family.

By this point, with no less than four distinct layers of theatricality in play (the actors of Propeller were playing Sly's wedding guests, who were masquerading as 'players', who were in turn playing the characters of *The Taming of the Shrew*, who were themselves divided into an onstage audience and their onstage 'show'), Propeller had already created a Russian doll of performances-within-performances and audiences-watching-audiences. It was here that they started to blur the already tenuous boundaries separating these layers. At the end of 1.1, Sly decided to enter the play-within-the-play himself. Slipping on a red leather jacket and stepping into a spotlight, he was handed a paperback copy of the script and woodenly declaimed Petruccio's first line. Thus, before an onstage audience of the company of players, Sly began to enact his first scene as Petruccio, reading at first, before warming to his role and starting to deliver Petruccio's commands and threats to Grumio as though they were his own words. This ambiguous Sly/Petruccio figure then remained off-script until Hortensio asked him, 'what happy gale/Blows you to Padua here from old Verona?' (1.2.47–8). Momentarily stumped, Sly realised the answer was in the script.

In its fluid transitions between layers of theatricality, Hall's production was staging a dynamic process of disengagement and re-engagement akin to Brechtian alienation. Propeller's interweaving of theatrical registers presented an ill-fitting jigsaw of different, overlapping, and frequently contradictory perspectives on Shakespeare's text, complicated by their logic-defying shifts between narrative frames. The influence of Brechtian performance modes upon the production was conspicuous: the all-male cast, of course, created a visible tension between the female characters of the *locus* and the male performers of the *platea*. The second half opened while the house lights were still up, with a non-Shakespearean song about Petruccio's motivations for marrying Katherine ('Did he marry her for money? Did he marry her for love?'). Petruccio's 'taming' of Katherine had been particularly brutal: at the wedding, for example, he had thrown her violently across the stage before dragging her away with him, and he had physically abused his servants in the scene which followed. When he explained his 'taming' tactics to the audience, he paused for an answer following his demand,

> He that knows better how to tame a shrew,
> Now let him speak. 'Tis charity to show.

(4.1.196–7)

'Anyone want to say anything?', he asked, to some laughter. After an uncomfortable pause, he shrugged, interpreting our silence as assent.[4]

Shakespeare may or may not have written a conclusion to the Sly narrative, but if he did, it was left out of the version of the play printed in the Folio. The anonymous 1594 version *The Taming of A Shrew*, however, ends with a short scene in which Sly awakes as if from a dream, and Hall's production drew upon this to restore the Sly frame during the play's final moments.[5] After Petruccio's last line, the whole cast began to discard their outer costumes, and to disappear back into the wardrobes from which they had emerged at the beginning. Hortensio and Lucentio – or were they simply players again by this point? – delivered their final lines with an edge of irony, removing their wedding attire and giving it to Petruccio/Sly, so that he was dressed in the same top hat and tailcoat in which he had started the play:

HORTENSIO. Now go thy ways, thou hast tamed a curst shrew.

LUCENTIO. 'Tis a wonder, by your leave, she will be tamed so.

(5.2.193–4)

The whole cast having disappeared into the wardrobes, Bruce-Lockhart was left alone onstage, clearly simply Sly once more. The closing dialogue was adapted from *A Shrew*:

> SLY.   The players, all gone . . . ? [*to the audience*] I have had
> The bravest dream tonight that ever thou
> Heardest in all thy life!
> [*The player of Katherine emerges from one of the wardrobes.*]
>
> PLAYER.   Ay, marry, but you had best get you home,
> For your wife will course you for dreaming here tonight.
>
> SLY.   Will she? I know now how to tame a shrew.
> I dreamt upon it all this night till now,
> And thou hast waked me out of the best dream
> That ever I had in my life. But I'll to my
> Wife presently and tame her too,
> An if she anger me.
>
> PLAYER.   How, art thou drunken still? This was but a play.
>   (Adapted from *A Shrew*, 15.8–21.)

Scardifield delivered these lines with a trace of Katherine's anger, before leaving Sly alone onstage once again. Unsettled, Sly held up his wedding ring as the lights faded to black.

The last five words ('This was but a play') were Propeller's invention. Scardifield's delivery and Bruce-Lockhart's response, however, indicated that this was not merely an invitation for the audience to relax in the knowledge that all they had witnessed was a harmless fiction. Propeller's fluid transition into the framing narrative highlighted the theatrical construction behind the play-within-the-play's ostensible moral, and Lucentio's description of Katherine's taming as 'a wonder' was rendered highly ambiguous. Sly's conclusion that he now knew 'how to tame a shrew' was met only with scorn and an accusation of drunkenness from the player, and a reminder that he had been watching, and participating in, an implausible patriarchal fantasy. Our onstage representative, Sly the spectator, had ultimately arrived at what was plainly an unsatisfactory reading of the play. Sly had failed, and the responsibility for a more challenging interpretation was now our own.

Some productions, of course, add further layers of Brechtian estrangement to the Shakespearean text. A fairly radical example of this strategy was evident in Thomas Ostermeier's *Hamlet* for the Schaubühne Berlin

(2008). The Schaubühne's official website describes the play as an 'analysis of the intellectual dilemma between complex thinking and political action' (Schaubühne 2012), and indeed the production drew multiple links between Hamlet's inactivity and the audience's own. When Hamlet (Lars Eidinger) spoke of 'guilty creatures sitting at a play' (2.2.591), the lights came up on the audience. During the play-within-a-play, Polonius (Robert Beyer) filmed the faces of spectators, and these images were projected onto a huge screen at the centre of the stage: just as Hamlet was observing the reactions of Claudius (Urs Jucker), so were we asked to watch ourselves. As Hamlet debated killing Claudius, prefilmed footage of an audience applauding played behind him. When I saw the production at London's Barbican theatre in 2011, Hamlet's speech descended into a torrent of action-movie clichés ('You killed my father, you're fucking my mother, and that's why you're going to die!'), before Eidinger broke off and asked the audience, 'Is this what you want to see?'. In a similar moment just before the play's climactic duel, Eidinger jumped from the stage into the auditorium, asking spectators whether they insisted on his going back onto the stage: 'Don't you know how this fucking play ends?' he asked, in English, with mock tears and incredulity. The subsequent tragic climax was played almost as parody, the over-the-top deaths of Claudius and Laertes recalling Bottom's Pyramus in *A Midsummer Night's Dream*. Upon his own demise, Hamlet ran his hand over his face to change its outward signifiers of 'emotion'. There could be no identification here, nor catharsis: we were being asked to reflect. I found myself remembering that Hamlet's actions in the final scene were described by Brecht as 'a piece of barbaric butchery' in which Hamlet makes what is emphatically the wrong choice of action (1977: 202). In a sense, we were being ushered *away* from the play.

Workshop 1: Ushering the audience (pp. 74–83)

Preparation:

Participants should be familiar with a particular Shakespearean play. The workshop leader should have photocopied a selection of Shakespeare's prologues.

Workshop:

1) In groups of three or four, participants should discuss ideas for a full-scale theatrical adaptation of the play on which they are working. They should be encouraged to think about the performance space and the role of the audience. It might

help for each group to chart their ideas in the form of a mind-map.

2) Once every group has developed the bare bones of an idea, the workshop leader should ask them to think specifically about the *beginning*. How would the adaptation start? How might they bring the audience into the performance space? How will they let the audience know that the performance is about to start? How will the audience know what sort of role will be required of them? Will a prologue be needed? Again, it may help if these ideas are jotted down by a group member.

3) Once each group has begun to develop answers to these questions, the workshop leader should set them a practical task: they must devise and perform the 'before-the-start' of their adaptation in such a way that this information is communicated to the audience. They can add text if necessary, but their performance must stop with the first line of Shakespeare's play (or the first line of the prologue, if it already has one).

4) Each group performs their 'before-the-start' sequence to the rest of the group.

5) Discussion. Did the audience respond in the ways they had hoped? If so, why did they? If not, why not? Are there any changes they might make?

6) Hand out copies of one or more of Shakespeare's own prologues. What sorts of cues are there for audience behaviour? Compare it with the groups' own 'before-the-start' sequences. Do Shakespeare's prologues show evidence of similar strategies?

Workshop 2: Estranging the audience (pp. 83–90)

Preparation:

Each participant should be working on a Shakespearean duologue with a partner.

Workshop:

1) Participants play out their duologues in front of the rest of the group. The workshop leader should encourage each pair to play their duologue as a self-contained scene, ignoring the presence of the audience.

2) After a brief discussion of each scene, the participants should be asked to play their duologues a second time, adding a line of third-person, past-tense narration to the audience before they say each sentence. For example:

> FRIAR LAURENCE.   Friar Laurence steeled himself to break the bad news.
> 'I bring thee tidings of the Prince's doom.'
>
> ROMEO.   Romeo threw himself onto the floor, and cried out,
> 'What less than doomsday is the Prince's doom?'
>
> (3.3.8–9)

Participants might benefit from a short trial-run in private before they perform the exchange to the rest of the group.

3) Discuss the effects of the added narration. Did it work? If so, why? If not, why not? What does it do to the actor's relationship with the audience? What does it do to the audience's perception of the character? What is the effect of separating actor from character in this way? Can it be read as a Brechtian estrangement effect? What might be *gained* from distancing the character in this way?

4) Participants are asked to play each scene a third time. This time, though, the additions should be in the first person, present tense. They should be played as asides and should explain the character's thinking to the audience. If a line is *already* an aside, or *can* be played as one, the actor need not improvise an additional line, but simply play the scripted line to the audience. For example, either of the following exchanges might work:

> FRIAR LAURENCE.   (I really hope he doesn't over-react.)
> Not body's death, but body's banishment.
>
> ROMEO.   (He has no idea how utterly awful that's going to be!)
> Ha, banishment? Be merciful, say 'death'...
>
> (3.3.11–12)

or

ROMEO. (*to audience*) Ha, banishment?
(*to Friar*) Be merciful, say 'death'...

(3.3.11–12)

Again, participants should probably be given the opportunity for a private trial-run before they perform to the rest of the group.

5) Discuss the effects of the asides. Did they work? If so, why? If not, why not? How do frequent asides change the actor's (and/or the character's) relationship with the audience? What are the advantages and disadvantages to this strategy? Does it work differently in comic scenes and in more serious ones? What does playing a *scripted* line as an aside do to the scene? Does the estrangement effect work differently when the separation between actor and character is less marked?

6
Playing with the Audience

Game-playing

One of the problems with the Brechtian account of Shakespearean performance is that in its focus on the impact of *locus/platea* interplay on the audience's meaning-making processes, it tends to underemphasise the same phenomenon's role in the creation of audience *pleasure*.[1] Theatre director Mike Alfreds has noted that critical discussions of performance tend to 'batten onto a play in literary terms', agreeing or disagreeing with a director's 'interpretation' while failing to describe 'what it was actually like to be there at that performance, what really happened between the actors and audience' (1979: 8). This is certainly as true in Shakespeare studies as it is in any other branch of theatre criticism, where it may be due in part to the fact that the productions which tour most widely and are thus available to the highest number of critics are precisely those which take the least notice of their audiences. In his book *New Sites for Shakespeare*, John Russell Brown suggests that major international productions often become fixed, consumable products; he criticises the polished but inflexible 'packaging' of Richard Eyre's *Richard III* (1990) for the way in which 'the audience was given a production by a director/dictator who had subdued individual freedom' (1999: 145–7).

Brown's book advocates a very different kind of Shakespearean performance. Having witnessed the intense audience engagement generated by certain Asian popular theatre styles (including Jatra and Kutiyattam), Brown suggests a more improvisatory Shakespearean theatre:

> The actors should be fully prepared, in that they have completely mastered the technical demands of comprehending and speaking the

text, but they should also be free to vary how they speak and what they do, according to how the play is coming to life and the audience responding.

He admits that such a style would certainly sacrifice 'many of the marvellous and affective possibilities of modern theatre productions', but suggests that performances of the kind he imagines might take actors and audiences 'into fresh imaginative engagement with the plays' (1999: 95). Brown shares some key concerns here with Alfreds, who founded the theatre company Shared Experience on the following principles:

> actors and audience in constant mutual awareness; the actor's vivid transformation; the dual nature of theatre; the shared act of imagination; the actor's freedom to create and respond freshly at each performance.
>
> (1979: 5)

The title of Alfreds' 2007 handbook for directors and actors – *Different Every Night* – indicates that the last of these has remained a central tenet of his theatre practice, while the contents of the book re-affirm the rest.

One director to have put Brown's proposal into practice is Patrick Tucker, whose Original Shakespeare Company staged unrehearsed performances of both full-length plays and short excerpts throughout the 1990s. Each actor would be given a 'cue script' consisting only of their individual lines and their cues, in what Tucker intended to be a recreation of Elizabethan performance practice. The actors were asked not to read the rest of the play in advance, so that they would discover the play, and their part in it, in the moment of performance. After seeing the company perform the first 600 lines of *The Two Gentlemen of Verona* in 1994, Peter Holland felt that their work

> proved conclusively that good actors pumped up with adrenalin can think fast and excitingly when, having learned their roles only from cue-scripts, they have no idea what the other actors in the scene may be about to say.
>
> (1997: 253)

Tucker himself, evoking 'that essential danger that a live performance brings', has suggested that the appeal of the company's work is that it is 'very like a circus, or a sports event': 'You know the format, but you absolutely do not know the result' (2002: 111).[2]

Tucker's metaphor of theatre-as-sport has been a popular one with exponents of semi-improvised Shakespearean performance. Brown had, in fact, suggested something similar many years earlier in his 1974 manifesto *Free Shakespeare*, in which he argued that Shakespeare's original audience was 'undoubtedly stimulated by the excitement of a game or contest', and that his plays 'were written for this immediate, shared sense of discovery and achievement' (1974: 80–1). More recently, the Globe's Mark Rylance has criticised highly polished, concept-driven Shakespearean productions on the grounds that watching one is 'a bit like going to see a football match where the two teams had practised an interpretation of the beautiful game' (2008: 106). His associate director Tim Carroll used the same analogy when he described 'the best theatre ensembles' as being like football teams, in that they 'develop their skills as a team, and try to reach a point where they can respond to any situation that might arise'. Both kinds of team, argues Carroll,

> train in accordance with certain principles, many of which are common to both: being in the moment, not dwelling on mistakes, remaining aware of everything around you, accepting offers, hiding or revealing your intention as the situation requires, variation of tempo and so on.
>
> (2006)

Key to the metaphor is the notion that when actors play Shakespeare's texts as a live game rather than a pre-planned recital, audiences and actors share in the thrill of the unexpected and in the moment of discovery. Describing a moment at the Globe in which Jasper Britton's Macbeth altered his delivery of the 'Out, out, brief candle' soliloquy (5.5.16–27) to acknowledge the presence of a pigeon which had flown onto the stage, Carroll suggested that the audience's delighted laughter indicated that 'they had shared with Jasper a moment of beautiful revelation, vouchsafed by the beauty of chance' (2008: 40).

Carroll's football analogy derives not from his writing on his work at the Globe, but rather from his introduction to *The Hamlet Project*. This was the inaugural project of The Factory, a London-based actors' ensemble formed in 2006 by Alex Hassell and Tim Evans. *The Hamlet Project* was a continuation of the work which Carroll had started in a production of *Hamlet* in Budapest in 2006, in which all of the roles except Hamlet had been learned by more than one actor, so that the casting line-up could be different each night. For *The Hamlet Project*, The Factory's ensemble undertook an eight-month process of training and exploration before beginning a series of public performances in 2007, each in a different location, with a cast which had been selected at random from the members of the ensemble (usually by a few rounds of the game Paper-Scissors-Stone). The only props used were those which had been either found in the venue or brought along by audience members. To ensure that there would be 'no recreating' from past performances – one of the golden rules of the project – either Carroll or a guest director would impose an arbitrary performance rule (an 'obstruction') at the beginning of each Act.

The ensemble's rigorous training ensured that while their performances were unplanned, they were far from chaotic, and frequently generated surprising and thought-provoking readings of the play. At a performance in a converted church in May 2008, for example, the Act 2 'obstruction' was that there must always be two actors downstairs in the nave, and one upstairs in the gallery (regardless of the number of characters in the scene): thus, Ophelia acquired a nameless female confidante in her scene with Polonius (2.1), and Hamlet delivered his soliloquy beginning 'Now I am alone' (2.2.551–607) while looking down at Claudius and Gertrude embracing. In both cases, the audience were left to deduce the possible meanings of these randomly generated but highly resonant stage pictures. Three months later, in a Hackney art studio, the same Act's obstruction was a rule that every time somebody started speaking, they had to do so before the previous speaker had finished. This time, as a consequence, Ophelia and Polonius seemed almost furious with one another, and Gertrude's 'More matter with less art' (2.2.96) was positively impatient; the whole Act seemed to be driven by agitation and unrest. Performers made the most of unlikely casting configurations: on one occasion, for example, a young Claudius and an older Gertrude turned what was a mere accident of casting into a persuasive reading of an older woman who had been emotionally and sexually manipulated by a young and ruthless new husband. In one particularly charged moment, the actor playing Hamlet picked up a real baby to illustrate 'What a piece of work is a man' (2.2.305), and his emotion was real.

It is striking that most of the directors cited above – Rylance, Carroll, Tucker, and Alfreds – have been drawn to direct work at Shakespeare's Globe.[3] The idea that the Globe is unsuited to 'pre-programmed' performances was a central one from the very beginning of Rylance's artistic directorship (Kiernan 1999: 69), and it seems to have stemmed partly from a sense, like Brown's and Tucker's, of the game-like nature of 'original practices', but partly also in response to the space itself (Carroll and Alfreds have also directed game-like work in modern shared-light spaces). Several of the actors involved in the theatre's first season described its atmosphere as being 'like a football match' (Kiernan 1999: 22, 134, 149), so it seems that the game-playing ethos extended from the stage to the audience, too.

In his book *Shakespeare's Clown*, David Wiles explores the ways in which Shakespeare's clown figures might be considered 'game-makers' who 'performed *with*, and not *to*, an audience constructed as equals' (1987: 179). His analysis is similar to that of the great teacher and theorist of clowning, Jacques Lecoq, who also understood clowning in terms of 'game' (or *le jeu*), and argued that it 'is not possible to be a clown *for* an audience; you play *with* your audience' (2009: 157).[4] The Globe has become famous for its lively interplay between stage and audience – Peter Thomson gives a detailed account, for example, of the scene-stealing nature of Jasper Britton's interactions with the groundlings as Caliban in *The Tempest* (2002: 138). A particularly anarchic example could be seen in the clowning of the Lecoq-trained actor Marcello Magni in 1998's *The Merchant of Venice*; Magni's Launcelot Gobbo improvised with audience members both before the show and during the interval, establishing a two-way rapport which made its way directly into the show during Launcelot's monologue in 2.2. Outlining his conflicting opinions about the 'fiend' who advises him to run away from Shylock, and the 'conscience' who commands him to stay, Magni turned to the audience to ask them what he should do:

> What should I do, huh? *[Pause. To a groundling:]* What should I do? *[Pause.]* PLEASE HELP! *[Mimics nonchalant pose of groundling. Audience laughter.]*[5]

Having solicited several contradictory responses from the yard, Magni's Gobbo decided to determine it by inviting a show of hands. In the performance videotaped for the Globe's archive, Magni makes much of the fact that while the groundlings seem overwhelmingly to favour the fiend, the playgoers in the galleries side with the conscience.

The interactivity of such moments seems to hold a huge appeal for modern audiences. In 2001, John Tulloch investigated audience responses to the Railway Street Theatre Company's production of *Much Ado About Nothing*, which played at the Q Theatre, Penrith, and on tour around New South Wales. Tulloch's initial questionnaire generated 273 responses and a number of follow-up interviews. Ninety-seven per cent of respondents reported that they found theatre 'special', and when asked what it was about theatre that they found special, a majority – ranging from 51% of under-17s to 70% of over 55s – emphasised 'liveness' (2005: 279). Tulloch's follow-up interviews revealed, in his words, 'a particular sensory pleasure in live physical proximity, even a sense of personal invitation, between actor and audience member' (2005: 280). He gives the response of one 16-year-old respondent as an example:

> I think *Much Ado* also worked well when they had the monologues, when the characters actually talked to the audience. It looked like they were talking to *you* instead of just . . . into a camera.
>
> (2005: 281)

One must be careful, of course, to note that Tulloch's findings document the responses of only a relatively small number of playgoers in New South Wales in 2001, and that those responses are specific to that context: the comment quoted above, for example, would seem to confirm Philip Auslander's thesis that 'liveness' is at least in part an after-effect of the mass media (2008: 56). Certainly, both Tucker and Alfreds also define the liveness of their performance styles in contrast to television and film (Alfreds 1979: 4; Tucker 2002: 110–11).

But whether it is a postmodern phenomenon or something encoded in the texts themselves, Shakespeare's plays offer multiple opportunities for such 'liveness' in performance. Ralph Alan Cohen, the co-founder of the American Shakespeare Centre and its reconstruction of the Blackfriars Playhouse, notes that productions work particularly well in the Globe and the Blackfriars when they 'acknowledge and collaborate with the audience' (2008: 218). He points out that the plays' numerous meta-theatrical references – Fabian's 'If this were played upon a stage, now, I could condemn it as an improbable fiction' (*Twelfth Night*, 3.4.125–6), for example, or Biron's 'Our wooing doth not end like an old play' (*Love's Labour's Lost*, 5.2.860) – are 'a joke shared with the audience, a joke about the collaborative work of making believe' (2008: 220). They signal, in Tim Carroll's words, a 'game' in which the audience is invited to participate.

Carroll's description is of Malvolio's gulling scene in *Twelfth Night*. In this scene, he argues, the 'box-tree' in which Sir Toby, Sir Andrew, and Fabian are hiding is so close to Malvolio, and their scripted interjections so frequent, that it is impossible to believe that Malvolio would not hear them. But this, he says, is the point: the scene asks its audience 'to be complicit in accepting something which is literally unbelievable' (2008: 38). A glance at the scene's production history reveals that actors and directors have felt free to stretch the audience's credulity to outrageous limits: in performance, it is usual practice to *augment* rather than to reduce the scene's implausible elements. Sir Andrew, Sir Toby, and Fabian regularly get too close to Malvolio, or speak too loudly, or move the objects behind which they are hiding, prompting ludicrous attempts at disguise in which, for example, they mimic bird noises (as in, for example, Kenneth Branagh's 1987 production) or pretend to be statues (as in Propeller's 2007 version). The more improbable, the better: it prolongs and extends the game.

There are generally two games being played concurrently during this sequence. The object of the onstage observers' game is to remain hidden from Malvolio while indulging in behaviours that jeopardise their cover; at the same time, the object of Malvolio's game is to persuade both himself and the audience that the words of the letter refer to him. Both projects are essentially playful, since the artificial prolonging of both involves a knowing complicity between actors and audience (were it not a play, in other words, both games would be over very quickly). Malvolio's reading of the letter has often been used as an opportunity for actor/audience interplay: in Ben Shaktman's production for the Pittsburgh Public Theatre in 1975, for example, Leonard Nimoy's Malvolio engaged in 'a five-minute improvisation, in which [he] good-humouredly seeks the help of audience members in deciphering the letter' (Favorini 1976: 270), while in Ian Judge's 1994 production for the RSC, Desmond Barrit appealed to the audience for advice upon the line 'What should that alphabetical position portend?' (2.5.116–17) (Schafer 2009: 157).

Donald Sinden gives an extraordinarily detailed account of his own performance as Malvolio in his chapter of *Players of Shakespeare 1*, documenting his performance in John Barton's 1969 production not only move-by-move but also laugh-by-laugh. His account uses a notation system for the size of each audience laugh, rating each one on a scale of 1 (the smallest 'worth trying for') to 9 ('the largest that can be expected'). Sinden scripts several exchanges with the audience – showing them the letter, responding to their presumed reactions, and so on (1985: 46). Thus, for example, when Malvolio reads the word 'steward' in the letter, he shows it to the audience:

> They obviously don't believe him, so he shows them the *very* word and mouths it a second time (laugh 3). Fools! He is patently wasting his time on them – they only laugh.
>
> (1985: 58)

Sinden's prediction of audience response (and his own counter-response) is surprisingly specific – he even anticipates a 'laugh 9 and round of applause' upon his exit from the scene, as if this outcome were pre-programmable and identical at every performance (1985: 59). As Jonathan Holmes notes, though, Sinden's account is almost certainly a retrospective one, documenting the typical response to a performance that undoubtedly grew attuned to its audiences' reactions over the course of a long run (2004: 28).

Sinden's own characterisation of his relationship with his audience is that he is 'controlling them' (1985: 46). Paul Chahidi, a regular performer at Shakespeare's Globe, notes too that an actor must 'try to bridle and control' audience laughter in order to retain control of the story itself (2008: 205). The language is distinctly reminiscent of that used in the discussions considered in Chapter 4 of *Shakespeare's* control of audience response, only the 'master' has changed: no longer Shakespeare, but the actor. The idea that one can modulate a performance to provoke specific and measurable responses from any audience once again casts the spectator in a role of complete passivity.

I wonder, though, whether Sinden's account overstates his level of control to some extent. Watching David Tennant's performance as Benedick in Josie Rourke's production of *Much Ado About Nothing* in 2011, I was struck by his ability to entice a whole sequence of different responses from the audience with little more than a series of gestures. The following transcript was written from memory shortly after the performance:

BENEDICK.   ... for I will be horribly [*throws up his arms and shouts*] in love with her!

AUDIENCE.   [*applause and cheering*]

BENEDICK.   [*bashful gestures: 'Oh, no, honestly, please don't cheer for me.'*]

AUDIENCE.   [*laughter*]

BENEDICK.   [*mock-modesty: 'No, no, really, it's nothing ... '*]

AUDIENCE.   [*laughter*]

BENEDICK.   [*mock-consternation: 'All right, shush now. I need to get on with my monologue.'*]

AUDIENCE.   [*laughter*]

BENEDICK. [*flattered: 'Fair play to you. I suppose I am quite brilliant.'*]

AUDIENCE. [*laughter*]

BENEDICK. [*mock-consternation: 'No, but really, we do have a play to perform.'*]

AUDIENCE. [*laughter*]

BENEDICK. I may chance have some odd quirks and remnants of wit broken on me because I have railed so long against marriage, but doth not the appetite alter?

AUDIENCE. [*laughter*]

BENEDICK. [*shrugs at audience as if to say, 'Exactly! You know I'm right, don't you?'*]

AUDIENCE. [*laughter*]

BENEDICK. A man loves the meat in his youth that he cannot endure in his age. Shall quips and sentences and these paper bullets of the brain awe a man from the career of his humour? [*Open arms, as if to invite response, which he vocalises himself:*] No!

AUDIENCE. [*laughter*]

BENEDICK. The world must be peopled.

AUDIENCE. [*laughter*]

BENEDICK. [*cocks head as if to say, 'You know what I'm saying, don't you?'*]

AUDIENCE. [*laughter*]

The version of this sequence which was filmed for Digital Theatre is similar to this, but not identical, suggesting that Tennant's counter-responses were indeed modified by the audience's reactions each night. Such brazen flirtation was not to everyone's taste: a post on the Shakespeare review blog *Margate Sands*, for example, complained of the way in which Tennant 'spent the entire performance crowdsurfing on an updraft of uncritical adulation wafting towards him from the stalls' (2011). But to my mind, it was an effective, even virtuosic display by an actor who was finely attuned to his audience's expectations and responses, and it created a powerful sense of conversation between stage and auditorium.

Talking to the audience

Central to Tim Carroll's notion of dramatic performance as 'game' is the idea of 'objectives'. This is, of course, nothing new in modern performance: the idea that actors should identify what a character wants from any given onstage exchange is central to Stanislavski's 'system', Strasberg's 'method', and countless other acting techniques grounded in psychological realism. David Mamet, in fact, has held that 'characterisation' itself becomes unnecessary when an appropriately cast actor speaks the words scripted for them with a clear sense of their 'intention toward the person to whom they are said' (1998: 55). Actors, in Mamet's view, should use the words of the script to perform (or at least attempt) an *action* upon their co-actors: a simple greeting, he suggests, might be 'an invitation, a dismissal, an apology, a rebuke' (1998: 55). In this sense, acting on stage, even naturalistic acting, is not a *representation* of behaviour – it is, as Richard Schechner put it, 'behaviour itself' (1985: 51). When actors play actions upon one another, something live is happening on stage for real.

But as the performance examples in the section above indicate, this 'game' is not necessarily limited to actions that can be played upon other actors. Holmes points out that in Donald Sinden's record of his performance as Malvolio, Sinden 'predicates his characterisation on the play-acting of those he is addressing, which as his account makes clear includes the audience as much as, and perhaps more than, his onstage addressees' (2004: 29–30). In such circumstances, both actor and character disappear into a single figure attempting a single task. Sinden describes himself in such scenes as 'one-hundred-per-cent myself, standing outside my character' (1985: 46), but as far as the audience are concerned, the figure onstage who is showing them the letter – persuading them, goading them, dismissing their responses and so on – is both Malvolio and Sinden, *locus* and *platea*, at once.

In the examples discussed above, Marcello Magni and David Tennant used extra-textual elaborations – namely ad-libs, facial expressions and gestures – to strike up a sense of live exchange with their audiences. It is just as possible, however, to converse with audiences using Shakespeare's text. Playing Orsino in the Globe's *Twelfth Night* in 2012, Liam Brennan opened the play by ordering the musicians to 'play on', before changing his mind, and shouting out, 'Enough, no more' (1.1.1, 7). At the performance I attended, several audience members laughed – amused, presumably, at Orsino's capriciousness. Brennan then looked around, as if he were slightly hurt at being judged in this way, before delivering his next line as an explanation to his critics: "Tis not so sweet now as it was before' (1.1.8). The line is not marked as an aside or even as part of a soliloquy, but playing it directly to the audience in this context made perfect sense: Orsino's line was a response to the audience reaction. There are many passages in Shakespeare's writing which can be played in this way. Indeed, the editorial convention which distinguishes 'asides' from other kinds of speech (a stage direction which has almost always been inserted by modern editors) sometimes masks the fact that Shakespeare's characters can be in near-constant conversation with their audiences throughout their time on stage.[6]

Some commentators deem such audience interaction incompatible with serious drama. Bert O. States finds it 'unthinkable' that Macbeth, Lear or Hamlet, for example, could 'peer familiarly into the pit', since the 'abridgement of aesthetic distance' which that would entail would make 'tragic character and pathos' impossible; States argues that 'the only characters in tragedy who "work" with the audience seem to be clowns and villains' (1983: 366). Similarly, for Peter Thomson, the comic actor 'distinguishes himself by a rapport with the audience which is denied to the "serious" actor, and which is altogether different from that of the "tragic" actor'. Thomson notes that though Hamlet or Macbeth may 'confide in us', they 'cannot play with us' (2002: 139). A fairly typical view is that the soliloquies of characters like Hamlet or Macbeth are examples of what Andrew Gurr has called the 'more naturalistic convention of thinking aloud', which Gurr contrasts with the 'less sophisticated' tradition of direct address to the audience (1992: 103). It is hardly necessary to cite examples of modern Hamlets or Macbeths who deliver their soliloquies into the empty space in the middle of a darkened auditorium, since the practice is widespread. Indeed, the word 'soliloquy' itself means literally 'to speak alone' (from the Latin *solus*, alone; and *loqui*, to speak).[7]

I am not convinced, though, that the speeches uttered by Shakespeare's characters when they are alone on stage are ever really 'soliloquies' in the strictest sense of the word (and Shakespeare certainly never used the word himself). Nor am I at all certain that direct address is in any way 'less sophisticated' or less compatible with tragedy than 'thinking aloud'. John Russell Brown has analysed a number of monologues by the very characters mentioned above – Macbeth (1999: 99–100), Lear (1999: 100–1), and Hamlet (2002: 19–21) – for examples of moments which might facilitate direct address, and he suggests that actors looking for 'opportunities to speak directly to their audience' will 'find them everywhere in Shakespeare's plays' (2002: 19). Tim Carroll, in fact, imagines soliloquies as a partly silent dialogue between actor and audience:

> The presence of the audience says, in effect, 'We are quite prepared to think, and even (in your imagination) say, anything that you need us to.' ... So the audience can silently say to Viola, 'You know about that ring, don't you?' To which she can respond, '[No!] I left no ring with her' (*Twelfth Night* 2.2.15). When Richard II is in prison, the audience may be thinking, 'Well, of course, a spoiled brat like you – you must be banging your head against the wall, wailing and complaining to the gods.' And he says, '[No, actually,] I have been studying how I may compare this prison where I live unto the world' (*Richard II* 5.5.1–2).
>
> (2008: 41; Carroll's insertions)

Rather similarly, Mark Rylance reports that following his delivery of the line 'To be or not to be, that is the question' at the Globe in 2000, he responded to the audience as if they had replied, 'What do you mean, that is the question?'. The conceit, he says, fostered 'a sense of dialogue with the audience', who were 'playing the role of Hamlet's conscience at that moment' (2008: 107). These imagined dialogues are inherently dramatic, charged with tension and with conflict, and every bit as interactive as the comic examples discussed above. But they are also impositions upon the audience: while spectators may, as Carroll suggests, implicitly give their consent to having their unspoken part in the conversation voiced for them by the actor, they are nonetheless 'spoken for' in the exchange. This all begins to change, though, if the audience's part in the conversation is left open.

A central idea in Bridget Escolme's book *Talking to the Audience* is what she calls the 'performance objective'. Escolme's premise is that

> whereas in the naturalistic theatre it is impossible for any character to desire or have an interest in anything outside the fiction, Shakespeare's stage figures have another set of desires and interests, inseparable from those of the actor. They want the audience to listen to them, notice them, approve their performance, ignore others on stage for their sake.
>
> (2005: 16)

Thus, for example, Ophelia's performance objective in 4.5 of *Hamlet* might be 'to stay on stage and to sing to us' (2005: 82).[8] *Richard II* can similarly be read as a 'competition for stage presence' between Richard and Bolingbroke; Richard's performance objective, argues Escolme, is 'to reach the point where his own presence in the theatre is more engaging than those who have set about to reduce his fictional power' (2005: 114, 123–4). Some characters, such as Coriolanus, might have an opposite objective: to absent themselves from the gaze of the audience as quickly as possible. It does not matter, in Escolme's model, whether characters succeed or fail in their attempts to 'act upon' the audience and achieve their performance objectives – the play is probably more interesting, in fact, if the audience are resistant to them in some way. The key is that actors find theatrical intentions for their characters which are not merely fleeting or mechanistic (making an audience laugh on a particular line, for example, before returning to the sealed-off fiction of the scene), but rather central to the structure of their roles in the plays.

Characters who attempt to 'act upon' their audiences, suggests Escolme, are likely to produce theatrical effects of a very different sort from those produced by characters whose existences are independent of their audiences. Frustrated with productions of *Troilus and Cressida* in which the heroine is presented as an objectified victim, Escolme speculates about the meanings that might be produced 'by a Cressida who makes eyes at us, who directly elicits the audience's approval for her actions or defies their disapproval of them' (2005: 39). Escolme observes that Cressida has a number of exchanges in which she satirises and subverts the words and behaviour of others, and notes that she can therefore be 'inscribed with clown-like performance objectives' (2005: 42). Exploring this approach with a group of students, Escolme found that when they were presented with a Cressida who spoke directly to them, the student spectators 'began to judge themselves rather than Cressida's morality, suddenly aware of their own role in the production of meaning':

> The idea that Cressida, or the performer – and the fact that it was unclear 'who' is significant – was flirting with them, was enjoyable rather than reprehensible as it had been when the character had been judged a flirt within a fictional *locus*.
>
> (2005: 45)

In such cases, the spectators become more than mere observers of a character's behaviour: they become the *cause* of that behaviour, and their role in the play becomes both more pleasurable and more complicated as a result.

Shakespeare's plays sometimes facilitate such interactivity to an extraordinary degree. Hamlet's soliloquy beginning 'Now I am alone' (2.2.551) is a notable example. Spoken to an audience, of course, what the opening line really says is 'Now *we* are alone': Hamlet considers himself free to engage the audience in an intimate dialogue now that his rivals for the audience's attention have left the stage. The speech then continues with a sequence of rhetorical questions, each of which can be posed directly to the audience:

> Is it not monstrous that this player here,
> But in a fiction, in a dream of passion,
> Could force his soul so to his whole conceit
> That from her working all his visage wanned,
> Tears in his eyes, distraction in 's aspect,
> A broken voice, and his whole function suiting
> With forms to his conceit? And all for nothing.
> For Hecuba!
> What's Hecuba to him, or he to Hecuba,
> That he should weep for her? What would he do,
> Had he the motive and the cue for passion
> That I have?
>
> (2.2.553–64)

The questions become increasingly difficult for both the audience, and indeed Hamlet, to answer; the last of them, suggests the actor and director Michael Pennington, 'hangs in the air' (1996: 75). Hamlet then attempts an answer (2.2.564–8), before returning to the audience with another series of questions:

> Am I a coward?
> Who calls me villain, breaks my pate across,
> Plucks off my beard and blows it in my face,
> Tweaks me by th' nose, gives me the lie i' th' throat
> As deep as to the lungs? Who does me this?
> Ha? 'Swounds, I should take it...
>
> (2.2.573–8)

The questions in this second round are more easily answered: so much so, argues Pennington, that Hamlet 'must surely have got an answer to some of them at the Globe', and 'even in these restrained days, the responses sit at the front of our mouths' (1996: 75). Indeed, Mary Z. Maher recounts that once, when David Warner delivered these lines in Peter Hall's 1965 production, a member of the audience shouted 'Yes!' in response to the first of these questions, responding again with his name on 'Who does me this?'; Warner apparently 'remembered this as one of the most exhilarating nights of his acting career' (1992: 41). Decades later at the reconstructed Globe, Mark Rylance's Hamlet regularly attempted to provoke a response to the question 'Am I a coward?', altering his delivery of the lines which followed according to the audience's answer: a 'yes' made him pugnacious, while a 'no' or a silence made him contemptuous of his audience's unwillingness to square up to him and offer a condemnation (which he evidently felt he deserved).[9]

We saw in Chapter 4 that studies which purport to analyse Shakespeare's control of audience response are often really examining his use of subject positioning: the *scope* which his texts allow for particular kinds of relationships with the audience. Certain characters are allowed a huge amount of time and text in which they can converse with their audiences; our relationship with a Hamlet may be very different from the one we may have with a Macbeth, or a Benedick, or a Falstaff, but in each of these cases the relationship is likely to be a substantial one, if only because these characters speak to us so often. Audiences may approve or disapprove of Petruccio in *The Taming of the Shrew*, but they are likely to understand his strategies in the play's central conflict far better than they will Katherine's, because he has two substantial monologues with which to explain them – whereas Katherine has none. Cleopatra may be the focal point of *Antony and Cleopatra*, but her relationship with the audience is complicated by the fact that she is never alone with them: she is only ever seen while she is 'performing' for her onstage audiences, and although her self-conscious performativity can make her enormously playful with a theatre audience, she is never allowed to communicate to them with the directness of, for example, Enobarbus.

In many cases, a character's level of contact with the audience varies over the course of a play. At the beginning of *1 Henry IV*, for example, Prince Hal lets the audience in on a secret – he is planning, after 'a while', to 'throw off' the 'loose behaviour' which we have just witnessed, and ultimately to reject the company of his debauched friends (1.2.192–214). He then concedes his position as the audience's closest ally in the play to Falstaff, who addresses us regularly; but our complicity with Falstaff is likely to be strained by the fact that we know that his young protégé is planning to reject him. Hamlet's withdrawal from the audience occurs in a different way. Hamlet generally builds a deep connection with spectators over the course of his seven major soliloquies, but suddenly retreats from them after his final one in 4.4 ('How all occasions do inform against me', 23–57). In fact, the latter appears only in the Second Quarto version of the text, and in the Folio, Hamlet's last substantial conversation with the audience occurs about halfway through the play in 3.3 ('Now I might do it pat', 73–96). In both speeches, Hamlet concludes by imagining an act of violence, and we are no longer party to his thoughts as he finally executes it in Act 5. Escolme describes this change in the character/spectator relationship:

> As a clown's skull is replaced in its grave, as Ophelia is newly laid in hers, it seems we must also say goodbye to the complex theatrical subjectivity of Hamlet, as he slips back into a simpler moral frame where there can be no questioning of man's inevitable fate.

In Mark Rylance's performance at the Globe, this shift was, suggests Escolme, nothing less than a 'bereavement of the spectator' (2005: 73).

Some plays give us the opposite arc. The title character in *King Lear* is initially one of its most distant: Cordelia, Edmund, Kent, and probably (though not certainly) the Fool all address the audience over the first few scenes of the play, but Lear's own speeches are usually spoken only to other characters on stage. This starts to change, though, as his sense of self-identity begins to crumble, and his questions in 1.4 may be asked directly of the audience:

> Does any here know me? This is not Lear.
> Does Lear walk thus, speak thus? Where are his eyes?
> Either his notion weakens, his discernings
> Are lethargied – ha, waking? 'Tis not so.
> Who is it that can tell me who I am?

(1.4.208–12)

Though he is never given a speech which is unambiguously spoken to the audience, the text allows an increasing amount of scope for flashes of contact with them as his mind deteriorates. Rather similarly, Coriolanus remains aloof from the audience for most of the play which bears his name, but is given to repeated metatheatrical self-reference: he complains to his mother halfway through the play that 'You have put me now to such a part which never/I shall discharge to the life' (3.2.105–6), and by the end, he laments that 'Like a dull actor now,/I have forgot my part' (5.3.40–1). When she directed a production of *Coriolanus* in Minnesota in 2006, Escolme found that a character who

> joins us to stand outside the fiction – physically, by coming away from a marked fictional *locus* or by refusing the social norms of the fictional world – is theatrically compelling even when morally repulsive.

A 'look from the man who, for most of the play, refused to look or be looked at', she argues, has 'a tremendous seductive charge' (2007: 177).

Shakespeare's most seductive figures, though, are often his most despicable. In several of his plays, Shakespeare developed upon the medieval tradition of morality drama, in which personified 'Virtues' and 'Vices' would battle for the soul of an 'Everyman'. The Vice characters of morality drama were generally enormous fun: they would confide their plans to the audience, make jokes, encourage participation, and attempt to trick the protagonist into sinning while the audience watched. Dramaturgically, the audience would become temporarily aligned with the forces of evil; typically, the Vice would almost triumph, but would ultimately be defeated by the forces of Virtue, and the audience with whom he had allied himself would be won back, alongside the Everyman figure, to morality. One might consider the anonymous 15th-century play *Mankind* as a particularly well-developed example of this formula, since its Vice characters repeatedly request the audience's complicity in executing their plans. Its chief Vice, Mischief, makes his *modus operandi* clear in his first scene: 'I am come hither to make you game'. As Wiles points out, the character is 'at once the villain, whom the audience learn to shun, and the welcome game-maker who makes the play possible' (1987: 1–2).

There are at least five Shakespearean characters who owe obvious debts to the Vice tradition. Four of them are very similar: *Titus Andronicus*'s Aaron, Richard of Gloucester (in both *3 Henry VI* and *Richard III*), *Othello*'s Iago, and *King Lear*'s Edmund. Each of these characters is a witty and articulate trickster who lets the audience in on a murderous scheme before allowing them to watch as he executes it; each takes delight both in his own ingenuity and in his victims' gullibility. Richard promises the audience that he will 'seem a saint, when most

I play the devil' (*Richard III*, 1.3.336), and makes his dramatic inher-
itance explicit in an aside later in the play: 'Thus like the formal Vice,
Iniquity,/I moralize two meanings in one word' (3.1.82–3). Iago explains
a similar strategy to the audience of *Othello*:

> When devils will the blackest sins put on,
> They do suggest at first with heavenly shows,
> As I do now.

> (2.3.342–4)

The latter speech is at times reminiscent of the Hamlet soliloquy discussed above: Iago begins by asking the audience, 'And what's he then
that says I play the villain?' (2.3.327), repeating 'How am I then a
villain?' halfway through (2.3.339). Unlike Hamlet's question, though,
Iago's is ironic: both he and we know that he is without doubt a 'villain',
and Iago often seems to expect the audience to enjoy this every bit as
much as he does himself. The actor Oliver Ford Davies reports that when
he was in rehearsals for the Almeida Theatre's *King Lear* in 2002, he gave
James Frain, the actor playing Edmund, the 'best advice' he had for such
roles:

> assume that the audience not only understand your position but
> are sympathetic to it. In other words, don't defy, or wheedle the
> audience; talk as if they're on your side.

> (2003: 126)

Directing *Richard III* for the RSC in 1984, Bill Alexander advised Antony
Sher to '[t]hink of the audience as a convention of trainee Richard
the Thirds' (Sher 1985: 177). Shakespeare's Vice characters ask their
audiences to undertake a diabolical imaginative exercise: to imagine
that they share their delight in evil. The game may well create an
extreme emotional tension in the audience, since it is likely that we
will be morally repulsed at precisely those moments when our theatrical
pleasure is at its deepest.

For David Troughton's Richard at the RSC in 1995, the audience
became an additional character. Troughton found himself fascinated by
Richard's crisis of conscience at the end of the play, when the character
recognises that

> My conscience hath a thousand several tongues,
> And every tongue brings in a several tale,
> And every tale condemns me for a villain.

> (5.5.147–9)

For Troughton, the implication of these lines was clear:

> [T]here they sit, these 'thousand several tongues', right in front of him – fifteen hundred on a good night! They have laughed with him, gone along with him, been amazed by him and finally have separated from him, forming two halves of the same character.
>
> (1998: 96)

Working backwards from this moment, Troughton found it possible to cast his audience as Richard's alter ego throughout. The audience became not only a confidante and an accomplice, but 'a character which had the power to influence and affect the direction that Richard takes during his murderous assault on the English crown' (1998: 89). The climax of the play, therefore, became the final showdown between Richard and this composite character; Richard's 'conscience' speech became 'a direct confrontation with the audience, with Richard seated at the front of the stage, daring them to criticize the life that he has led' (1998: 95). The audience's role was not merely incidental, but central to the very shape of the plot.

The other key Shakespearean Vice character follows a very different trajectory. Sir John Falstaff, like Richard, is likened to a Vice quite explicitly: in this case, Prince Harry calls him 'that reverend Vice, that grey Iniquity, that father Ruffian, that Vanity in Years' (*1 Henry IV*, 2.5.458–9), listing the sorts of abstract nouns which medieval Vices often had for names. Like Richard, Falstaff has a close relationship with the audience, and the three plays in which he appears are peppered with funny monologues for the character. Unlike Shakespeare's more sinister Vice-descendants, however, Falstaff is far from murderous: his sin is merely that of self-indulgence. Charged with being an 'abominable misleader of youth', Falstaff defends himself on the grounds that as a man who is 'old', 'merry' and 'fat', he is representative of 'all the world' (*1 Henry IV*, 2.5.471–85). In this sense, he is more a carnival figure than a villain.

Falstaff's seductions of the audience, then, are not quite so straightforwardly condemned by their contexts. As the armies prepare for battle at the end of *1 Henry IV*, Falstaff is left alone on stage, having been told by Hal, 'thou owest God a death' (5.1.126). He turns and speaks directly to the audience:

> 'Tis not due yet. I would be loath to pay him before his day. What need I be so forward with him that calls not on me? Well, 'tis no matter; honour pricks me on. Yea, but how if honour prick me off when I come on? How then? Can honour set-to a leg? No. Or an

arm? No. Or take away the grief of a wound? No. Honour hath no skill in surgery, then? No. What is honour? A word. What is in that word 'honour'? What is that 'honour'? Air. A trim reckoning! Who hath it? He that died o' Wednesday. Doth he feel it? No. Doth he hear it? No. 'Tis insensible, then. Yea, to the dead. But will it not live with the living? No. Why? Detraction will not suffer it. Therefore I'll none of it. Honour is a mere scutcheon. And so ends my catechism.

(5.1.127–40)

At Shakespeare's Globe in 2010, Roger Allam regularly solicited the reply 'no' from the audience in response to some of these questions, especially at 'But will it not live with the living?'. When the play was performed in Spanish by the Mexican Compania Nacional de Teatro at the Globe to Globe festival in 2012, Roberto Soto's delivery of the speech produced exactly the same sorts of responses from a number of Spanish-speaking spectators. Falstaff's deconstruction of 'honour' is evidently persuasive, and in contrast with the Vice characters considered above, his behaviour does not result in a tragic outcome which might force the audience to reconsider their allegiance. Falstaff's friendship with the audience thus opens the play up to all sorts of potentially subversive meanings. As David Wiles argues, 'the Tudor Vice/clown tradition was never more complex than when, under pressure for dramaturgical change, it spawned Falstaff' (1987: 116).

Casting the audience

In Tim Carroll's production of *Richard III* for Shakespeare's Globe in 2012, the audience were not merely Richard's addressees: we were cast in a number of fictional roles within the world of the play. In 3.7, for example, Roger Lloyd-Pack's Buckingham made use of our collective silence to cast us, with a dismissive gesture, as the unresponsive citizens of London:

RICHARD.   How now, my lord, what say the citizens?

BUCKINGHAM.   Now, by the holy mother of our Lord,
The citizens are mum, speak not a word.
[…] when mine oratory grew to an end
I bid them that did love their country's good
Cry 'God save Richard, England's royal king.'

RICHARD.   And did they so?

BUCKINGHAM.   No, so God help me, they spake not a word;
But, like dumb statues, or breathing stones,
Stared each on other, and look'd deadly pale.

$$(3.7.1–26)^{10}$$

After audience laughter, Buckingham continued with his tale, explaining that he had planted 'some followers of mine own/At the lower end of the hall', and that these collaborators had cried 'God save King Richard!' (3.7.34–6); when he recounted this, Lloyd Pack worked to solicit this response from a number of nearby groundlings. The scene went on, and Mark Rylance's Richard reappeared on the balcony, dressed as a monk, before the Lord Mayor and the 'citizens of London'. Buckingham insisted to Richard that 'we heartily solicit/Your gracious self to take on you the charge/And kingly government of this your land' (3.7.130–2), and made a gesture to the audience which invited an affirmative cheer. 'Would you enforce me to a world of care?' said Rylance's Richard (3.7.213), and once again, spectators cheered in response. 'I am not made of stones,' he replied (3.7.214), with glorious mock-reluctance, and the audience laughed. Finally, when Buckingham declared 'Long live Richard, England's worthy king!' (3.7.230), he encouraged many more in the audience to join in. The participating audience members were playing at least three separate, but overlapping, roles: partly the ignorant citizens of London, crying for Richard when we were manipulated to do so; partly Buckingham's unscrupulous plants, helping him to orchestrate events; but we were also partly ourselves, an amused and probably sceptical theatre audience who were entirely aware of Richard and Buckingham's audacious ruse. We could not have laughed at it if we were not.

Rylance's Richard had built a kind of playful reciprocity with the audience from the opening moments of the play, smiling, laughing and stuttering as he admitted to us, almost casually, that he had laid 'plots' and 'inductions dangerous' (1.1.32); when he complained that 'dogs bark at me as I halt by them' (1.1.23), several playgoers voiced a mock-sympathetic 'Aah!'. As the performance progressed, though, Richard's relationship with the audience shifted. Once we had cheered for him to become King, the implications of our complicity became clear: he ordered the young princes' deaths with a chilling calmness, and gave a public instruction to 'Rumour it abroad/That Anne my wife is sick, and like to die' (4.2.52–3) while the terrified Anne stood right next to him. By the time he was confronted by a furious Queen Elizabeth (Samuel Barnett) in 4.4, the allegiances of the majority of the audience had clearly shifted: there was incredulous laughter at his dismissive responses to her grief, and she exited to applause, during which Richard glared at the groundlings with a kind of betrayed fury. When James Garnon's Richmond made his first appearance in 5.2, he welcomed us as 'Fellows in arms, and my most loving friends' (5.2.1), and now we had a new ally onstage. His oration to his soldiers was directed straight at us, whereas Richard's was delivered almost to nobody. Clearly we were being offered a new role within the fictional world, as Richmond's, rather than Richard's, soldiers: despite our previous sympathy for the devil, now, finally, Richmond could assure us with sincerity that 'God, and our good cause, fight upon our side' (5.5.194). In such circumstances, one could see perfectly how the play's dramaturgical strategies might once have worked to reinforce hegemonic Tudor accounts of English history.

In shared-light spaces like the Globe, it seems natural to play such passages to the audience. As Ralph Alan Cohen argues,

> [s]uch moments as Antony's funeral oration, King Henry exhorting his troops at Agincourt, and Claudius addressing the court at Elsinore are obviously moments in which Shakespeare has transformed the house into a part of the play.
>
> (2008: 219)

Indeed, an average-sized modern professional cast cannot hope to convincingly embody the 'many-headed multitude' of *Coriolanus* (2.3.16–17), the mob which Cassius fears and which Brutus so badly underestimates in *Julius Caesar* (3.2), or the charging English army of *Henry V* (3.1). There was evidently a similar problem in Shakespeare's own theatre: Thomas Platter's account of watching 'the tragedy of the first Emperor Julius Caesar' in 1599 is clear that the play had 'a cast of some fifteen people' (Gurr 2004: 256), and if this is (as is widely believed) a description of Shakespeare's play, then the onstage crowd during Brutus and Antony's all-important funeral orations cannot have numbered more than about seven or eight (Cassius leaves the stage with a substantial group of citizens at the beginning of the scene). *Henry V*'s Chorus addresses this problem directly in his opening prologue, when he asserts that 'a crooked figure may/Attest in little place a million' (15–16). Faced with a tiny cast, he suggests, the audience must fill in the numbers with their imaginations.

The effect of this in *Henry V* is often to ask the audience to assume a temporary imaginary identity as Henry's loyal soldiers. Henry's famous speech beginning 'Once more unto the breach, dear friends, once more' (3.1.1–34) is a potentially show-stopping piece of rhetoric in which an English audience – cast as 'dear friends' – can be whipped up, like Henry's soldiers, into patriotic fervour. The speech was frequently met with applause at the Globe in 1997, and at the same theatre in 2012, Jamie Parker's delivery climaxed in a genuine invitation to the audience to cry 'God for Harry! England and Saint George!' (3.1.34). Performed during a summer which had been suffused with British patriotism – Queen Elizabeth's Diamond Jubilee and the London Olympics were at the forefront of the national consciousness – a significant number of audience members took up Parker's rallying call. Parker told *The Independent*'s Alice Jones, in fact, that at one performance, 'two guys in the gallery turned up with a St. George's flag' (19 July 2012). Ko reports similarly nationalistic responses to the speech in the 1997 production, adding that while the English characters were cheered, the French were repeatedly booed (1999: 115). Cynthia Marshall describes a moment later on in the latter production when Mark Rylance's Henry invited any members of the audience/army with 'no stomach to this fight' to 'depart' (4.3.35–6); one spectator in the gallery cried out 'We're with you, Harry!', to 'the delight and apparent approval of most everyone else' (2000: 360).

I am not sure, though, that all such superficially jingoistic responses can be read as unambiguous endorsements of Henry, or indeed of real English nationalism. Henry's speech is immediately followed by a parodic inversion, in which the drunkard Bardolph enters repeating Henry's words – 'On, on, on, on, on! To the breach, to the breach!' (3.2.1) – before his companions agree to hang back from the fighting. In the 2012 Globe production, the audience's responses to Henry's speech were undercut even further in this scene, as the actor playing Bardolph imitated 'the action of the tiger' with a comic growl, and added a series of misquotations of Henry's famous speech; many spectators laughed at this moment of subversion. Later, when Henry ordered the killing of the prisoners (4.6.37), the audience's silence was all the more conspicuous because of their previous noisiness; Ko describes the same moment in the 1997 production as having 'left many in the audience visibly and audibly at a loss' (1999: 117). 'If shuffling and looking about are any indication,' he continues, 'the audience I was a part of not only felt disappointment but also underwent that disconcerting experience of being taken out of the moment during the Agincourt sequence' (1999: 118).

Ko concludes by identifying in such audiences 'some degree of self-consciousness about participating in theatrical illusion' (1999: 118).

In both productions, the audience's performance of English patriotism was clearly a playful and temporary one – their assumed identity was often, as it were, in ironic quotation marks (usually, in fact, a significant proportion of audience members at the Globe are not English). When Rylance delivered Henry's challenge to 'attest/That those whom you called fathers did beget you' (3.1.22–3) directly to the audience, it was met with laughter. Parker's Henry identified an individual spectator as a 'good yeoman/Whose limbs were made in England' (3.1.25–6), clasping him on the shoulder, and once again, the effect was to make the audience laugh. We were being reminded of the fundamental silliness of pretending that we were the English army; our fictional identity did not coincide to any great extent with our real one as members of a theatre audience. Of course, audience members who are so invested in seeing the play as an expression of English patriotism that they have planned ahead and brought St. George's flags to wave are unlikely to have their minds changed by the nuances of performance. Spectators who have a more casual relationship with the play's nationalism, however, may find themselves in a different position.

The fictional crowds which Cohen lists have an important factor in common: they are all manipulated by powerful speakers into a collective endorsement of morally questionable behaviour. Antony uses his public oration in order to provoke 'Domestic fury and fierce civil strife' (3.1.266); Claudius uses his in order to legitimise a claim to authority which he has achieved by murder. Even Henry's is a glorification of violent action, and if it does rouse an audience to the point where they momentarily forget their scepticism, it demonstrates all the better the dangerously seductive power of heroic speechmaking: upon his very next appearance, Henry threatens the people of Harfleur with merciless violence, mass rape, and the brutal murder of infants (3.3.84–126). We might add the Roman citizens of *Coriolanus* to Cohen's list, since they are repeatedly addressed by public speakers. Their collective opinion is the site on which the play's ideological battle between the patricians and the tribunes is fought – although unlike their counterparts in *Julius Caesar*, the plebeian crowd in *Coriolanus* also debate among themselves.

These fictional crowds do not realise that they are being manipulated, but the real-life audience generally do. The act of watching such crowds, therefore, is very different from pretending to be part of one. In Gregory Doran's *Julius Caesar* (RSC, 2012), Antony's funeral speech was delivered to an onstage crowd of around 30 actors, who became increasingly vocal, unified and aggressive as the scene went on; the theatre audience, sat around the periphery of the stage, could only look on in impotence as Antony's oratory worked its terrible effects. Deborah Warner's production of the same play for the Barbican International Theatre Event in 2005 recruited a cast of 100 supernumeraries for the crowd scenes, and while the effect of watching such a large crowd erupt into violence was both visceral and thrilling, the audience in the theatre clearly shared none of its responses. Interestingly, Escolme notes that when she saw the same production at the more intimate Teatro Español in Madrid, the crowd scenes 'worked differently':

> I was less inclined to judge the plebeians, as I was closer to them and to those attempting to inspire and persuade them. I was, after all, part of a theatre crowd, being persuaded of all kinds of things myself.
>
> (2007: 173)

Escolme's analysis highlights one of the key questions facing any company attempting *Julius Caesar*: to what extent should one invite one's audience to stand aloof from the play's crowd, and to what extent should one invite them to be part of it?

The text itself seems to suggest a certain correspondence between the audience and their onstage counterparts. When, at the beginning of the play, Casca describes the Roman crowd's responses to Caesar, he says that they 'clap him and hiss him, according as he pleased and displeased them, as they use to do the players in the theatre' (1.2.260). David Thacker's 1993 production for the RSC exploited this parallel by staging the play in promenade, so that all of the action took place among a crowd who were both a theatre audience and, when necessary, the people of Rome.

Sarah Hemming's account of the production's rehearsal process indicates that the company were keenly aware of the potential problems inherent in the audience's double role: Kenn Sabberton, the actor playing Casca, pointed out that a play which begins by ordering its audience to 'get you home' will render them rather uncertain as to what is being asked of them, while Barry Lynch (Antony) emphasised the importance of making the audience 'feel very comfortable' (*Independent*, 28 July 1993). Ultimately, the production appears to have got the balance more-or-less right; despite his stated aversion to promenade performance, Peter Holland felt that

> Thacker staged the Forum scene brilliantly, with the promenading audience and a few actors mingled among them staring up at

Brutus or Antony on their towers as the light gently accentuated the crowd's rapt faces; helped by the hard-working concentration of the crowd-actors, the audience was bound together into a group, if not a mob.

(1997: 160)

According to Hemming, a 'straw-poll' of the production's early test-audience revealed that 'most would now book for a promenade ticket rather than a conventional one' (*Independent*, 28 July 1993).

Push the audience/crowd parallel too hard, though, and it starts to fall apart. A theatre audience is composed not of Shakespeare's Roman citizens, but rather of people who have paid to come and see a play, and an overt emphasis on their fictional role is likely to serve merely to remind them of this. This was particularly evident in Mark Rylance's 1999 production of *Julius Caesar* at the Globe. Shakespeare's play may align the audience with the people of Rome during the funeral orations, but the parallel ends there – it is the onstage citizens, not the audience, who become the dangerous mob which murders Cinna the Poet. In an attempt to implicate the audience in this moment, however, the Globe production planted actors in modern dress among the groundlings (the rest of the production was in Elizabethan dress). Stirred to violence by Antony's rhetoric, these groundling characters leapt onto the stage to beat Cinna violently before dousing him with petrol; Rylance apparently characterised this stage invasion during rehearsals as an attempt 'to *challenge* the audience to *do something about it*' (Bessell 2000: 24; emphasis original). But however ethically committed spectators are, they are unlikely to feel moved to leap onto the stage during a play in order to prevent what is very obviously a fictional murder. Consequently, as Catherine Silverstone reports, audience members tended to laugh at the sequence in performance (2005: 44). Writing in *The Sunday Times*, John Peter termed the production's audience involvement 'phoney':

I call it phoney because, when actors, playing citizens in modern clothes, mingle with the audience and harangue the politicians onstage, the audience is not really involved: people tend to smirk uneasily, watch how others react, giggle like schoolboys – everything except feel that the 'citizen' is one of them and that they are taking part in the action.

(30 May 1999)

Audiences can be implicated in a play's narrative by their actual spectatorial choices, as this chapter has shown, but direct coercion from the actors is likely to remind them simply of the pretence.

Numerous productions have fallen victim to this over the years. Peter Hall's 1984 *Coriolanus* for the National Theatre sold on-stage tickets to audience members who were, in Holland's words, 'willing, as needed, to be shepherded around the stage by a few actors'. For Holland, though, the strategy backfired:

> Clutching their shopping and often looking distinctly embarrassed, this mob proved only the gap between Coriolanus's Rome and the moment of the performance. Never a starving, angry, politicised, vulnerable group of citizens, they shared with Shakespeare's crowd only their confusion.
>
> (2008: 148)

Kristina Bedford's account of the production reports that Ian McKellen's 'threatening charges' as a sword-brandishing Coriolanus were 'met with nervous titters from individuals worried at the prospect of being caught up in the stampede' (1992: 44). McKellen himself has complained that conventionally seated spectators came away talking about 'the odd characters they have spent the evening looking at, instead of talking about the production' (2003). Hall gradually reduced the amount of audience involvement over the production's run, partly at the behest of his frustrated actors – but Bedford notes that even after this cutback, 'the self-conscious reactions of individuals embarrassed to find themselves in the public eye still led to a diffusion of tension in the dynamic of the action' (1992: 44).

Other examples abound. Holland describes the forced audience involvement during the wrestling scene in John Caird's 1989 *As You Like It* with some distaste: spectators were encouraged by the cast to stand up for Duke Frederick's entrance, and while most did as they were told, Holland reports that he was 'made to feel curmudgeonly for sitting firmly in my place' (1997: 56). As the scene continued, various cast members planted in the audience tried to goad the spectators into cheering for Charles, the antagonist of the scene. For Holland, the sequence 'brought the play's momentum to a complete halt' (1997: 56). Similar problems were evident in Iqbal Khan's 2012 *Much Ado About Nothing*, when audience members were invited onto the stage to become guests at Claudio and Hero's wedding. While their presence was amusing at the beginning of the scene, when they shared nibbles and interacted with the actors, it became jarring when the scene took its darker turn: as Claudio denounced Hero and the characters around them responded with shock and horror, a handful of self-conscious and embarrassed audience members could be seen in the thick of the action, grinning from ear to ear. In all of these cases, the audience members' fictional roles within the play world were directly in conflict with their roles as spectators.

In some productions, of course, this is precisely what is being aimed at. Shakespearean parodies frequently employ audience participation in order to establish a sense of disjunction from the official discourses of the Shakespearean text: thus the Reduced Shakespeare Company, for example, cast the entire audience in the role of Ophelia's subconscious in their version of *Hamlet* in *The Complete Works of William Shakespeare (abridged)*, while in shows like the Edinburgh Fringe's annual *Shakespeare for Breakfast*, or Oddsocks theatre company's Shakespearean pantomimes, audience participation is a recurring feature. The epitome of this strategy was perhaps to be found in Mark Rylance's authorship-conspiracy play *I Am Shakespeare* (2007), the climax to which featured the whole audience being encouraged to stand-up, Spartacus-like, and assert their authorship of Shakespeare's plays; Michael Billington described the moment as 'nonsensically liberating' (*Guardian*, 3 September 2007). Insincerity may be the aim, or it may be a means to an end. Icelandic company Vesturport's 2003 *Romeo and Juliet* issued their audiences with bubble-blowing kits, so that spectators could participate in the wedding celebrations which concluded the first half; this fostered a jokey atmosphere at the time, but it also set a tone which the production's tragic conclusion directly subverted. It was all the more powerful because of it.

Casting the audience is inherently carnivalesque, and this can sometimes complement the text. In a 2008 *Twelfth Night* by the theatre company Filter, Sir Toby Belch (Oliver Dimsdale) and Sir Andrew Aguecheek (Jonathan Broadbent) slowly enlisted the audience into their debauched coterie, encouraging spectators to join in with a rowdy song, to come up onto the stage and drink tequila shots, to share takeaway pizza in the auditorium, or to throw a number of fabric balls across the length of the theatre at Sir Andrew's Velcro helmet (Figure 6.1). The sequence climaxed in glorious anarchy, the entire theatre a site of playful activity; when Ferdy Roberts' Malvolio interrupted the chaos with a furious 'My masters, are you mad?' (2.3.83), his question was clearly directed not just at Sir Toby and Sir Andrew but at the whole house. As Billington put it in his *Guardian* review, the production allowed its audience 'to

Figure 6.1 Oliver Dimsdale (Sir Toby Belch) and Nicolas Tennant (Sir Andrew Aguecheek) in Filter's *Twelfth Night*. Still: Ellie Newbury, from *Twelfth Night*, a Filter Theatre production in association with the Royal Shakespeare Company, as featured in *What You Will*, a film by Filter/Guy de Beaujeu/Simon Reade, 2012

become participants in a feast of misrule' (3 September 2008). A similar effect was evident in Michael Boyd's 2006 production of *2 Henry VI*, when Jack Cade's followers cast the audience as the ruling-class intelligentsia against whom they were rebelling. Here, the audience was playfully antagonised by everyone onstage. One audience member (who turned out to be a plant) was threatened with execution, and upon Dick the Butcher's exhortation to 'kill all the lawyers' (4.2.78), the whole company sprung into the auditorium in an attempt to find a lawyer among the spectators. The audience plant was then sentenced to death because he was in possession of an RSC programme ('He's a book in his pocket with red letters in't!'; 4.2.91). The sequence generated a carnivalesque inversion of both theatrical and political order, at once hilarious and rather dangerous, and drew satirical attention to issues of social class and privilege both inside and outside the fiction.[11]

In these last two examples, the casting of the audience is of a different order from the play-acting requested of spectators in the Hall *Coriolanus* or the Khan *Much Ado*. Here, the audience were not asked to assume a fictional identity, but rather they became implicated in the conflicts of the plays through their actions and identities as spectators. In this sense, it is sometimes where the attempt to coerce an audience into a particular kind of role or behaviour *fails* that a play's power structures become most exposed, and perhaps most vulnerable. Peter Holland's refusal to stand up for Duke Frederick, or the Globe audience's evident disunity with the people of Rome in the 1999 *Caesar*, are moments which, in Escolme's words, 're-engender the audience as audience' (2005: 119): for a moment, the Duke must have lost some of his already-tenuous authority, the Roman mob some of their collective force. The audience's refusal to be interpellated in such instances may well be uncomfortable and even jarring, but it is dramatically charged. Whether these stage figures succeed or fail in their attempts to persuade us to 'do something', the complicity, or the conflict, is real.

Workshop 3: Game-playing (pp. 94–102)

Preparation:

Participants should be familiar with a particular Shakespearean play. The workshop leader should have selected a number of scenes from that play in which particular 'games' are played, or in which characters are depicted improvising. The workshop is designed for the exploration of comic set-pieces, but it might also work with less obviously playful scenes.

Workshop:

1) Play the well-known improvisational game 'Freeze'. Two players improvise a scene based on a scenario suggested by the group; at any point during the scene, an audience member shouts 'Freeze!', and the performers freeze in whichever pose they find themselves. The new player taps one of the performers on the shoulder, replacing them in the freeze-frame, and begins a new scene from this pose. The game continues until every group member has played.

2) Discuss the game. When was it funniest? Why? What is the role of the audience in this game? How important is it that we recognise each new scenario as soon as it starts? How have particular players successfully extended the game? If there is time, the group might explore other improvisation games.

3) Participants should be divided into small groups (typically of 2–4, though this will depend on the number of characters in each scene). Each group should be given a Shakespearean scene in which some sort of 'game' is played, and asked to identify the 'rules'. For example, a group studying *Twelfth Night* might look at:

- Viola's first meeting with Olivia (1.5.211–88);
- Malvolio's discovery of the letter (2.5.22–137);
- Viola and Sir Andrew's abortive fight (3.4.213–302);
- Feste's impersonation of 'Sir Topas' (4.2.1–72).

Participants should work out the 'rules' for themselves, but examples might include 'Get as close as possible to Malvolio without being discovered', 'Make a complete coward look as terrifying as possible', and so forth. There might be different rules for different characters, or in different parts of the scene.

4) Each group should perform their scene in such a way that the rest of the group should be able to guess what the 'rules' of the game are. Remember: the easier the game is, the less interesting it is. Groups should be encouraged to add sequences of play which extend or prolong the game; games are likely to be more

appealing if they develop in some way. Groups should think about the extent to which the audience is co-opted into each game.

5) Discuss. Were the scenes funny? If so, why? Did the audience members spot the 'rules'? What is the effect of being allowed to spot the rules early on in the scene? What was the role of the audience in each game? Can we identify games being played both on the dramatic and meta-dramatic levels? Can we identify similar elements of 'play' in scenes which are not obviously comic?

Workshop 4: Talking to the audience (pp. 103–13)

Preparation:

Participants should be working on Shakespearean monologues. Ideally, these should be speeches in which the character speaks alone with the audience, but the exercise can also work with speeches in which a character addresses an onstage group.

Workshop:

1) As a group, develop a list of verbs which describe actions one can perform upon somebody else *by speaking to them*. The workshop leader should write these words on a whiteboard or flipchart where everyone can see them. Try to come up with more verbs than there are group members. Examples might include: *belittle, charm, command, excite, frighten, impress, intimidate, offend, persuade, surprise, teach, warn.*

2) These words are all actions that a character might play upon an audience. Try them out by asking each participant to improvise a short speech in which they perform one of the actions upon the rest of the group.

3) If the monologues are in verse, it may help to ask the participants to 'improvise' a verse speech by simply repeating the phrase 'a-one-a-two-a-three-a-four-a-five' *as if* they were performing a particular speech action. Discuss the physical and vocal strategies they use in order to achieve their intended action.

4) Now turn to the speeches which the participants have prepared. Ask them to pick a verb from the list, and to
use their speech to perform that action upon the audience. They should feel free to invade the audience's space
if they wish, but they might prefer to remain physically
separate.

5) Discuss the effects of this direct address. What sorts of strategies did the speakers adopt in order to achieve their intended
actions? Did they succeed? Consider the effects of success, failure, and partial failure. Does the strategy cast the audience in
a particular role? Did the audience feel that they were or were
not inclined to adopt this role?

6) Try the exercise again. This time, participants must pick at least
two contrasting verbs from the list, playing them in different
sections of the speech.

7) Discuss the effects of this. How does this strategy implicate
its audience in the speaker's actions? Are we listening to an
actor, to a character, or both? Does this approach work better
for comic characters than it does for tragic characters?

An alternative workshop might try a similar exercise with a series
of duologues (and might usefully follow on from the boxed
exercise above titled 'Estranging the audience'). Does presenting
a duologue as a 'public conversation' open up any possibilities? Might it work as a competition between speakers for the
audience's sympathies?

Workshop 5: Casting the audience (pp. 113–23)

Preparation:

Participants should be familiar with one of Shakespeare's scenes
of public oratory (for example, Antony's funeral oration, or one
of Henry V's battle speeches). This exercise will work best with a
group of 12 or more. The scene might need to be cut for length.

Workshop:

1) Read through the scene as a group, and discuss the ways
in which the speaker's words might work upon the onstage

crowd. Identify specific turning points, and any moments which *require* a particular response.

2) Cast all of the named speaking parts. The rest of the group should play the fictional crowd, improvising responses as well as voicing those implied or scripted in the text.

3) Briefly discuss the scene, identifying which moments of crowd behaviour were dramatically effective, and why.

4) Divide the group into two. One group should perform the onstage crowd, while the other sits down and watches the scene. The speaker should be encouraged to address both audiences.

5) Switch over, so that the group who were performing in part 4) now become the audience.

6) Discuss the different effects of being part of a crowd and of watching a crowd. Did participants notice different things at different times? Did they prefer being members of the onstage crowd, or members of the audience? Why? Did the speaker address the two audiences in different ways? If so, what was the effect of this? If not, how did the offstage audience feel about being addressed alongside the onstage one?

7
Immersion and Embodiment

Immersing the audience

In its discussion of 'ushering the audience', Chapter 5 mentioned the induction to Ian Rickson's production of *Hamlet* at the Young Vic in 2011. Susannah Clapp's review for *The Observer* described it as follows:

> The audience approach their seats...through a backstage maze of corridors, passing a gym, a library and a number of long-faced functionaries scribbling notes; we could be in a dreamthinkspeak production – let no one say that immersive theatre has not changed things.
>
> (13 November 2011)

Indeed, a great deal of the theatre considered in the previous two chapters owes a debt to 'immersive theatre', a phenomenon which has become increasingly popular (in British theatre, at least) since the turn of the millennium. Sophie Nield defines immersive theatre as that 'in which the audience inhabit the space of the play alongside the actors' (2008: 531), while Andrew Eglinton understands the term as referring to 'a type of performance that engulfs its audience in a responsive environment' (2010: 49). It might be useful here to distinguish between immersive theatre and promenade productions, in which spectators follow a set path around a series of locations: examples of the latter might include not only the Thacker *Julius Caesar* and Cooke *Pericles* mentioned above, but also Frantic Redhead's long-running production of *Macbeth* (1998–2007), in which spectators followed the action of the play around Edinburgh's Old Town, or Demi-Paradise's annual Shakespearean productions in and around Lancaster Castle (2000 onwards). Immersive productions, on the other hand, typically allow their audiences to move around the performance site at their own pace, and often to interact with its contents.

The company mentioned by name in Clapp's review, dreamthinks-peak, describe themselves as specialists in 'site-responsive works'. They have twice produced what might be called 'immersive' adaptations of *Hamlet*: *Who Goes There?* in 2001 and *The Rest is Silence* in 2012. *Who Goes There?* premiered at the Brighton Festival before touring to Holland and then being adapted for London's Battersea Arts Centre in 2002; the company's official website explains that

> [e]ach venue was transformed into the court of Elsinore, allowing the audience to promenade through corridors, galleries, basements and performance areas, witnessing and eavesdropping on the action around them.

The production was part-drama, part-installation, mixing live action and film. Audience members were invited to become guests at Claudius and Gertrude's wedding reception, sharing wine and cake. They could eavesdrop on Polonius as he expounded his plans. Other scenes were less obviously representational and more dream-like, as Rhoda Koenig's review for *The Independent* indicates:

> In one darkened room the floor and a television showing a man and child playing are covered with billowing white muslin, and a woman sits, her back to us, washing her hands. . . . A man taps and scrapes in the scenery workshop, having just made a coffin. In a loft opening above us, a worried-sounding man reads lines from the play printed on little strips of paper before letting them slip down to us, like rejected fortune-cookie mottoes.
>
> (24 June 2002)

The text of *Hamlet* was cut up and re-arranged, manifesting itself in unusual configurations, both as speech and as visual symbolism. Lyn Gardner described the experience as being 'like seeing the play from several different angles, and with different mindsets, simultaneously' (*Guardian*, 22 June 2002).[1]

When dreamthinkspeak returned to *Hamlet* a decade later, they adapted their earlier strategy to a more confined format. *The Rest is Silence* trapped its audience in a large, dark, square, mirrored room, confronting them for the first few minutes with nothing but the space itself:

when I saw it, the initial absence of people who were obviously performers made me aware both that I was looking for signs of 'performance' in
my fellow audience members (were any of these people 'acting'?), and
that I was probably being looked at in this way myself. The production's
director, Tristan Sharps, told a Radio 4 documentary what he imagined
he would do if he were an audience member in this situation:

> I'm confronted by mirrors. I'd find that quite funny, I think – I'd be
> doing a few experiments, seeing how often I can see myself in the
> mirror, and checking out if I could see myself in infinity. I would
> definitely go up to the mirrors; I would probably touch them ... And
> then I'd think, "Well, where's the performance going to happen?"
>
> (Hemming 2012)

As the play started, the lights came up behind one of the mirrors, revealing it to be one-way glass: we were looking into a modern bedroom
and its adjacent bathroom from the perspective of their own mirrors,
as a naked man (who turned out to be Claudius) emerged from the
bed, used the bathroom sink, and rehearsed his first line ('Though yet
of Hamlet our dear brother's death/The memory be green ... ', 1.2.1–2)
into the mirror. Various 'rooms' then lit up behind the mirrors all
around us, showing a number of solitary characters looking into their
own reflections – Ophelia nervous and image-conscious, Laertes preen-
ing and flexing his muscles, Gertrude coolly applying make-up, Hamlet
impassive and introspective. We were positioned as voyeurs, staring
into intimately private spaces, choosing for ourselves the characters
upon whom we most wanted to spy. The semi-reflective surfaces of
the windows gave us back our own ghostly reflections as we did so
(Figure 7.1).

Spying became one of the central motifs of the production. The performers behaved, even in soliloquy, as if they could not see us; the sense
of voyeurism was increased by the fact that the dialogue was electron-
ically amplified and slightly distorted, as if mediated through hidden
microphones. In a neat echo of the play's own motif of mirrors and
reflections, nearly all the scenes in the play were viewed as if from the
perspective of a mirror. At one point, three identical sets of Hamlet's
bedroom were set up in parallel behind three of the windows. At once,
a single character entered each space – Polonius the first bedroom,
Gertrude the second and Claudius the third – and each set about snoop-
ing through Hamlet's private papers (Polonius with curiosity, Gertrude
with emotion, and Claudius furtively, wearing gloves). Once Polonius

Figure 7.1   Ophelia (Bethan Cullinane), Polonius (Richard Clews), and Laertes (Ben Ingles) in dreamthinkspeak's *The Rest is Silence*, 2012. Photograph by Jim Stephenson

left the space and returned to his office (behind a fourth mirror elsewhere in the space), Rosencrantz and Guildenstern entered the vacant bedroom to discover cut-up fragments of paper. Hamlet appeared in yet another room to give Ophelia what seemed to be love letters. All of these characters, each framed by a different 'mirror', then read aloud what turned out to be the 'To be or not to be' speech (though Rosencrantz and Guildenstern's delivery muddled up the word order). Faced with multiple versions of the speech from which to choose, the audience started to wander around the space almost as if they were in an art gallery.

Katie Mitchell's video installation *Five Truths*, which premiered in 2011, took this approach to the play even further. Created for the Victoria and Albert Museum, *Five Truths* featured the actor Michelle Terry in five different short films of Ophelia's suicide, each in the style of a different 20th-century theatre practitioner (Stanislavski, Brecht, Brook, Artaud, and Grotowski), all playing simultaneously in a gallery space. The viewer was thus presented with an array of Ophelias – some controlled, some chaotic, some victimised, some nightmarish – in a disorienting and visceral jumble. Each film read differently in relation to the others: as I watched the naturalistic and understated Ophelia of the 'Stanislavski' film, the songs of the 'Brecht' Ophelia to the left and the screams of the 'Grotowski' Ophelia to the right became, for me, the noises of a single character's troubled subconscious; the assertive 'Brecht' Ophelia, meanwhile, was so totally different from her passive 'Brook' counterpart that it was hard not to read them as polarised and incompatible interpretations of the character. *Guardian* critic Matt Trueman's write-up echoed his colleague Lyn Gardner's thoughts on dreamthinkspeak: calling the installation 'a visceral, immersive experience', he noted that '[l]ike reflections caught by a shattered mirror, *Five Truths* shows Ophelia from every possible angle at once' (21 July 2011).

When the installation visited Leeds, its host, Opera North, commissioned the local company Invisible Flock to create a companion piece. The resulting performance, *Who is Ophelia?*, was 'a digital, online and live encounter' which took participants 'on an interactive modern retelling of the story of Ophelia' (Opera North 2012). Audience members followed a trail through Leeds city centre, led both by text-massages sent directly to their mobile phones, and a series of interactive video screens which had been installed in shop windows. The experience, which played with the visual iconography of the drowning Ophelia, was advertised as being 'best appreciated after dark' (Opera North 2012). The journey also allowed participants to unlock online content which could be viewed live on a smartphone. Invisible Flock's Richard Warburton described the piece as a 'city wide interactive game', and explained that a key aim was to 'encourage participants to re-envisage their immediate surroundings and look at public spaces through a different lens' (Warburton 2012).

These various 'immersive' adaptations of *Hamlet* indicate some of the possibilities of the form. Spectators are typically given a role which involves physical activity and an element of decision making; their experience of the performance will be in no small part determined by the extent to which they choose to participate, by their own preferences, and by accidents of chance. The spectatorial frame through which they approach the piece is likely to be influenced as much by those of the art gallery and the video game as by that of the proscenium-arch, giving a greater sense that meaning is in the hands of the spectator rather than inherent in the production: in Barthes' formulation, the audience's role in an immersive piece is likely to be more 'writerly' than 'readerly' (1974: 4–5). Different, even conflicting meanings may compete for the spectator's consideration, and these ideas might present themselves in surprising configurations (immersive pieces are often said to be 'dreamlike'). The immersive form is also likely to focus its audience's attention on the processes (and in some cases the problems) of spectatorship itself.

Perhaps the most famous and influential makers of 'immersive' performance over the first decade of the 21st century were the theatre company Punchdrunk, who have produced a number of Shakespearean adaptations: *A Midsummer Night's Dream* (2002), *The Tempest* (2003), *The Firebird Ball* (an adaptation of *Romeo and Juliet*, 2005), and their enormously successful adaptation of *Macbeth*, *Sleep No More* (2003, 2009, and 2011). They describe their style as 'a game changing form of immersive theatre in which roaming audiences experience epic storytelling inside sensory theatrical worlds' (Punchdrunk 2012). Certain practices have become definitive: they typically create an intensely detailed set of themed installations within a large disused building; inside these spaces, actors and dancers perform sequences of movement which are highly symbolic but not always directly connected with narrative. Until some of their more recent shows, it was usual practice for the company to issue audience members with plain white carnival masks, instructing them that they were free to wander the space at their own pace and to follow performers around it, but that they were neither to touch the performers, to remove the masks, nor to speak to one another. Actors and dancers generally perform in 'looped' sequences, during which they ignore spectators; in between 'loops', they pick spectators for 'one-on-one' improvisations.

The format makes it difficult to describe a Punchdrunk show, since each audience member's experience will be different. Clapp's review of *The Firebird Ball* gives one account of the show:

> Pacing in the dark past rows of abandoned shelving and a suddenly deserted office, it looks as if nothing is happening. Then you start to see things. Figures, which from behind look like fellow spectators, turn out to be petrified models, reaching to the sky or bowed among the filing cabinets. A bird-like girl in crimson scampers past, pursued by a young man. Trying to follow her, you climb a flight of stairs and find a white wood, a forest of canvas columns; one tree bears a blossom of feathers.
>
> (*Observer*, 27 March 2005)

The Times' Donald Hutera, meanwhile, found nothing happening in the 'forest of cloth trees', but did catch 'Romeo and Mercutio's lovely duet, springing off the furniture and walls of a free-standing half-room', and spotted 'the Friar weeping quietly in a field of brutally broken effigies' (11 March 2005). In a retrospective essay, Andrew Eglinton describes having found Tybalt 'guarding a purple-lit doorway, contorting his body to the angular confines of the frame'; he notes that the majority of critical writing on the production 'was devoted to accounts of personal "moments" in a similar vein' (2010: 48). The show's 'purposefully ambiguous signifiers and absent text', he suggests, 'proved elusive for critiques of plot, staging, and character portrayal – the mainstay of play reviews' (2010: 48).

The masking of the spectators is, as Gareth White puts it, 'the most decisive and radical' of Punchdrunk's audience strategies (2009: 219). It has numerous effects: spectators become easily identifiable to one another as fellow audience members, allowing them to become 'invisible' rather than taken for part of the performance; their facial expressions are hidden from one another, making collective responses less likely; it has also been suggested that the relative anonymity of the mask enables spectators to lose any inhibitions they may have about taking part. White reports that the one Punchdrunk performance he saw which did not mask its audience (2004's *Woyzeck*) was 'less immersive, and more self-conscious', since audience members grouped together and laughed at their discomfort in a way that their masked counterparts at other Punchdrunk shows did not (2009: 225). White notes, moreover, that 'when performers try to take off the participants' masks, as they often do in the isolated, one-on-one interactions, they produce the strongest reactions': spectators apparently respond with 'tears, confessions, and sometimes anger' (2009: 228). W. B. Worthen's detailed account of *Sleep No More* describes his own experience of having his mask removed – it feels, he says, 'astonishingly intimate' (2012: 93).

One of the company's central claims is that their format 'rejects the passive obedience usually expected of audiences' (Punchdrunk 2012). In an interview with *Time Out*, artistic director Felix Barrett described the Punchdrunk approach as being about 'putting the audience in control of their destiny' (9 February 2005), and variations on this theme are among the most dominant in accounts of 'immersive' work. A number of commentators, though, have queried the extent to which such productions really do put their audiences in control. Following Jacques Rancière, Robert Shaughnessy (2012a) has questioned the assumption that an audience's physical inactivity necessarily equates to passivity or that physical engagement automatically increases individual agency. Theatre critic Michael Coveney has gone further, denouncing the 'fascistic sense of coercion' he has identified at performances by Punchdrunk and other immersive companies; Coveney gives the company's insistence that the audience always wear masks as one example. In his discussion of another immersive production (the long-running *You Me Bum Bum Train*), he complains that the style 'pretends you're the centre of attention, but deprives you of any freedom to dominate or re-organise the proceedings' (*whatsonstage.com*, 19 July 2010). Worthen's description of *Sleep No More* hints at a similar critique of Punchdrunk's work:

The performance's three cycles are carefully managed and we wander through a densely totalized, retro environment operated through a concealed technological apparatus. Throughout the space, black-masked minders in black T-shirts and jeans, occasionally in black suits, intervene to police the spectacle...As Brecht might have said, that is the realist theatre's closest approximation to the reproduction of social life: a prison, in which the guards are barely visible and in which we "choose" to be cabined, cribbed, confined to a "nature" we assent to, assent through, produce.

(2012: 95)

White summarises this position neatly when he suggests that the company 'produce experiences in which we appear to forget ourselves as social subjects' (2009: 228).

Not all immersive productions serve such unashamedly escapist ends. Mike Pearson and Mike Brooks' *Coriolan/us* (National Theatre Wales, 2012) was a conflation of Shakespeare's play with Brecht's unfinished Marxist rewrite, and its immersion of its audience was much more politically charged.[2] Performed in a gigantic former RAF aircraft hangar in rural Wales, it gave its spectators similar latitude to roam freely. Here, though, spectators were issued not with masks but with headphones: these ensured that however far away from the main action they positioned themselves, they would be able to hear the actors' dialogue, as well as John Hardy's atmospheric score. The actors, in modern dress, merged with the crowd, often speaking directly to them; a number of camera operators also occupied the space, and footage of the action was displayed live on the two large screens which hung from the hangar's ceiling (Figure 7.2). While public scenes were played out in the open spaces of the hangar, private conversations such as Coriolanus's confrontation with Volumnia generally took place in a car or in one of the three caravans positioned around the periphery of the space. Spectators thus had a number of choices as to how they were to experience the play's events: live, as either participants or voyeurs; as the audience of the live film; or incidentally, over their headphones. Frequently they were faced with different dramas in different parts of the space: Alun Thomas's review notes that as Menenius begged Coriolanus not to destroy Rome, half the audience were 'surrounding the car to hear the negotiations', while the other half witnessed 'the silent fear of Coriolanus' wife and mother through the windows of a caravan' (2013: 53).

Figure 7.2   Coriolanus (Richard Lynch), First Citizen (John Rowley), and Second Citizen (Gerald Tyler) in *Coriolan/us*, 2012. Mark Douet/National Theatre Wales

Where *Sleep No More* did its best to help its audience disappear, *Coriolan/us* made them highly present. 'Everyone in this production', noted *The Guardian*'s Andrew Dickson in a preview article, 'will be watching everyone else' (30 July 2012). Thomas's review highlights the production's 'striking use of the spectators' as Coriolanus commanded the audience to join him in his attack on the Volscians; nobody joined in, and this conspicuous inactivity became a spur to Coriolanus's contempt. Audience self-consciousness was not something this production wished to avoid. Spectators could frequently catch images of themselves on the gigantic screens, caught in the act of spectating – in many cases, the live footage showed audience members peering through windows into the characters' private (or not-so-private) dramas. This mediatised audience, conspicuously consuming images of war, reminded several commentators of current world events: Michael Billington found himself recalling media images of the Arab Spring (*Guardian*, 12 August 2012), while Dickson noted 'the unsettling sensation that permeates coverage of many 21st-century conflicts, from Libya to Egypt to Syria: that of geopolitical distance combined with the often stomach-churning intimacy of rolling news and amateur footage' (*Guardian*, 30 July 2012).

In this respect, *Coriolan/us* was developing a theme which had been established in one of the most influential Shakespearean productions of recent years. Ivo van Hove's *Roman Tragedies* (Toneelgroep Amsterdam, 2007) was a Dutch-language adaptation of *Coriolanus*, *Julius Caesar*, and *Antony and Cleopatra* in which the action of all three plays took place over nearly six hours, on a huge stage which had been dressed to resemble a modern corporate conference centre (Figures 7.3 and 7.4). Dozens of sofas were arranged in a grid around a number of plasma television screens, and audience members were invited during regular breaks to come up and watch the performance from within its enormous set. The characters of Shakespeare's plays, cast here as 21st-century politicians and celebrities, were followed around by television crews, and their words and actions were transmitted live to the TV screens across the space: as in *Coriolan/us*, audience members were thus invited to choose between the onstage action and its mediatised representation onscreen. In the performance I saw at London's Barbican Theatre, the majority of audience members chose the latter – primarily, I imagine, because the screens were where the English-language subtitles were displayed, though the reasons might have been more complex than this.

Figure 7.3   Mark Antony (Hans Kesting) speaks directly to the camera during his funeral oration in *Roman Tragedies*, 2010. Toneelgroep Amsterdam, copyright Jan Versweyveld

Figure 7.4 Audience members onstage during Ivo van Hove's *Roman Tragedies*, 2010. Toneelgroep Amsterdam, copyright Jan Versweyveld

Whatever the motivation behind their choice of medium, the spectacle of hundreds of onstage audience members watching television screens while live action occurred around them was a hugely resonant one. While it was possible for spectators to watch the events of the play uncensored, a visible majority opted to follow the version which had been edited; those of us who did were willingly and publicly submitting to media control. Christian M. Billing reports that the official edit was even playing on screens in the theatre foyer: '[t]here was no escaping the version of events that the technicians, stage right in the video-editing suite, wanted audience members to see' (2010: 421). Van Hove had cut all of the scenes featuring crowds, so the audience to whom the tribunes, Antony, Brutus and their compatriots were appealing was very clearly the media audience who were visible onstage. The public debates in *Coriolanus* were staged in the style of a modern political enquiry, and *Julius Caesar*'s funeral orations as a press conference: speeches were made into microphones, and cameras were ever-present. Antony delivered parts of his funeral speech directly into the camera, which seemed perfectly natural when viewed on screen, but decidedly calculated as live action.

Like many immersive productions, *Roman Tragedies* allowed its spectators a superficial multiplicity of choices which masked a strong element of control. Spectators could choose where to sit, purchase drinks and food onstage, pick up one of a number of international newspapers, or even check their email from one of the stage-side computer terminals. But as Natalie Corbett and Keren Zaiontz's review points out, their participation was 'entirely proscribed': amplified announcements made it clear when and where spectators were allowed to move, and the timing of these intervals was displayed in an onscreen, second-by-second countdown. 'The implicit (and explicit) contract for the audience to be visible yet silent observers,' they note, 'was quite rigid' (2011: 119). As the play's televised wars broke out, a passive audience of media consumers could be seen calmly snacking in the background. Of course, there is nothing inherently passive about watching a screen rather than live action, about following a theatre company's instructions, or indeed about eating: but the *image* of an inactive and manipulable media audience was a powerful one, and central to the production's meanings. Billing suggests that van Hove 'wanted to explore how technologically mediated channels of political representation (which became a scenographic focus) militate against meaningful dialogue between social groups in the modern world' (2010: 415).

Affecting the audience

It is easy, in discussions of spectatorship, to get caught up in questions of ideology, agency and control at the expense of the subject of emotional and embodied responses. Punchdrunk's claims about the agency of its audiences are evidently dubious, but the debate surrounding them can serve to mask what is remarkable about the company's work: its thrillingly visceral effect. Gardner describes emerging from the 2003 incarnation of *Sleep No More* feeling 'disoriented and punch-drunk' (*Guardian*, 17 December 2003), drawing attention to the affective response which is implicit in the company's name: according to the *OED*, the word 'punch-drunk' originates from boxing, describing the condition in which participants became 'dazed or stupefied from taking punches to the head'. In an interview with Sarah Hemming on Radio 4, Felix Barrett described his artistic aims in similarly physiological terms:

What I'm trying to do is make an audience member as present, so that all their senses are heightened and their synapses are firing as quickly as possible – so that the experience becomes more potent.

(Hemming 2012)

This intensely embodied effect cannot, of course, be adequately described in print, and this is perhaps the primary reason for its critical neglect.

This is not to say that critics have not tried. W. B. Worthen's essay on *Sleep No More*, alternating as it does between a rich and personalised present-tense description of the performance and a past-tense semiological and cultural analysis, indicates by its very structure that the phenomenological experience of a performance is just as important to an understanding of its effects as a textual 'reading' might be. Worthen suggests at one point that *Sleep No More*'s 'abstract, detailed, blank-faced movement' was both 'astonishing' and 'difficult to characterize precisely', since it was 'not about character': ' "what the *actor* is *doing*" is what we attend to' (2012: 91). In her book *(Syn)aesthetics: Redefining Visceral Performance*, Josephine Machon discusses Punchdrunk's work as a key example of 'visceral performance', a broad genre which 'places emphasis on the human body as a primary force of signification' and which 'enables practitioners and audience members alike to tap into pre-linguistic communication processes' (2009: 1). Such performances, she argues, affect audiences on a 'primordial' level, producing 'a response of disturbance that can be simultaneously challenging and exhilarating, at once unsettling and pleasurable' (2009: 1). Her title, *(Syn)aesthetics*, describes the experience of art which combines sensation and perception. To experience synaesthetically, she argues, 'means to perceive the details corporeally' (2009: 17).

For Machon, the 'Shakespearean and Jacobean theatre' provides an important historical example of 'visceral' performance (2009: 1). Beyond contemporary accounts and scholarly hypotheses – and, perhaps, archaeological remains and reconstructions – all that is left to us of this phenomenon is the written playtext. But even this can be experienced corporeally. In an interview with Machon, Barrett explains that as a director, his approach to Shakespeare is one of 'feeling', since 'you *feel* the text and you translate that to movement' (2009: 96; emphasis original). As Bruce R. Smith has argued, the sounds of Shakespeare's spoken language, 'whether consciously attended to or not, have their effect on epidermis and nerves' (2010: 164). Discussing the spitting and explosive sounds of the language used by Lear in his curses to Goneril (1.4.254–69), Smith notes that in modern productions, 'the actor playing Goneril often recoils under the force of Lear's words: she bends over and wraps her arms and hands around her body' (2010: 164).

Quite aside from their sonic properties, Shakespeare's plays make particular demands of actors' bodies. Hermione must stand very still, if she is to be taken for a statue; Mercutio and Tybalt must fight; Coriolanus, if the text's stage direction is followed, must hold Volumnia *'by the hand, silent'* (5.3.183, s.d.). Touch plays a central role in Shakespeare's dramaturgy: as Raphael Lyne has shown, the endings of numerous plays can be read as tantalising extensions, and ultimate satisfactions, of the audience's innate desire to see characters come into physical contact with one another (Lyne 2011). (That an audience *will* desire to witness such touching is assumed by Lyne on the basis of the cognitive theory of 'mirror neurons' discussed in Chapter 2.) At the end of *The Comedy of Errors*, for example, two long-lost brothers finally come face-to-face with one another after two hours of physical separation and near-misses, and hold hands (5.1.429–30). The audience of *The Winter's Tale* are denied the spectacle of the reconciliatory embraces between Leontes, Polixenes, Florizel, and Perdita which are narrated in 5.2, and Perdita and Leontes' attempts to kiss Hermione's statue are rebuffed by Paulina in the following scene; the audience's (presumed) desire is finally satisfied as the statue *'slowly descends'* and takes Leontes' hand, and the latter exclaims, 'O, she's warm!' (5.3.109). Similarly in *Twelfth Night*, Viola and Sebastian's protracted recognition scene is left cruelly unresolved, as Viola insists that her brother should *not* embrace her until her story has been verified by witnesses (5.1.249–54). This tension is finally resolved by proxy, with Orsino's 'Give me thy hand' (5.1.270) and 'Here is my hand' (5.1.322) satisfying the desire for a concluding embrace. All such moments, of course, anticipate the joining together of the audience's hands in applause.

In performance, it does not always work like this. Violas and Sebastians frequently embrace following the very speech which seems to preclude such action, presumably in order to satisfy this anticipated audience desire. Afghan company Roy-e-Sabs' production of *The Comedy of Errors* at the 2012 Globe to Globe festival climaxed in an explosion of physical embraces well before the final hand-hold, with virtually all the characters on stage hugging and kissing one another; the audience, many of whom were Afghan expatriates, responded with cheering and applause (my own article on the production for *Shakespeare Beyond English* considers this scene in light of the Afghan cultural taboo surrounding physical displays of affection between the genders; 2013: 282–6). In all-male casts like those of Propeller, Cheek by Jowl, or Shakespeare's Globe, a final embrace between a fictional heterosexual couple can be complicated by the simultaneous homoerotic embrace between two male performers, and certainly at the Globe there is often an audible reaction which seems to suggest that at such moments audiences are reminded of the actors' actual genders. But however Shakespeare's concluding touches are staged, it seems likely that their effects will be felt on some level in spectators' bodies.

An embodied effect of a very different sort might be produced in the trial scene of *The Merchant of Venice*. Shylock has clearly produced a knife and begun to sharpen it on his shoe by the time of his exchange with Bassanio and Gratiano at 4.1.120–2. The knife stays onstage as Shylock anticipates using it to cut a pound of flesh from Antonio's breast, and in performance, most Antonios follow Portia's instruction to 'lay bare your bosom' at 4.1.249. The audience is thus presented with an actual knife and a real, exposed human body, and primed to anticipate an incision: the tension may well be a sustained and physical one for actors and audiences alike. Shylock's act of violence seems imminent for more than 50 lines, and some productions insert a further moment of hiatus before Portia's 'Tarry a little' (4.1.302) finally disrupts his actions. In Rupert Goold's production (2011), the moment was lingering and almost unbearable: in silence, Shylock (Patrick Stewart) made a mark with a pen on Antonio's (Scott Handy's) chest before approaching him with a large knife, hands shaking, as if he were simultaneously both determined and reluctant to carry out the sentence. Antonio's body was tense and trembling, and he panted loudly through a muffle as Shylock's knife approached him. Even as an audience member who knew perfectly well that the violence was about to be averted – and moreover, that Patrick Stewart was certainly not going to mutilate Scott Handy in actuality – I found the scene extremely disquieting. Bodies respond to other bodies in ways that defy the intellect.

'Cruelty,' says Smith, 'because it engages the human body in such visceral ways, heightens an effect that is always present in dramatic performance' (2010: 171). Certainly many of Shakespeare's plays are crowded with displays of violent physical exertion and simulated pain: *Titus Andronicus* alone features numerous fights, multiple onstage deaths (most of which are bloody), the appearance of Lavinia with '*her hands cut off and her tongue cut out, and ravished*' (2.4.0 s.d.), the cutting off of Titus' hand and subsequent delivery of his sons' heads in 3.1, and the retaliatory revelation of Chiron and Demetrius' heads in 5.2. *Macbeth* adds to this catalogue not only further instances of onstage combat and violent death, but the spectacle of child murder; *King Lear*, the gouging out of a man's eyes. *Macbeth* in particular calls for copious amounts of stage blood: Duncan's first line identifies the captain by his 'bloody' state (1.2.1), while the captain primes the audience to anticipate a Macbeth whose sword 'smoke[s] with bloody execution' (1.2.18); the dialogue of 2.2 requires both Macbeth and his wife to have blood-stained hands; the first murderer has Banquo's blood on his face in 3.4, and in the same scene Macbeth describes Banquo's ghost as shaking his 'gory locks' (3.4.50); the second apparition in 4.1 is a '*bloody child*', anticipating, perhaps, the stabbing of a child in the following scene; Macbeth's severed head is presented in the play's concluding moments.[3] In performance, of course, such moments can be presented in ways which avoid gruesome spectacle: 'blood' can be provided simply by the audience's imaginative collaboration as it is evoked in the dialogue, or staged non-representationally – both Peter Brook's *Titus Andronicus* of 1955 and Yukio Ninagawa's of 2004 used flowing red ribbons. But where something resembling real blood is used, the effect is often extremely visceral.

Lucy Bailey's work at Shakespeare's Globe has become particularly associated with such effects. After her relatively innocuous *As You Like It* (1998) staged the wrestling scene in the yard, her subsequent productions at the theatre exploited the venue's physical immediacy even further. *Titus Andronicus* (2006) had a great deal of its action performed on wheeled platforms among the spectators, and Bailey's gruesome staging of Lavinia's mutilation caused so many audience members to feel faint – and often actually to faint – that the Globe had to issue advance warnings of the production's 'graphic nature' (*BBC News*, 2 June 2006). In her *Timon of Athens* (2008), a vast black net was extended across the roof of the theatre, from which the performers swooped like vultures or crawled like spiders, clicking and rattling ominously; when Timon smeared his excrement over the faces of the Painter and the Poet and threw it across the stage, his actions once again produced bodily reactions in the audience. Bailey's 2010 *Macbeth* repeated the trope which had caused such controversy in 2006, adding a scene in which the Thane of Cawdor's tongue was cut out onstage; this and other instances of onstage violence prompted the Globe to post notices in the foyer warning that 'this is a gruesome portrayal of a brutal play'. The oppressive sense of claustrophobia engendered by the play's tolling bells (demanded by the text in 2.1, 2.3, and 5.5) and repeated knocking (continuous through 2.2 and 2.3) was augmented in Bailey's production by the slitted fabric canopy which was stretched across the yard, through which groundlings were encouraged to poke their heads.

Penelope Woods' research on the audience reactions to these productions notes some highly embodied responses. Audience members at the 2010 *Macbeth*, for example, 'fainted in record numbers': in one case, 47 audience members were 'taken ill' at the same performance, and the Globe's Front of House Show Reports lead Woods to estimate that around 360 audience members fainted over 64 performances (2012: 233–4). Though spectators often faint at Globe shows regardless of the performance content, only 82 fainted over 83 shows in the same season's *As You Like It*. The fact that the Globe's previous record had been set by Bailey's *Titus Andronicus* (271 fainters over 47 shows) leads Woods to conclude that 'there was some connection between the presentation of extreme violence on stage and the extreme and unusual visceral response manifested in the audience' (2012: 234). Fascinatingly, the phenomenon appears to be contagious: Woods reports higher concentrations of fainters among groups and people standing close to each other, and in one performance, Ken Shorter, the actor playing Cawdor, felt dizzy at exactly the moment which also provoked audience members to faint (2012: 241). Most intriguingly, these responses were not simply due to audience members being duped into thinking that the violence was 'real': when spectators who had been distressed by the fake blood or excrement were comforted by stewards or actors, attempts to show them that the substances were merely stage make-up were ineffective (2012: 205). The audience members knew the substances were illusory, but were viscerally affected nonetheless.

Woods draws a parallel between Bailey's work at the Globe and that of Punchdrunk, and notes that one actor (Frank Scantori) has worked repeatedly with both (2012: 213). Robert Shaughnessy has made a similar comparison, suggesting that the Globe and the 'immersive' theatre movement share many of their core values: 'in particular, the idea that participation is enabling, empowering, democratic and even transformative' (2012a). As we have seen, the political implications of this idea must be subject to serious scrutiny; but when the Globe or an 'immersive' company make claims for a more engaged spectator, it is not an empty boast. The engagement may not be a primarily intellectual one, but involvement in a performance which leaves the heart racing and the adrenalin surging has very real effects on a spectator's moment-by-moment experience, including the process of making meaning. Mark Rylance once described 'the physical activeness' of the spectator's body at the Globe as leading to 'a quite different state for the heart and mind': '[t]he elements add to an awakened and sometimes drenched sense of the physical body' (Kiernan 1999: 132). His metaphor is one of heightened perception through immersion – and while I would hesitate to make such grand claims for some of the gorier elements of Bailey's work at the Globe, the extremity of spectators' visceral reactions to it suggests that an analogous process may be at work, on a subtler level, in any performance at the theatre.

Workshop 6: Affecting the audience (pp. 139–45)

Preparation:

Each participant should be working on a Shakespearean duologue with a partner.

Workshop:

1) Begin the workshop with a physical warm-up.
2) Following this, the workshop leader should ask all participants to lie down on the floor, relaxing every muscle and draining their bodies of physical tension. Ask them to get up from the floor very slowly, in as relaxed a manner as possible. They should begin to move around the space, slowly increasing the level of tension in their bodies: from slouching, to floating, to springing, to tip-toeing, to the point where their bodies are starting to freeze up with tension.
3) Discuss the emotional effects of these different bodily states. At which stage of the exercise did they feel happiest? At which did they feel most defensive?
4) Divide the group into pairs. Each participant should hold one hand up towards their partner and imagine that the two of them hold an invisible football between their palms. They should move around the space as a pair, being careful never to 'drop' the football; they should experiment with pushing, pulling, and staying still.
5) Discuss the emotional effects of pushing and pulling, and of being pushed and being pulled. What happens when there is conflict?
6) Turn to the scenes on which the participants have been working. Ask them to identify lines or moments in the scene which hint at particular states of tension: of internal tension, of

relaxation, of pushing, of pulling, of stasis, and so forth. Each pair should find a way of playing the scene which expresses these states physically. Encourage each pair to push particular physical states to an extreme (for example, a stand-off between two characters might involve both characters invisibly 'pushing' against one another to the point that it becomes exhausting for both actors).

7) Ask pairs to perform their scenes twice, once in silence, and once with the dialogue.

8) Discuss the effect of these dynamic changes in physical tension upon an audience. How did watching the scene make participants *feel*?

8
Constructing the Audience

The focus of the last few chapters has largely been on the ways in which the practice of being an audience might be influenced by the practices of the stage. It is not merely from a production and its performance, however, that audiences derive their cues for their own 'performances' as spectators. Ideas about the nature of Shakespearean spectatorship circulate widely in culture more broadly, and audiences will inevitably arrive at a Shakespearean performance with certain preconceptions about what their role is likely to involve. They may be or may not be seasoned playgoers. Experiences at school may well have taught them to associate Shakespeare with authority, with difficulty, with the institution, with literature, or with English history; a different sort of education might have contested some of these constructions or provided alternative ones. Audience members who are frequent visitors to Shakespeare's Globe are likely to have ideas about spectatorship which are very different from those who are more used to the West End, cinema, rock concerts, or live sporting events. Responses to a given production, then, will be strongly influenced by the extent to which it either confirms or challenges those expectations.

Presentations of theatrical spectatorship in popular culture give some indications as to the sorts of competing models which are at play. In London over the summer of 2012, a poster for Mastercard's 'Priceless London' campaign featured a close-up photograph of a woman with expensive jewellery and immaculately coiffed hair, sitting in the stalls of a Victorian theatre and looking up at the stage with tears in her eyes; the text promised 'exclusive theatre experiences in the city you love'. Elsewhere in the city, posters for Shakespeare's Globe's 2012 season featured long shots of several hundred audience members enjoying a performance together as a varied and colourful group. This tension between exclusivity and inclusivity, private experience and public event, is evident too in fictional film and television portrayals of Shakespearean spectatorship. A recurring trope is the transformative power of the live Shakespearean performance: Kenneth Branagh's *In the Bleak Midwinter* (1995), John Madden's *Shakespeare in Love* (1998), and Tommy O'Haver's *Get Over It* (2001), for example, all depict a climactic theatrical triumph, a standing ovation, and a sense of restored community among actors and spectators. In each case, the film's fictional audience is socially diverse, physically active, vocal, and responsive. Shakespearean audiences of a more sedentary though no less involved nature are depicted in Andy Cadiff's *A Bunch of Amateurs* (2008), Richard Linklater's *Me and Orson Welles* (2008), and the finales to each of the three seasons of the Canadian TV series *Slings and Arrows* (2003–2006), where in each case, once again, a fictional Shakespearean performance is rapturously received. Elsewhere, Shakespearean spectatorship is depicted as a rather more stuffy, socially exclusive affair, often in dire need of livening up: a 1980s TV advertisement for Carling Black Label showed a performance of *Hamlet* breaking out into a game of football, while Charles Lane's comedy *True Identity* (1991) culminates in a performance of *Othello* being disrupted by a mob showdown. The finale to the third season of NBC's *The West Wing* (2002) takes place against the backdrop of a gala performance of Shakespearean adaptation *The Wars of the Roses*, at which President Bartlet (Martin Sheen) is accused by a political rival of being 'an academic elitist and a snob'. In all three, the fictional spectators sit in the dark and wear evening dress.

Audiences are literally as well as metaphorically 'constructed' by the processes which bring them to the theatre: pricing, scheduling, advertising campaigns, marketing, theatre architecture, Front of House routines, and so forth. These are what Gérard Genette would describe as 'paratexts' – systems, communications, and material items which contribute to the process of ushering an audience into the text itself. Such paratexts 'surround and extend' the text and influence the public's reading of it, working 'at the service of a better reception for the text and a more pertinent reading of it' – more pertinent in the eyes of its producers, at least (1997: 1–2). By way of illustration, it may be useful to contrast the paratextual framing of two productions of *Much Ado About Nothing* which played in London over the summer of 2011: Josie Rourke's at the Wyndham's Theatre and Jeremy Herrin's at Shakespeare's Globe. For Rourke's production, in the heart of the West End, it was difficult to get a ticket for less than £50; for Herrin's, 700 £5 tickets were available at each performance. Due to the extremely high demand for tickets, most audience members at the Wyndham's Theatre would have booked months in advance, while it was generally possible at the Globe to buy a ticket on the day of the performance. Advertising material for Herrin's production tended to emphasise photographs of the Globe building and its Elizabethan-style costumes, while the publicity images for Rourke's simply featured close-ups of its two leading actors, David Tennant and Catherine Tate (Tate and Tennant had recently starred together in the fourth series of the television programme *Doctor Who*). The Globe marketed itself, as always, as a replica of Shakespeare's theatre, emphasising the collaborative nature of its space (shared light, visible audience, thrust stage, and so forth) and its claims to 'Shakespearean' authority. The Wyndham's, meanwhile, is a traditional Victorian proscenium-arch theatre with typically ornate interior decoration, which evokes not only an aura of 19th-century luxury, but also an acute awareness of economic hierarchy (audiences are separated in the foyer according to the tier of seating for which they have paid). In light of all this, it was hardly surprising that Rourke's production staged a 'star entrance' for David Tennant in order to solicit audience applause, and exploited his popular appeal throughout the show; spectators who had been primed at every stage to anticipate a 'good night out', and had paid significant sums of money and probably planned months in advance in order to see a production which had been sold largely on the basis of Tennant's celebrity, would surely have expected nothing less.

Surveying reactions to the West End production, I was struck by the disparity between different sorts of responses. The frequently rather lukewarm reviews in the press and on theatre blogs did not tally at all with the overwhelmingly positive responses which were evident in the theatre itself. I found myself reminded of John Tulloch's research into audience reactions to English Touring Theatre's *The Cherry Orchard* (2000), which showed that spectators who had been attracted by the play or the writer responded much less positively (56% approval) than those who had been attracted by the presence of particular famous actors (81% approval), or those who had booked in order to celebrate a special occasion (91% approval) (2005: 205). Chekhov aficionados, suggests Tulloch, are likely to come to a performance 'with very clear expectations of the kind of artistic and symbolic conventions for which they "love Chekhov"', and are thus more likely to disapprove when their expectations are not met (2005: 207). The same is probably true of Shakespearean specialists and enthusiasts, though more research would need to be done in order to confirm this.

At the Globe, meanwhile, audience activity is shaped by a very different set of expectations. W. B. Worthen has coined the phrase 'Globe performativity' to describe the nexus of 'modes of conduct, expression, communication, and acknowledgement' that characterises behaviour at the Globe (2003: 25). Suggesting that the Globe 'occupies a performative horizon shared at one end by theme parks and at the other by a range of living-history restorations', Worthen argues that its audience's behaviour must be in part 'shaped by expectations, modes of attention, and habits of participation learned at these venues of popular performance' (2003: 86). Indeed, several commentators have noted the performative nature of spectatorship at the Globe: in her book on the theatre, Pauline Kiernan prefers the term 'audience performance' to 'response' or 'participation', since she feels it allows a greater sense 'of the audience being both proactive and reactive' (1999: 28), while John Russell Brown has written more critically of the Globe audience's 'self-conscious air...playing their parts as "groundlings" with stereotypical behaviour' (2002: 13). Gordon McMullan likewise describes the Globe audience as 'one self-consciously *playing* at being a Globe audience' and argues that when Tim Carroll writes of 'the audience's ability to play the role required of it' (2008: 43), the director speaks 'as if he were directing everyone in the theatre, not just those on the stage' (2008: 232). There is certainly an element of truth in this, as the analysis in Chapter 6 has shown. But what McMullan's analysis perhaps underemphasises is that similar behaviours characterise the workings of *most* theatrical organisations. All audiences play at being audiences, whether self-consciously or not, by the very fact that they adopt certain behaviours as a group and in response to that group (what could be more performative, for example, than the act of applause?). Theatre professionals, moreover, will almost always have some sense of the ways in which their practice will affect the formation of that group identity, and construct their practice accordingly; theatre practitioner Chris Goode, for example, writes of 'the phantom audience that we, as makers, project, out of an admixture of experience, hearsay and blind anxiety' (2011: 467).

This section of the book has explored in detail some of the ways in which this can be done: by ushering the audience, by estranging them, playing with them, talking to them, casting them, 'immersing' them, or affecting them viscerally. These are, of course, just a few examples. They are, moreover, all actions which are attempted by the stage *upon* the audience. But as we have seen, audiences are under no obligation to acquiesce. Audience members frequently resist the stage's attempts to steer their behaviour: Tulloch, for example, describes a group of teenagers in the audience of *The Tempest* at the Barbican in 1999 who were engaged in 'their own popular cultural performance', chatting to one another and waving their arms in time with the music they were playing on their Walkmans as they defied the institutional pressures on them to engage with the stage performance (2005: 3–4). I witnessed similar resistance when I sat behind a school party in the audience for Teatr Pieśń Kozła's *Macbeth* at The Point, Eastleigh in 2010, where most of the students in front of me spent the evening muttering to one another, fidgeting noisily, and playing with their phones. The disconnect was evident on both sides of the stage: in the theatre bar afterwards, I found myself reassuring two very dejected members of the company that their work would not be treated with the same kind of dispiriting indifference at every performance (Eastleigh was the Polish company's first stop on a UK tour). Teatr Pieśń Kozła's production was a disciplined, musical, highly serious, and ritualistic exploration of Shakespeare's play, and audience members from elsewhere on its tour have testified to its haunting and rhythmic power. At this particular performance, though, neither stage nor audience seemed to have had very much to say to one another.[1]

Sometimes the resistant spectator feels herself or himself in the minority. In her chapter on 'Audiences' for *Shakespeare and the Making of Theatre*, Sarah Werner recounts her dismay at what she perceived as a collective endorsement of misogynistic stereotypes when the audience at Shakespeare's Globe laughed loudly at Albany's line 'Shut your mouth, dame' (5.3.145) in 2008's *King Lear*, and again at Rosalind's 'Do you not know I am a woman? When I think, I must speak' (3.2.244–5) in the following year's *As You Like It* (2012: 171–3). *The Financial Times'* theatre critic, Alastair Macaulay, has repeatedly articulated his impatience with 'the Globe audience', writing about crowds of which he was evidently a member in the third person, as if 'it' were a separate entity: 'it' is, apparently, composed of 'plebs' (28 May 1999), 'never so happy as when it can boo, hiss, cheer or roar with laughter' (1 June 1998), and 'clutches at anything it can find to laugh at' (7 July 2004).[2] But this unified audience of philistines, to which Macaulay imagines himself an adversary, is of course just another construction; Macaulay himself seems to recognise this in his review of the Globe's *Hamlet*, when he notes that 'most of the audience laughs a great deal less than the nearest standees' (13 June 2000). Collective laughter can create a powerful sense of an in-group and its outsiders, but it generally masks a much more nuanced set of responses.

Audience response will almost always be divided, of course. The existence of user-submitted reviews on websites such as *london-theatreland.co.uk* and *whatsonstage.com* have made the fiction of the unified audience response more impossible to sustain than ever before: the *whatsonstage.com* page for the RSC/Wooster Group collaboration *Troilus and Cressida* (2012), for example, lists 40 user-submitted reviews, of which 30 award the production the lowest possible rating of one star, four the highest rating of five stars, and four a very positive four stars, while only one audience member awards the performance either two or three stars respectively. Thus, while the 'average' rating is an indifferent two stars, the vast majority of *whatsonstage.com* users either condemned the production or strongly endorsed it. Audience responses to Rourke's *Much Ado* on *london-theatreland.co.uk* are similarly divided, although the weighting is the opposite: of 84 reviews, 74 awarded either four, four-and-a-half, or five stars, while eight users awarded either one or two, and only two users gave a middling rating. We should hesitate, of course, before reading such statistical breakdowns as a measure of over-all audience response: audience members with strong opinions about a production will be much more motivated to write a review than those who are ambivalent, and not all users employ star ratings in quite the same way (some five-star reviews voice serious criticisms, for example, while some one-star reviews outline redeeming features).

An obviously divided audience is often an interesting one. A friend and I bought tickets to the same performance of the Globe's *The Merchant of Venice* in 2007; I got a seat in the lower gallery, while he bought a standing ticket for the yard. A miniature Venetian bridge jutted out into the yard, and it was from this position, among the groundlings, that Salerio and Solanio mocked and impersonated Shylock in 2.8. The playgoers who surrounded them most immediately tended to laugh at this cruel and anti-Semitic sequence; from my seat in the gallery, however, the audience laughter was as remote as the fictional world of Venice. Speaking with my friend afterwards, I found that we had reacted to the moment in completely different ways – his proximity to the laughing group had made him profoundly uncomfortable, while my distance from them had led me to view the moment as one which was problematising rather than celebrating the Christians' mockery. Like *Roman Tragedies* and *Coriolan/us*, this was, perhaps, a production which was dividing its audience in order to make us look at one another more closely.

The actual responses of modern Shakespearean audiences remain largely undocumented. Archive recordings allow researchers to identify communal responses such as laughter and applause, but this rarely allows for an analysis of individual reactions. Professional reviews by academic and press critics are a useful source of information, but are inevitably biased towards the responses of a particular kind of spectator.[3] User-submitted reviews on internet sites also provide a wealth of material, but as we have seen, the self-selecting nature of the sample makes this problematic, too; casual reviewers, moreover, might not provide answers to the sorts of questions in which academic critics are interested. Audiences are frequently surveyed for marketing purposes by theatre companies anxious to identify particular kinds of tastes and preferences, but this kind of feedback is generally solicited in the form of multiple-choice questionnaires. Surveys of this sort allow for the identification of broad trends, but tend to obscure the nuances of individual response. Audiences are rarely asked for their opinions by academic researchers, but this is beginning to change: as we saw in Chapter 3, John Tulloch (2005), Willmar Sauter (2010), and Penelope Woods (2012) have led in-depth surveys of modern Shakespearean audiences, while online projects such as *Year of Shakespeare* and the University of Warwick's *Re-Performing Performance* have collected audio and video recordings of audience interviews.[4]

The last four chapters, then, have explored just some of the identities that modern Shakespearean audiences have been asked to assume, considered the extent to which these requests derive from text, production, or performer, and hinted at some of the ways in which particular audiences have responded. But if 'the audience' is a role projected by the stage, it is a nebulous one, hard to define precisely; the task of audience researchers keen to identify the extent to which this role is either taken up or resisted by actual spectators therefore becomes very complicated. This chapter has suggested that 'audience' is a role which we start to formulate well before we step into the theatre, and which continues to resonate long after the particular group of spectators that constitutes it has disbanded. At the same time, 'the audience' is an identity to which individual spectators might never fully subscribe at all: they may understand their individual responses both in parallel and in contrast to those of the shadowy group called 'audience' from which they stand apart.

Part IV
Debate and Provocation

9
Pocket Henry V: A Collaborative Debate

Audience response is a slippery and often elusive object of study. The individual spectator's experience of an audience's group response is inevitably highly subjective: attempts to describe that response, let alone analyse it, are heavily influenced by the spectator's own context. On the very simplest level, the audience response in one section of the theatre building might be very different from the reactions evident only a few metres away; on a broader level, the social and cultural frames of reference within which a spectator makes sense of his or her neighbour's reactions might be very different from those of the neighbours themselves. In Chapter 1, I made a case study of the audiences of a particular Shakespearean production using a number of different methodological approaches, but the analysis was all my own: the resulting narrative was thus the product of my own cultural priorities and reference points. What might somebody else have made of the same data? This question was the impetus for a second experiment in accounting for audience response, in which I invited a colleague to accompany me to another Shakespearean production. Our brief was simple: each of us would independently write an account of the production and its reception, and we would use these accounts to initiate a collaborative debate between us.

On Tuesday, 25 September 2012, the audience researcher Dr Penelope Woods and I went to a London secondary school to observe Propeller theatre company's *Pocket Henry V* in action. The production is an adaptation of *Henry V*, based on Propeller's own full-scale, all-male touring production, but cut down to one hour and performed by a cast of six. It toured schools, theatres, and a Spanish theatre festival in late 2012, and was described in its advertising copy as a 'pocket-sized show for young audiences'. Our initial accounts are below; the debate, which was conducted via email, follows.

Penelope Woods

Large men with guns and partial uniform patrolled the assembly hall as we filed in. The sixth-form students whom I was with discussed, with some excitement, how nervous this performance strategy made them feel. It was a focus-pulling and alienating device that effectively re-codified the familiar school hall and injected it with possibility. This was the possibility of something shocking or strange that might rip a small hole in the fabric of expectations sewn up by the otherwise familiar school routine. The device functioned as an immersive shorthand for 'war'.

The 300-strong audience in the hall on this afternoon was a mixture of Year 9 pupils studying *Henry V*, a local primary school contingent right at the front wearing luminous bibs, a sixth-form Theatre Studies group, and a handful of staff. The rectangular hall seated students in two adjacent blocks with a central gangway. There was a balcony about 60 feet back from the stage from which more students looked down on the action. Audience and performers shared the same afternoon lighting. The school clock above the stage had stopped at a quarter to nine.

The soldiers entered from the back of the hall singing *A Pair of Brown Eyes*, the Irish folk song by Shane McGowan. The close harmony of the singing soldiers suggested the male comradeship of this 'band of brothers', while the lyrics described blood and war and body parts. A change in gear was effected by a sudden amplified crash through the sound system, a simultaneous lighting change, the tolling of bells, the swift formation of a tableau with the King centre stage and spot-lit, and the scattering of blood-red petals. The song morphed to a more lugubrious rendition of the *Kyrie Eleison* litany and there was some dispersed chatting among the students as the play opened with Henry's discussion with the archbishops. Henry (Chris MacDonald) pulled the focus back with direct address to the audience, seeking out and holding eye contact with the students to assert: 'yours the noble sinews of our power' (1.2.223).

The noble ambassador of France was announced by kazoo. His chest of tennis balls opened and spilled off the stage and down into the hall among the students. The scattered bouncing picked up on the repetitive 'mock', 'mock', 'mock' of Henry's response to the Dauphin's insult (1.2.281–86). The students, particularly the very young students closest to the rolling balls, followed them with their eyes, their rubbery attention skittering across the hall. Gathering the focus back posed a challenge but MacDonald engaged the audience again in direct address.

The royal 'we' of his concluding speech became an inclusive 'we' that co-opted the students in his/'our' military endeavour.

This radically cut production then skipped us over many scenes to land us in the French King's court, with the throne now draped with a *fleur de lys* cover, and love songs played on a ukulele, to produce a different court dynamic. I was unsure how readable this scene was, or consequently how successfully it established the character of Henry's 'enemy'. Cannon sounds and machine-gun fire shortly announced that we were in the thick of the siege. Harry, wearing grubby singlet and crucifix, was enthroned in a siege tower. The audience were cast by MacDonald as 'yeomen' and exhorted to 'show us here/The mettle of your pasture' (3.1.26–7). The end of the speech was abrupt, in a way that felt it could have cued laughter, but none came. Instead the 'Mayor' of Harfleur entered from the back of the assembly hall with an umbrella and a loudspeaker, a slightly comic figure, who conceded the city to Henry's army. The sound of rain underscored Henry's subdued acceptance and for me suddenly manifested the floods that were devastating the country. I wondered whether the recorded sound of the rain was experienced in this associative way by the students.

The soldiers reprised the *Pair of Brown Eyes* refrain as Alice (Thomas Padden) entered from the back and had her clothes and make-up done semi-visibly behind a makeshift screen at the front of the hall. Acknowledging the student audience's scrutiny of her drag, she pointed ostentatiously to her outfit and exclaimed 'Ma jupe? C'est de *Marks & Spencer's*.' The exaggerated stereotypes of femininity served to emphasise by contrast the monotonously homosocial world of church, court, and battlefield we had seen so far. Alice described Princess Catherine (played here by Neal Craig) as 'a bit like Kate Middleton' except that she 'wore clothes on both her bottom and her top half'. There was some laughter at this section.

Having cut the Eastcheap characters and Captain Fluellen, there was none of the pathos and comedy of the lower orders to offset the jingoistic militarism of Henry's war. Making the dragged-up foreign Alice function as the comedic lynch-pin for the whole play was a choice that was somewhat problematic. This section, played as a risqué bathing scene, did not consistently produce the laughs that it seemed to have been constructed to get. There was a bit with a suggestive loofah that generated 'oohs' from the students and some nervousness, engendering a notably charged atmosphere. Alice went to shave Kate's armpits and then stopped herself, saying: 'Non, ce n'est pas Francais'. This fell rather flat. The fact of laughter more generally at this scene, however, was something of a relief, since there had been none thus far.

A snare drum roll returned us to the army camp and the men singing around a 'camp-fire'. This was signified with torchlight playing across faces and some dry-ice standing in as smoke. The dry-ice was another spectacle, like the tennis balls, that dispersed attention as much as it startled and awoke it. As the smoke fanned out across the hall, the students waved it away, and some coughed. The delight of the smoke that entered into their own immediate horizon of attention and play prompted further laughter, discussion, and coughing among the students. I wondered how this was being experienced by those students seated above us in the balcony area looking down.

A harmonica played while Harry, loosely disguised with a cloak, talked to his men. I found it hard to gauge how apparent this disguise was to the student audience. Their spectatorial and imaginative labour had been drawn on consistently in this small-cast production to help re-inscribe the actors in their doubled and re-doubled character parts. While MacDonald's Henry enumerated his perspective on the legitimacy of the war and the King's integrity and humanity, a student behind me yawned audibly, and the primary school students at the front turned around restlessly in their seats to look at the rest of the audience.

We plunged back into the more familiar theatrical languages that had been established for the play with the sounds of thunder and hooves and the appearance of men in Riot Police uniforms. The roar of a soundtrack of crackling flames and burning was overlaid on top. I wondered how immediately or viscerally this staging evoked the London Riots of the year before (my immediate association) and how the students felt about those riots.

Henry ordered his men to cut the throats of all their prisoners (4.6.36–8) and a soldier onstage slit a bag of 'blood' which gushed into a white bucket. This visual language of swirling red echoed the opening scene of red petals. The announcement that the day was Henry's, after all, was followed by a long silence and then a bugle call played softly on a low pipe. Drumming gradually swelled as the scene switched from battlefield to court.

The French and English kings sat side by side, one enthroned, the other in a wheelchair. Craig's Kate, with painted lips but unpainted cheeks, arrived to greet Henry. The students did not laugh at her 'I cannot speak your England', or at Henry's response; instead Alice 'did' the laughs for us onstage, perhaps revealing a response that the company sought or had anticipated, but were not getting in this performance.

Kate, with her shaved head and painted face, was haunted-looking and serious. Her family and her country had been ravaged and torn apart by this impulsive and greedy warrior king. It felt as though the students responded to her hopeless gravity rather than to other indications in the production that there was licence or room to laugh at this bit.

As the scene warmed up, Henry's failed attempts at French generated some laughs, while Kate's unyielding response to Henry's 'Canst thou love me?' – 'I cannot tell' – prompted a spontaneous round of laughter. The build-up to Henry and Catherine's kiss, with Henry kissing Kate's hand first and then proposing a kiss on the lips, escalated tension in the school hall about whether or not we were about to watch two men kiss. The kiss that this section culminates with was executed with a sleight of hand (literally) which proposed that the kiss had taken place, but did not stage the men's lips meeting. This resulted in a restless rumbling and muttering among an audience clearly nervous about onstage kissing, particularly in its complex cross- and transgender enactment by this company. The cast began a rendition of the *Te Deum Laudamus*, swelling to a nostalgic, grieving, celebrating chorus that broke off abruptly with a crack of lighting and tableau formation that echoed the theatricality of the opening scene. This was a mausoleum of Henry V into which I read the futility of the brief reign of this famous King. The cast joined in with an 'Amen' and a final boom of war resounded through the hall.

Stephen Purcell

We had attached ourselves to a class of friendly Year 12 BTEC students, who led us to the hall where the performance was to take place. The route was policed by actors in military combat gear, each of whom wore a balaclava and carried a large wooden baton. They stared at us in threatening silence as we passed.

We, of course, were far from silent. Students and teachers alike giggled nervously and muttered comments to those around them; as we entered the cavernous school hall, the excited hubbub continued. 'Make sure you remember this bit', one of the teachers instructed a group of Year 9 boys as they filled the rows of seats near me, intimating that the performance's frame would be an important element in their subsequent follow-up in class. Some of her pupils laughed as a masked soldier advanced towards her, and she skipped away in mock terror. When Propeller's cast of six entered from the back of the hall, singing in unison, the students fell to well-behaved silence and attended to the production with what seemed to be genuine interest and curiosity.

The actors made their way towards the small stage that stood at the end of the hall and remained on it for most of the production. The primary reason for this was presumably practical – it was the only space in the hall from which the action could be seen by the whole audience, who were arranged in straight rows facing the front. It did, however, place the actors in a strongly demarcated 'authority' space, where King Henry's throne sat only a few feet away from a small lectern: the students were thus confronted with adjacent symbols of both theatrical and pedagogical authority. A good 20 minutes passed before one of the actors re-entered the audience space; this occurred when Chris MacDonald's Henry, rallying his troops at Harfleur, leapt into the central aisle to address the audience as his 'good yeomen,/Whose limbs were made in England' (3.1.25–6). It was his fellow actors, though, to whom he referred as standing 'like greyhounds in the slips' (3.1.31), and he returned to the stage within a few seconds. The sense that MacDonald was attempting to forge a more powerful connection between Henry and the students was strong; so, too, was the sense that he had not entirely succeeded. Indeed, MacDonald mentioned in a question and answer session afterwards that he had found the size and shape of the school hall problematic in this respect.

It was shortly after this that the production seemed to ignite the space between stage and audience with a more tangible charge. Until this point, the dialogue had been entirely Shakespeare's, and direct address had been limited to occasional asides rather than full speeches. Now, however, Thomas Padden's Alice entered in a pleated skirt and addressed the audience in a sitcom-style French accent with a distinctly non-Shakespearean monologue. 'You are probably wondering what a beautiful woman like me is doing in a play like this', said he/she, flirting with the audience and soliciting mocking laughter from the hall. The Year 9 boys near me were especially amused when Alice made reference to the Duchess of Cambridge's recent topless photograph scandal. They seemed less keen, though, to participate in a more directly prompted moment, as Alice asked us to join her in calling the Princess ('Où estu, Catherine?'), and to applaud her as she entered. This particular audience-within-an-audience seemed happy to participate on its own terms, but not so much under explicit coercion from the stage.

The scene that followed was similarly broad. Catherine's English lesson took place while the Princess took a bath, and the students seemed to enjoy the scene's innuendoes and cartoonish characterisation. After such a profound sense of disconnection between stage and audience in the early scenes, the students' responses here made me reflect upon the practical function served by characters such as Pistol, Bardolph, Mistress Quickly, and Fluellen in the uncut text: their scenes provide actors with an opportunity to re-engage with their audiences on a very direct, anachronistic and meta-theatrical level. In this production, where the more obviously comic characters had been cut, this dramaturgical function fell to Alice and Catherine.

The production did not regain this charge between stage and audience until Catherine's reappearance in the final scene. This time, though, the audience's energy took a more hostile form. As Henry and Catherine's conversation neared its conclusion, it became increasingly clear that the scene might require its male performers to kiss one another; from 'Then I will kiss your lips, Kate' (5.2.255) onwards, an undertone of mumbling and shuffling sounded in the rows around me. When this sequence was interrupted by the King's return, the sense of relief was palpable: loud murmurs broke out across the hall. Henry's subsequent request, 'bear me witness all/That here I kiss her as my sovereign Queen' (5.2.352–3), provoked audible groans: perhaps because the student audience thought they had escaped the prospect of having to perform a response to a homosexual kiss, only for the possibility to present itself again, and perhaps because the line itself was a very specific request for them to 'bear witness' to the act. As it happened, the kiss itself was very carefully staged – the performers kissed their own fingers and then each other's. Both production and audience seemed intensely aware that in a secondary school, a romantic kiss between two men is highly taboo.

When the actors bowed at the end of the show, the applause was warm and generous. Whoops and cheers sounded from elsewhere in the hall; near me, the Year 9 boys merely applauded politely.

Debate

SP: Reading our two accounts side-by-side, I'm really struck by the moments in which we've accounted for audience response rather differently. There seem to be three key discrepancies:

1. Our feelings about the relationship between the 'Inner Frame' of the performance and the 'Outer Frame' of its presentation within an educational context. You argue that the performance 'recodified the familiar school hall' in a rather liberating way, whereas I felt that the performance was working much more in tandem with the trappings of institutional authority.

2. Our sense of Henry/Chris MacDonald's connection with the student audience. You suggest that he succeeded in co-opting the students 'into his military endeavour', whereas I felt his attempts to establish a direct relationship with the students had not quite worked.

3. Our readings of the students' responses to the bathtub scene. You've emphasised some of the ways in which it failed to generate the laughter it was clearly aiming for, while my account suggests it was more successful (though both of our accounts, in fact, register its hit-and-miss nature).

We were, of course, sat with very different constituencies within the hall: the responses of the Year 9 boys near me were clearly rather different from those of the mixed-gender group of sixth-formers near you.

I wonder to what extent the performance's institutional context accounted for some of the evident mismatches between the company's expectations of audience response, and the actual reactions of the students. With the sexual humour, for example, I think perhaps it may have been the context, rather than the humour itself, which made the students nervous about responding: institutionally sanctioned innuendo disrupts all the normal rules about 'appropriate' school discourses, and while this may have been liberating for some students, it might have been unsettling for others. I notice that we both used the word 'charged' in relation to the bathtub scene, and I wonder whether we've used this term as a metaphor for the tension between the different discourses and horizons of expectations which were underlying the scene and its reception?

PW: I think the identification of a tension between the inner and outer frame in this production is really helpful. The two moments where the incompatibility of these frames felt like it was most at stake seemed to be the opening pre-performance section and the bathtub scene – we both pay attention to these sections in our accounts. I felt that the framing device of having the six actors patrol the space menacingly to begin with was effective. It surprised the students I was with and seemed to offer a very different codification and use of this space to the one with which it is usually inscribed. As you point out, this was the only time the actors really used the audience space, so this initial practice felt like an unfulfilled promise that anticipated a slightly different production to the one we actually got.

I very much agree with your assessment of the bathtub scene and the reasons it was 'charged' in this context. There was an anxiety on the part of the students about how they 'could' or 'should' respond to this scene, and a simultaneous anxiety on the part of the teachers, generally sitting at the end of rows and monitoring behaviour. I'm interested that you think this 'charge' was different among the Year 9s to the sixth-form students and I suspect you are right about this; the stakes are different for these different demographics. In this scene, I felt that the humour on offer through the stereotyping of the French, and particularly French women, was not seized on by the students. Instead, the complexity of dragged-up male bodies pretending to be scantily dressed, slightly saucy female bodies generated a kind of nervous tension among the older students I was sitting with.

I felt a frustration with this section, as with any young people's theatre in which the reductive humour regimes of stereotype (which so easily collapse into sexism, racism, homophobia) are employed. For me, this betrays an anxiety about not being able to hold students' attention with the 'serious' stuff. These cheap laughs seem choreographed to secure, or regain, attention, bespeaking an anxiety about the inevitability of it having been lost in the first place. As we both point out, the cut-down version that removes the Eastcheap characters places a burden of comedy on the Alice and Catherine scenes. In an all-male production of a play predominantly concerned with homosocial scenarios, making the only cross-dressed female characters the keystone of light relief is problematic. I point out that the students resisted the available humour in the final scene and registered instead something that seemed more interesting about the vulnerability and gravity of Kate's situation here.

Where the inner and outer frame did have a fleeting moment of rewarding symbiosis was, I felt, in the foreign-language lesson in which Alice teaches Kate English. This reaped the benefits of being framed by a school-hall setting. The students who were embedded in familiar routines of pedagogy responded knowingly to the scenario of the enthusiastic but hapless pupil trying and not always succeeding with her language lessons.

I note that the school hall clock had been stopped for the performance. This was an indication of the rupture in merging performance and institution. Clocks are a 'sign' of institution, its regime, schedule, and organisation of bodies in space through time. However, you will rarely find clocks in theatres – except in a set signifying something about organised daily life – because performance likes to propose that

it is outside of time. This seemed a potent metaphor for the disconnection we have registered about performance and audience in this
setting.

SP: I'm not sure I found the Alice and Catherine scenes problematic in
quite the same way. While they certainly relied on some crudely stereo-
typed jokes, their overall function seemed much more progressive to
me: in a play-world dominated by nationalistic machismo, it was a pair
of foreign women (who were also men in drag) who made contact with
the audience most directly and satirised the discourses of the main plot.
As your own account shows, Catherine's comic treatment did not preclude the possibility of the audience taking her seriously in the final
scene.

I hadn't noticed the clock, but I like your sense that it symbolised
a 'rupture'. In many ways it was the ruptures that interested me most
about this theatre event – the sense of licensed naughtiness, and the
students' uncertain reactions to it; the blend of official and unofficial
histories; the anachronistic clash of past and present; and the feeling
that this was an 'adult' production re-tailored for a school audience.
I found myself wondering, for example, whether any of the students
would have recognised the Shane McGowan song, and the joke about
French women's personal grooming habits was not only a bit xenopho-
bic but also rather dated. I found myself especially interested in the
students' performances of resistance at various points. We both noted
their responses to the kiss, for example, and I was especially interested
by your account of the students near you yawning. Were these yawns
'performed', do you think?

PW: I think audience yawning is often more complicated than it is
given credit for, particularly among visible and/or young audiences.
The audible yawning that took place around me in response to King
Henry's campfire 'disguise' scene seemed an appropriate performative
response, on one level, to the unpersuasive and self-aggrandising claims
Henry makes in this section. However, it also manifested restlessness,
effectively establishing a shared microcommunity among the immediate audience I was sitting with. I think the students were resisting being
asked to *listen* to the matter of the play. The theatrical strategies up until
this point – heavy underscoring, props, smoke, and so on – had incul-
cated a regime of reactive (as opposed to active) attention. When it came

to asking the students to use a more active independent attention to listen to Henry's words and his arguments (and assess these within the conflicting narratives of 'war' in the play), this audience activity was at odds with the reactive attention pattern that had been established.

This seems like a good opportunity to address the second discrepancy you highlight, and to think about the issue of direct address. We both reference the explicit direct address strategies employed by MacDonald, as Henry, and Padden, as Alice, in particular. However, whether this successfully connected with students or not is less clear. I think this issue also comes under your useful delineation of the students' 'performances of resistance' on this afternoon. In his promotional video for this cut-down production, Propeller's Artistic Director, Edward Hall, places emphasis on the direct address, arguing that in an educational context, it has a social agenda:

> In Shakespeare's plays the characters talked to the audience [...] Propeller like to engage with the audience in this way because we like younger people to come into the theatre and feel like they can express themselves, that it is *their* afternoon or their evening and they can enjoy it or not in the way they wish to.
>
> (Propeller 2012)

For Hall, direct address is a strategy for explicitly enabling *audience* expression and ownership. Neither of us, though, felt that student expression had been successfully encouraged or enabled in this performance. The moments of direct address for Henry were about co-opting the students into his dubious military endeavour, but I'm not sure how engaged, enthused or even comfortable students were with this. Perhaps this registers something further about the particular synthesis of these two frames. Within that institutional framing, I suggest, students are habituated to having people address them directly but without any sense that this might instantiate meaningful reciprocity. Here your point about the mapping of the performance space onto the authority space is significant. These authority structures and practices may have needed to be more successfully disrupted or recodified for the direct address, and particularly that of the 'king', to be experienced as 'enabling' student expression and engagement in the way Hall desired. It seems significant that the moments of energetic engaged encounter were with the direct claims on space and attention made by the tennis balls and the smoke that entered the assembly space and hailed the students' immediate and local attention but posed no threat to pedagogic strictures governing what to do when someone addresses you.

SP: 'What to do when someone addresses you' – I've felt that anxiety myself in the theatre! In many ways, I think, the uncertain status of the actors in the school environment compounded what is a fairly perennial problem when a fictional character talks directly to a group of real spectators. How are we meant to react? It's rarely an exchange in the manner of a real conversation.

But this is also a play which is about the legitimacy – or otherwise – of authority. Perhaps the students' unwillingness to be co-opted into Henry's army was an entirely appropriate response – an active refusal rather than simply a failure to engage. As an authority figure, Henry was heavily aligned in this particular staging with the institution; maybe the tension we've talked about was a manifestation of a healthy scepticism about such figures.

I'm fascinated by your inference that modes of attention are produced by the stage – that the students had not been allowed enough space to acclimatise to long verse speeches, but that if they had, their responses would have been different. Do you think the production's reliance on sound effects, bouncing balls, dry-ice, and so forth underestimated the students' receptive capabilities?

PW: It did perhaps reveal anxieties about engaging and sustaining the attention of young audiences. But it may also have responded to the material limitations of touring performances in schools, enabling some control and consistency in directing attention and producing atmosphere in otherwise variable spaces and circumstances which do not allow much time for rehearsal or reconfiguration. The conventional direction of attention through lighting technologies is disrupted in most school performance spaces in which, as in this assembly hall, we all share the same lighting. The company employed a minimal ground rig, but focus was directed by the use of underscoring and sound effects in conjunction with the sort of precise and spectacular blocking and choreography that makes a sudden impact. I describe several moments in which the company expertly achieved these spectacular tableau scenes. These set up an iconography of kingship and of war that was vivid and memorable. I wondered what you made of this?

However, the production was perhaps not as successful as it sought to be in implicating students actively in the performance text. Ultimately it established a more passive kind of attention, so that when verse-speaking required active listening, the students disengaged. My concern is that this then corroborates latent anxieties about the students' inability or lack of desire to attend to the speaking. The doubling necessitated by this small company production had additional implications for the ways in which students engaged with and attended to it. If we had had the opportunity, this would have been interesting to follow up. I suspect there were strategies for staging direct address and interaction that might have scaffolded the students' listening and thinking more successfully. However, I also appreciate the difficulties that MacDonald articulated in the subsequent Q&A: in that assembly hall, with its front-on proscenium-arch-type stage and students in rows (and further back up in a balcony), it was hard for the actors to generate the kind of atmosphere that would facilitate inclusivity and engagement.

SP: I agree that the visual elements of the production were very effective, though I did feel that they were sometimes rather 'framed' – aside from the tennis balls and the Harfleur sequence, most of the visual imagery was confined to the small stage at the end of the large hall, and was effectively rendered in only two dimensions. As you've argued, the interactive opening sequence was something of an unfulfilled promise: it suggested that the production would have a strongly immersive element, but in fact it made only token gestures towards immersion, which, as you've pointed out, tended to momentarily scatter attention rather than focus it.

I also agree that the end-on configuration was problematic. With an in-the-round or thrust staging in the centre of the hall, the students would have been able to see each other watching and responding, and the actors would have seemed more part of their world. I'd have been interested to see a sequence like the bathtub scene much earlier in the show – something that effectively told the students, 'don't worry – we're interested in your presence, and we're glad you're here'. I think both the Chorus's prologue and the first Eastcheap scene often do that in full-length productions, but the former was heavily cut and the latter cut entirely here. I can imagine that Henry's first speech to the audience might also have had this sort of effect in a different space and might well have established the kind of active attention that the character would require from spectators again later in the play. MacDonald is evidently a very capable actor, and I wonder whether, if he had persisted a little longer in his foray into the audience space in 3.1, or even tried the same thing a little earlier, he would have more readily established a dynamic in which it was clear to the students that it would be worthwhile for them to reward him with their close attention.

I realise that this rather undermines what I said above about the students' unwillingness to engage with Henry being a valid political choice. This makes me wonder about the politics of the play's dramaturgical structure. Does Henry need to be 'engaging' – to successfully co-opt his audience into his military project, in other words – in order for the play to *work*?

PW: It seems to me that something is emerging here about the aesthetics of the production and their conjunction with the politics of the play as performed within this setting. I agree with your sense that the imagery was 'framed'; deliberately put on display. The question for me is whether these images were closed or open (I'm thinking, in particular, of that first tableau of monarchical power in the English court, of the siege scene, and of the concluding 'memorial' image of the victorious Henry). The very static nature of these tableaux, in such a heavily cut production, might provoke a complex reflective spectatorial dynamic that asks: 'Is this it?'. On the other hand, these tableaux may propose an iconographical summation of power.

I think it is interesting that I concluded my account of the production with the 'boom' of the final tableau, whereas your account extended to include the students' response. I responded, perhaps, to the closed finality of the last tableau and left out the applause. Perhaps I answer my own question there in feeling that this imagistic aesthetic closed down debate around power in the play rather than presenting it for further thought. I wonder how you read the students' enthusiastic response to the production that you usefully noted, or why you thought those immediately in your vicinity were more subdued?

I particularly agree with your sense that a very different dynamic would have informed this production if the students could have seen each other watching, rather than having to face the front. I suspect this would have made the engagement with the performance feel more actively negotiated. My interest in what those students in the balcony above us might have made of watching this performance and its audience from their distant bird's-eye perspective was provoked by the potential of a multi-layering of perspective to complicate the readings of the production that we identified. In fact, the more I think about it, the more interested I am in the ways that the seating configuration

produced the particular moments of student response we have discussed here. Given this complex institutional coding and the way it
was reinforced by the seating arrangement, it was perhaps even more
important that the production made the students feel 'we're interested
in you', 'your presence is important', if it sought to produce a meaningful engagement with the play and its politics. I think Henry *does* have to
be engaging, and seductive, for there to be tension between the desire to
be persuaded by his charisma, on the one hand, and the play's currents
of doubt and scepticism about war, on the other.

The most seductive performer was, in fact, Padden's Alice. Would you
agree? This might go against my evident personal frustration with the
scene. However, the part of Alice in this version of the play gave him
the most licence to explore a direct relationship with the audience and
engage them in a relationship not simply delimited by codes of power
and authority. His explicit acknowledgement of the students and invitation to them to contribute (although this felt coerced and was resisted
at some points) stood out in the production.

One final thing I am interested in is the associations the students may
have been making and that the production explicitly drew on. Reference to the 'real world' is a dramaturgical practice that acknowledges
the complexity of the spectator's horizon of response and association
in ways that can be rich and powerful. My experience of talking to students about productions they have seen – and perhaps that would have
been the case here if we had been in a position to talk to these students – is that their response is negotiated through a layering of readings
of narrative and performance within a dense set of immediate signifiers. The indexing of war and the London riots, for instance, I thought
was provocative. The sound of rain accompanying Henry's self-pitying
speech, which I think was meant to evoke sadness, hardship, loneliness,
nostalgia perhaps, mostly reminded me of the really serious and terrible
rain that was affecting the country at that moment. My own associations and responses, furthermore, were permeated with a reflexivity
about what sorts of associations everyone else was bringing to bear.

SP: I often find myself noting the nature of audience applause, because
it's one of the most performative acts that spectators generally undertake
at a play. So while I agree that the production's tableaux tended to be
fairly authoritative, 'closed' images, the final word of the performance
belonged to the students. The enthusiastic response did seem to indicate
(and once again I'm going back on myself here) that the production had
indeed 'recodified' something about the institutional setting, allowing

the normal patterns of school activity to be productively and creatively disrupted. But I think the more subdued response near me may have been performative, too. Fear of homophobic abuse can be a fairly strong drive among male teenagers, and I suspect that some of the Year 9 boys might have wanted to distance themselves from the transgression of gender and sexual norms which had been performed in the play's final scene. I certainly agree that Padden's Alice was 'seductive' – so too was Craig's Catherine – and this probably exacerbated this aspect of the audience response.

I notice that our discussion is tending now towards speculation about the students' cultural associations, priorities, and allegiances. We should really be asking the students themselves about these things! Of course, that was not a planned part of this particular project, and as we both know, interviewing a substantial number of audience members is a major logistical undertaking. But it would seem to be the logical next step....

PW: Applause is a key site of consideration in any work on audience, and while some work has emerged in performance studies, yet more has been done on applause at political rallies by psychologists and conversation analysts. Applause is interesting as an expressive and physical activity that performs and reveals complexities of dynamics within the audience. But applause is also an entrenched cultural convention. It is a legitimate and required behaviour in both a school context and a theatre context, and it would be highly unlikely for students not to clap at all. However, interpreting what is signified by their applause is problematic. While I suspect students will clap hard or excitedly if they have particularly enjoyed something, I also think they might clap enthusiastically at rather unengaging performances because this convention offers them a safe and legitimate space to contribute. Furthermore, the release of clapping is enjoyable in itself. The microcommunities of applause behaviours in different parts of an auditorium are significant and pose challenges for audience researchers to identify and evaluate. As you suggest we are beginning to chart out some ideas for possible future audience research work here.

SP: And on that note, perhaps we should take a bow, and leave the stage! Thank you so much for the discussion.

Notes

Prologue

1. The Porter in *All Is True* comes close when he complains that 'no audience' is able to endure the 'youths that thunder at a playhouse' (5.3.58–9), but the surrounding lines show that he uses the word in the sense of a more general assembly of listeners. There are a few similar uses: Biron refers to the other characters onstage witnessing his humiliation as 'this audience' (*Love's Labour's Lost*, 4.3.208); Polonius uses the word to describe himself as he plans to eavesdrop on Hamlet's conversation with Gertrude (*Hamlet*, 3.3.31), while Hamlet himself addresses the bystanders who are 'but mutes or audience to this act' upon his death (5.2.287).

2 Making Sense of the Stage

1. The reader might wish to view the scene on DVD or via the clip on the BBC's tie-in website at http://www.bbc.co.uk/programmes/p011lpqg.
2. Modern Shakespearean scholarship, however, has not been blind to the political dimensions of spectatorship; the notion that drama always performs an ideological function has been the fundamental idea behind both New Historicism and Cultural Materialism. Stephen Greenblatt's work, for example, explores the many ways in which Shakespeare's plays are 'centrally and repeatedly concerned with the production and containment of subversion and disorder' (1994: 29).

3 Agency, Community, and Modern Theatre Practice

1. Canetti describes theatre audiences, though, as 'stagnant' crowds:

   > Everything is fixed: the play they are going to see, the actors who will perform, the time the curtain will rise, and the spectators themselves in their seats....There they all sit, like a well-drilled herd, still and infinitely patient. But everyone is very well aware of his own separate existence.
   > (1962: 36)

2. Bennett (1997: 217) notes that the idea of interpellation by ideology is from Althusser (1971: 172–183).
3. Transcribed from Brian De Palma's film of *Dionysus in '69* (1970).

4   Controlling the Audience?

1. See, for example, the reviews by Dominic Cavendish (*Daily Telegraph*, 24 September 2012), Alex Needham (*Guardian*, 1 October 2012), Ben Dowell (*The Stage*, 19 November 2012), and Alexandra Coghlan (*The Arts Desk*, 19 November 2012).
2. Most modern stand-up comedians, however, eschew the simple set-up–gag–laugh formula; the days of stand-up comedy as a platform for 'telling jokes' are largely over, and the most celebrated and successful comedians today tend to structure their routines in much more imaginative ways.

5   Framing the Stage

1. Requests for 'patience' are made in *Romeo and Juliet* P.13, *2 Henry IV* E.9, *Henry V* P.33, 2.0.31, *All's Well That Ends Well* E.5, *Pericles* 18.44, 22.124, and *The Winter's Tale* 4.1.15; pleas for 'pardon', meanwhile, occur in *A Midsummer Night's Dream* E.8, *2 Henry IV* E.3, *Henry V* E.8, E.15, *Pericles* 5.40, 18.5, and *The Tempest* E.19. Spectators are described as 'gentle' in *A Midsummer Night's Dream* E.7, *2 Henry IV* E.12, *Henry V* E.8, 2.0.35, *All's Well that Ends Well* E.6, *The Winter's Tale* 4.1.20, *The Tempest* E.11, *All Is True* P.17, and *The Two Noble Kinsmen* E.18.
2. Hall and his textual advisor, Roger Warren, adapted elements from the inductions to both Shakespeare's play and the anonymous 1594 play *The Taming of A Shrew*, a text whose exact relation to Shakespeare's is the subject of much debate. This is the first line of the latter.
3. Adapted from *The Shrew*, Induction 1.103–31. This and all subsequent transcriptions from Propeller's production were transcribed live by this author at two separate performances during the production's run at the Old Vic, London, 11 January – 17 February 2007.
4. In Bogdanov's production (1978), Jonathan Pryce paused after ''Tis charity to show' for 'as long as 1½minutes' (Shaughnessy 2012b: 218).
5. See Schafer (2002: 233–5) for details of productions which have done the same.

6   Playing with the Audience

1. Brecht, in fact, stressed the *importance* of audience pleasure in his 'Short Organum for the Theatre' (1977: 180–3).
2. Once again, there is a similarity here with Brecht, who considered the sporting audience 'the fairest and shrewdest audience in the world', and believed that if theatre audiences were allowed to smoke (as spectators at boxing matches were), they might develop a more detached and critical perspective (1977: 6, 8). Describing the dominant German theatre of the time, he complained that 'there is no possible way of getting any *fun* out of this ... There is no "sport"' (1977: 7).
3. Carroll was an Associate Director at the Globe from 1999–2005, during which period he directed numerous productions there; Tucker's company

performed *As You Like It* (1997), *King John* (1998), and *Cymbeline* (1999); Alfreds directed *Cymbeline* (2001) and *A Midsummer Night's Dream* (2002).

4. Lecoq's ideas about clowning and 'game' have been more fully developed by his former colleague Philippe Gaulier.

5. Transcribed from the video recording in the Globe's archive. This performance, and Magni's Shakespearean performances more broadly, are the subject of my article in the *Routledge Companion to Actors' Shakespeare* (2012: 158–173).

6. Alan C. Dessen points out that 'Shakespeare apparently did not use the term as part of his working vocabulary' (1995: 52).

7. Bridget Escolme critiques Gurr's 'post-nineteenth century assumption about theatrical progress' (2005: 7), and points out that States' description of an actor 'peering' into the pit assumes modern rather than Elizabethan theatrical conditions: 'audience in darkness, actor with bright lights shining into his/her eyes' (2005: 70).

8. Indeed, the desire of the characters in *Hamlet* either to remain onstage or to return to it has been a recurring trope in creative responses to the play, and is frequently used as a metaphor for mortality. At the end of Tom Stoppard's *Rosencrantz and Guildenstern Are Dead*, Rosencrantz pleads, 'Couldn't we just stay put? I mean no one is going to come on and drag us off' (2000: 116–17). Harold Rosenberg's *Act and the Actor*, meanwhile, characterises the play's ghosts and corpses as having similarly metatheatrical aims: 'Dig and there are skulls. Stick a sword through a wall that is a curtain and a voice will cry out, "I am slain!" ... Those ejected from the scene struggle to return to it. ... This lighted rectangle is all there is' (1970: 75). The Thomas Ostermeier production, discussed above, might be read in a similar way.

9. Rylance's performance of this speech, and his responses to audience interjections, are discussed in Carroll (2008: 40), Conkie (2006: 38), Escolme (2005: 71), and Worthen (2003: 106).

10. All quotations from Tim Carroll's production of *Richard III* are from the prompt copy in the archive at Shakespeare's Globe.

11. This sequence is discussed in much greater detail in my book *Popular Shakespeare* (2009: 56–9).

7   Immersion and Embodiment

1. A similar approach to this play was staged well before the boom in 'immersive theatre', by Vancouver's Tamahnous Theatre, who produced *Haunted House Hamlet* in 1986. Written by Peter Eliot Weiss and directed by Kate Weiss, this production allowed its audience 'to roam about the three floors of the house at will, flitting in and out of scenes'. The result, explains Baṇuta Rubess, was 'an infinite number of new plays', since every audience member 'creates and re-creates the play for themselves' (1986: 131). Like both of dreamthinkspeak's *Hamlet* adaptations, *Haunted House Hamlet* also reassigned the 'To be or not to be' speech to multiple characters.

2. Pearson, a foundational figure in British site-specific theatre, is ambivalent about his influence on the boom in 'immersive' productions, expressing particular reservations about what he calls Punchdrunk's 'acolytes'. He told *The*

Guardian's Andrew Dickson: 'I didn't want it to become the brand' (30 July 2012).

3. Interestingly, it is the sight of a character bleeding which prompts one of the only contemporary descriptions of Shakespeare's own audience's responses. Thomas Nashe's *Pierce Penilesse* (1592) writes of *1 Henry VI*:

> How would it have joyed brave *Talbot* (the terror of the French) to thinke that after he had lyne two hundred yeares in his Tombe, hee should triumphe againe on the Stage, and have his bones newe embalmed with the teares of ten thousand spectators at least, (at severall times) who, in the Tragedian that represents his person, imagine they behold him fresh bleeding!
>
> (Quoted in Gurr 2004: 251)

8 Constructing the Audience

1. We should be wary, though, of assuming that all disruptive behaviour is a performance of resistance. Peter Holland reports that when Joe Papp's 1965 *A Midsummer Night's Dream* went on a tour of school playgrounds in deprived suburbs of New York, a report by researchers from Columbia University recommended the employment of 'social controllers' or 'professional "shooshers" ' in order to 'reinforce the norm of quiet' among noisy spectators (2002: 199). Holland, however, questions the 'assumption that an audience must be taught to be quiet because that indicates attention', noting that 'audiences plainly did enjoy the performances and expressed that enjoyment in part by not being silent' (2002: 200).
2. Prescott (2005) writes at some length about the descriptions of Globe audiences in reviews by the major London newspaper critics.
3. See Prescott (2005) and my own article for *Shakespeare* (2010).
4. See Prottey (2012) and University of Warwick (2008).

Reading List

For a **general overview** of the study of theatre audiences, see Bennett (1997), or – for a short but provocative update – Freshwater (2009). For approaches from **theatre semiotics**, see Aston & Savona (1991), Barthes (1972), Carlson (2007), Counsell (1996), De Marinis (1987, 1993), Eco (1977), Elam (2002), Kowzan (1968), Rebellato (2009), or Ubersfeld (1999). For approaches that stress the **cultural** nature of spectatorship, see Abercrombie & Longhurst (1998), Barthes (2000), Case (1988), Fish (1980), Hall (1980), Kennedy (2009), Lilley (2010), or Sauter (2000). For an emphasis on **phenomenology and corporeality**, see Fensham (2009), Smith (2010), or States (1983, 1985, 2007). Widely cited studies from **cognitive science** include Fauconnier & Turner (2002), Gallese (2001), Gallese et al. (1996), Jacob & Jeannerod (2003), and Niedenthal et al. (2005); for an application of these ideas to the study of theatrical spectatorship, see Cook (2010), McConachie (2007, 2008), or Ralley & Connolly (2010). Studies documenting **empirical research** into theatre audiences include Bakhshi, Mateos-Garcia & Throsby (2010), Coppieters (1981), Eversmann (2004), Fearon (2010), Fitzpatrick (1990), Fitzpatrick & Batten (1991), Gourdon (1982), Reason (2004, 2010), Sauter (2002, 2010), Schälzky (1980), Schoenmakers (1990), and Tulloch (2005).

For optimistic ideas about the transformation of audience members into a **collective**, see the writings of theatre practitioners Alfreds (1979), Brook (1987, 1990), or Grotowski (1975), or those of theorists Bakhtin (1984), Dolan (2005), or Turner (1969, 1982). Theorists who are more **sceptical** about the unified audience include Auslander (2008), Blau (1990), Brecht (1977), Canetti (1962), and Rancière (2007, 2009). For accounts of practitioners who have sought to empower their audiences politically through **participation**, see Boal (2000), Callaghan (2003), Kattwinkel (2003), Kershaw (1992), Mitter (2005), or Stourac & McCreery (1986); for discussions of the more recent phenomenon of **immersive** performance, see Eglinton (2010), Hemming (2012), Machon (2009), Nield (2008), Shaughnessy (2012a), White (2009), or Worthen (2012).

Important studies of the **historical Shakespearean audience** include Cook (1981), Dawson & Yachnin (2001), Gurr (1992, 2004), Harbage (1941), and Low & Myhill (2011); useful ideas about **Shakespeare's own theatre practice** can be found in Bruster & Weimann (2004), Dessen (1995), Lopez (2003), Stern (2009), Weimann (1987, 1992), and Wiles (1987). Studies situating Shakespeare's practice within its broader **cultural context** are numerous; some of those cited here include Greenblatt (1994), Holderness (1985), and Jardine (1983). Brown (2002) considers audiences, theatre practices and cultural contexts – both historical and modern – in his study of Shakespeare and the 'Theatrical Event'. For studies of **cues for audience response in the Shakespearean text**, see Bilton (1974), Cartwright (1991), Hapgood (1988), Honigmann (1976, 2002), Howard (1980, 1984), Kernan (1982), Slater (1982), and Sprague (1935).

Studies of **modern Shakespearean audiences** include Brown (1999), Escolme (2005, 2007), Kennedy (2009), Tulloch (2005), Werner (2012), Woods (2012), and Worthen (1997, 2003). For a more general analysis of **modern Shakespearean theatre practice**, see, for example, Holland (1997), Purcell (2009), Hampton-Reeves & Escolme (2012), or Wells & Stanton (2008); for a broader consideration of **modern cultural constructions of Shakespeare**, see Bristol (1996) or Holderness (2001). Performance histories of **specific plays** can be found in series such as *Shakespeare in Production* (Cambridge University Press), *Shakespeare in Performance* (Manchester University Press), *Shakespeare at Stratford* (Arden Shakespeare), and *The Shakespeare Handbooks* (Palgrave): examples cited here include Dymkowski (2000), Holderness (1989), Lindley (2003), Loehlin (2002), Marshall (2004), Schafer (2002, 2009), Smallwood (2003), Smith (2002), and Tatspaugh (2002), while Maher (1992) provides a stand-alone study of modern Hamlets.

Specific productions are best researched through reviews in journals and newspapers, or the materials held in theatre archives, but productions are occasionally also documented in book-length studies (e.g. Bedford 1992). Theatre practice at the reconstructed **Shakespeare's Globe** is the subject of numerous studies, including Bessell (2000), Carson & Karim-Cooper (2008), Conkie (2006), Kiernan (1999), Ko (1999), Marshall (2000), Silverstone (2005), and Woods (2012). Accounts by modern Shakespearean **theatre practitioners** are especially useful: some are published in books and essay collections (such as the long-running *Players of Shakespeare* series published by Cambridge University Press), while others are available online, in newspapers and journals, or in theatre programmes. Examples by **directors** include Alfreds (1979), Barton (1984), Brook (1987, 1990), Carroll (2006, 2008), Cohen (2008), Hall (2003), and Tucker (2002), while some of the **actors** cited here include Chahidi (2008), Davies (2003), Downie (2003), McKellen (2003), Naiambana (2005), Pennington (1996), Rylance (2008), Shaw & Stevenson (1988), Sher (1985), Sinden (1985), and Troughton (1998). Holmes (2004) provides a book-length analysis of actors' accounts of performing in Shakespeare.

Abercrombie, Nicholas and Brian Longhurst (1998) *Audiences: A Sociological Theory of Performance and Imagination*, London: Sage Publications.

Alfreds, Mike (1979) *A Shared Experience: The Actor as Story-teller*, Dartington: Department of Theatre, Dartington College of Arts.

Althusser, Louis (1971) *Lenin and Philosophy and Other Essays*, trans. Ben Brewster, New York and London: Monthly Review Press.

Artaud, Antonin (1993) *The Theatre and its Double*, translated by Victor Corti, London: Calder.

Aston, Elaine and George Savona (1991) *Theatre as Sign System: A Semiotics of Text and Performance*, London: Routledge.

Auslander, Philip (2008) *Liveness: Performance in a Mediatized Culture* (2nd edn.), Abingdon: Routledge.

Bakhshi, Hasan, Juan Mateos-Garcia and David Throsby (2010) *Beyond Live: Digital Innovation in the Performing Arts*, National Endowment for Science, Technology and the Arts, http://www.nesta.org.uk/library/documents/Beyond-Live-report.pdf.

Bakhtin, Mikhail (1984) *Rabelais and His World*, trans. Hélène Iswolsky, Bloomington: Indiana University Press.

Barrett, Felix and Maxine Doyle (2009) 'Colliding Worlds: Shakespeare, Hitchcock and Punchdrunk', *Sleep No More* programme note, London: Punchdrunk.

Barthes, Roland (1972) 'Literature and Signification: Answers to a Questionnaire in *Tel Quel*', in Roland Barthes, *Critical Essays*, trans. Richard Howard, Evanston: Northwestern University Press, 261–279.

Barthes, Roland (1974) *S/Z: An Essay*, trans. Richard Miller, New York: Hill & Wang.

Barthes, Roland (1977) *Image-Music-Text*, trans. Stephen Heath, London: Fontana.

Barthes, Roland (2000) *Mythologies*, trans. Annette Lavers, London: Vintage Books.

Barton, John (1984) *Playing Shakespeare*, London: Methuen.

Bedford, Kristina (1992) *Coriolanus at the National: 'Th'Interpretation of the Time'*, Cranbury, London, & Mississauga: Associated University Presses.

Bennett, Susan (1997) *Theatre Audiences: A Theory of Production and Reception*, London: Routledge.

Bessell, Jaq (2000) 'The 1999 Globe Season: The Red Company: *Julius Caesar*', *Research Bulletin 15*, London: Shakespeare's Globe.

Billing, Christian M. (2010) 'Shakespeare Performed: *The Roman Tragedies*', *Shakespeare Quarterly* 61:3, 415–439.

Bilton, Peter (1974) *Commentary and Control in Shakespeare's Plays*, New York: Humanities Press.

Blau, Herbert (1990) *The Audience*, Baltimore: John Hopkins University Press.

Boal, Augusto (2000), *Theatre of the Oppressed*, trans. Charles A. and Maria-Odilia Leal McBride and Emily Fryer, London: Pluto Press.

Brecht, Bertolt (1965) *The Messingkauf Dialogues*, trans. John Willett, Chatham: W. & J. Mackay & Co.

Brecht, Bertolt (1977) *Brecht on Theatre*, trans. J. Willett, London: Eyre Methuen.

Bristol, Michael D. (1996) *Big-Time Shakespeare*, London: Routledge.

Brook, Peter (1987) *The Shifting Point: Forty Years of Theatrical Exploration 1946–1987*, London: Methuen.

Brook, Peter (1990) *The Empty Space*, London: Penguin.

Brown, John Russell (1974) *Free Shakespeare*, London: Heinemann.

Brown, John Russell (1999) *New Sites for Shakespeare: Theatre, the Audience and Asia*, London & New York: Routledge.

Brown, John Russell (2002) *Shakespeare and the Theatrical Event*, Basingstoke: Palgrave Macmillan.

Bruster, Douglas and Robert Weimann (2004) *Prologues to Shakespeare's Theatre: Performance and Liminality in Early Modern Drama*, London & New York: Routledge.

Callaghan, David (2003) 'Still Signalling through the Flames: The Living Theatre's Use of Audience Participation in the 1990s', in Susan Kattwinkel [ed.] *Audience Participation: Essays on Inclusion in Performance*, Westport, CT: Praeger, 23–36.

Canetti, Elias (1962) *Crowds and Power*, trans. Carol Stewart, London: Victor Gollancz Ltd.

Carlson, Marvin (2007) 'Semiotics and its Heritage', in Janelle G. Reinelt and Joseph R. Roach [eds] *Critical Theory and Performance* (2nd edn.), Ann Arbor: University of Michigan Press, 13–25.

Carroll, Tim (2006) 'Introduction to *The Hamlet Project*', *The Factory Theatre*, http: //thefactory.wetpaint.com/page/Tim+Carroll%27s+Introduction+to+The+ Hamlet+Project.

Carroll, Tim (2008) 'Practising Behaviour to His Own Shadow', in Christie Carson and Farah Karim-Cooper [eds] *Shakespeare's Globe: A Theatrical Experiment*, Cambridge: Cambridge University Press, 37–44.

Carson, Christie and Farah Karim-Cooper [eds] (2008) *Shakespeare's Globe: A Theatrical Experiment*, Cambridge: Cambridge University Press.

Cartwright, Kent (1991) *Shakespearean Tragedy and its Double: The Rhythms of Audience Response*, Pennsylvania: Penn State Press.

Case, Sue-Ellen (1988) *Feminism and Theatre*, New York: Methuen.

Chahidi, Paul (2008) 'Discoveries from the Globe Stage', in Christie Carson and Farah Karim-Cooper [eds] *Shakespeare's Globe: A Theatrical Experiment*, Cambridge: Cambridge University Press, 204–210.

Cohen, Ralph Alan (2008) 'Directing at the Globe and the Blackfriars: Six Big Rules for Contemporary Directors', in Christie Carson and Farah Karim-Cooper [eds] *Shakespeare's Globe: A Theatrical Experiment*, Cambridge: Cambridge University Press, 211–225.

Conkie, Rob (2006) *The Globe Theatre Project: Shakespeare and Authenticity*, New York: The Edwin Mellen Press.

Cook, Amy (2010) *Shakespearean Neuroplay: Reinvigorating the Study of Dramatic Texts and Performance through Cognitive Science*, New York: Palgrave Macmillan.

Cook, Ann Jennalie (1981) *The Privileged Playgoers of Shakespeare's London, 1576– 1642*, Princeton: Princeton University Press.

Coppieters, Frank (1981) 'Performance and Perception', *Poetics Today* 2:3, 35–48.

Corbett, Natalie and Keren Zaiontz (2011) 'The Politics of Distraction: Spectatorial Freedom and (dis)Enfranchisement in Toneelgroep's *Roman Tragedies*', *Canadian Theatre Review* 147, 117–120.

Counsell, Colin (1996) *Signs of Performance*, London: Routledge.

Crouch, Tim (2011a) *I, Shakespeare: I, Malvolio, I, Banquo, I, Caliban, I, Peaseblossom*, London: Oberon Books.

Crouch, Tim (2011b) *Plays One: My Arm, An Oak Tree, ENGLAND, The Author*, London: Oberon Books.

Dachel, Kimberley (2006) '*Pericles, Prince of Tyre/Children of the Sea* Performance Review', *Theatre Journal* 58:3, 495–498.

Davies, Oliver Ford (2003) *Playing Lear*, London: Nick Hern.

Dawson, Anthony B. and Paul Yachnin (2001) *The Culture of Playgoing in Shakespeare's England: A Collaborative Debate*, Cambridge: Cambridge University Press.

De Marinis, Marco (1987) 'Dramaturgy of the Spectator', trans. Paul Dwyer, *The Drama Review* 31:2, 100–114.

De Marinis, Marco (1993) *The Semiotics of Performance*, trans. Áine O'Healy, Bloomington & Indianapolis: Indiana University Press.

De Palma, Brian, Robert Fiore and Bruce Rubin [dir.] (1970) *Dionysus in '69*, USA: Performance Group Stage Productions & Sigma III Corporation.

Dessen, Alan C. (1995) *Recovering Shakespeare's Theatrical Vocabulary*, Cambridge: Cambridge University Press.

Dolan, Jill (2005) *Utopia in Performance: Finding Hope at the Theatre*, Ann Arbor: University of Michigan Press.

Downie, Penny (2003) 'Steeped in History' (video interview), *Stagework*, http://www.stagework.org.uk/webdav/harmonise@Page%252F@id=6012& Document%252F@id=2705.html.

Dymkowski, Christine [ed.] (2000) *Shakespeare in Production: The Tempest*, Cambridge: Cambridge University Press.

Eco, Umberto (1977) 'Semiotics of Theatrical Performance', *The Drama Review* 21:1, 107–117.

Eglinton, Andrew (2010) 'Reflections on a Decade of Punchdrunk Theatre', *TheatreForum* 37, 46–55.

Elam, Keir (2002) *The Semiotics of Theatre and Drama*, London: Methuen.

Elam, Keir (1986) 'Theatre of Consciousness', *The Times Literary Supplement*, 7 March, 250.

Escolme, Bridget (2005) *Talking to the Audience: Shakespeare, Performance, Self*, London & New York: Routledge.

Escolme, Bridget (2007) 'Living Monuments: The Spatial Politics of Shakespeare's Rome on the Contemporary Stage', *Shakespeare Survey* 60, 170–183.

Eversmann, Peter (2004) 'The Experience of the Theatrical Event', in Vicky Ann Cremona, Peter Eversmann, Hans van Maanen, Willmar Sauter and John Tulloch [eds] *Theatrical Events: Borders, Dynamics, Frames*, Amsterdam & New York: Rodopi, 139–174.

Fauconnier, Gilles and Mark Turner (2002) *The Way We Think: Conceptual Blending and the Mind's Hidden Complexities*, New York: Basic Books.

Favorini, Attilio (1976) 'Review of *Twelfth Night*', *Educational Theatre Journal* 28:2, 270.

Fearon, Fiona (2010) 'Decoding The Audience: A Theoretical Paradigm for the Analysis of the "Real" Audience and Their Creation of Meaning', *About Performance* 10, 119–135.

Fensham, Rachel (2009) *To Watch Theatre: Essays on Genre and Corporeality*, Brussels: P. I. E. Peter Lang.

Fish, Stanley (1980) *Is There a Text in this Class? The Authority of Interpretive Communities*, Cambridge, MA & London: Harvard University Press.

Fitzpatrick, Tim (1990) 'Models of Visual and Auditory Interaction in Performance', *Gestos* 9, 9–22.

Fitzpatrick, Tim and Sean Batten (1991) 'Watching the Watchers Watch: Some Implications of Audience Attention Patterns', *Gestos* 12, 11–31.

Freshwater, Helen (2009) *Theatre & Audience*, Basingstoke: Palgrave Macmillan.

Gallese, Vittorio (2001) 'The "Shared Manifold" Hypothesis: From Mirror Neurons To Empathy', *Journal of Consciousness Studies* 8, 33–50.

Gallese, Vittorio, Luciano Fadiga, Leonardo Fogassi and Giacomo Rizzolatti (1996) 'Action Recognition in the Premotor Cortex', *Brain* 119, 593–609.

Genette, Gérard (1997) *Paratexts: Thresholds of Interpretation*, trans. Jane E. Lewin, Cambridge: Cambridge University Press.

Goode, Chris (2011) 'The Audience is Listening', *Contemporary Theatre Review*, 21:4, 464–471.

Goold, Rupert [dir.] (2009) *Macbeth*, BBC/Thirteen/Illuminations in association with wnet.org.

Gourdon, Ann-Marie (1982) *Théâtre, Public, Perception*, Paris: Éditions du Centre National de la Recherche Scientifique.

Grant, Stuart (2010) 'Fifteen Theses on Transcendental Intersubjective Audience', *About Performance* 10, 67–79.

Greenblatt, Stephen (1994) 'Invisible Bullets: Renaissance Authority and its Subversion, *Henry IV* and *Henry V*', in Jonathan Dollimore and Alan Sinfield [eds] *Political Shakespeare: Essays in Cultural Materialism* (2nd edn.), Manchester: Manchester University Press, 18–47.

Grotowski, Jerzy (1975) *Towards a Poor Theatre*, London: Methuen.

Guntner, J. Lawrence, Manfred Wekwerth and Robert Weimann (1989) 'Manfred Wekwerth and Robert Weimann: "Brecht and Beyond"' in J. Lawrence Guntner and Andrew M. McLean [eds] (1998) *Redefining Shakespeare: Literary Theory and Theatre Practice in the German Democratic Republic*, London: Associated University Press, 226–240.

Gurr, Andrew (1992) *The Shakespearean Stage, 1574–1642* (3rd edn), Cambridge: Cambridge University Press.

Gurr, Andrew (2004) *Playgoing in Shakespeare's London* (3rd edn), Cambridge: Cambridge University Press.

Hall, Peter (2003) *Shakespeare's Advice to the Players*, London: Oberon Books.

Hall, Stuart (1980) 'Encoding/Decoding', in Stuart Hall, Dorothy Hobson, Andrew Lowe and Paul Willis [eds] *Culture, Media, Language*, London: Hutchinson, 128–138.

Hampton-Reeves, Stuart and Bridget Escolme [eds] (2012) *Shakespeare and the Making of Theatre*, Basingstoke: Palgrave Macmillan.

Handke, Peter (1997) *Offending the Audience*, in Peter Handke, *Plays 1*, London: Methuen, 1–32.

Hapgood, Robert (1988) *Shakespeare the Theatre-Poet*, Oxford: Clarendon Press.

Harbage, Alfred (1941) *Shakespeare's Audience*, New York: Columbia University Press.

Hemming, Sarah (2012) 'It's Fun, But Is It Theatre?', BBC Radio 4, 28 May.

Holderness, Graham (1985) *Shakespeare's History*, Dublin: Gill & Macmillan.

Holderness, Graham (1989) *Shakespeare in Performance: The Taming of the Shrew*, Manchester: Manchester University Press.

Holderness, Graham (2001) *Cultural Shakespeare: Essays in the Shakespeare Myth*, Hatfield: University of Hertfordshire Press.

Holland, Peter (1997) *English Shakespeares: Shakespeare on the English Stage in the 1990s*, Cambridge: Cambridge University Press.

Holland, Peter (2002) 'Touring Shakespeare', in Stanley Wells and Sarah Stanton [eds] *The Cambridge Companion to Shakespeare on Stage*, Cambridge: Cambridge University Press, 194–211.

Holland, Peter (2008) 'Peter Hall', in John Russell Brown [ed.] *The Routledge Companion to Directors' Shakespeare*, Abingdon: Routledge, 140–159.

Holmes, Jonathan (2004) *Merely Players?: Actors' Accounts of Performing Shakespeare*, London & New York: Routledge.

Honigmann, E. A. J. (1976) *Seven Tragedies: The Dramatist's Manipulation of Response*, London: Macmillan.

Honigmann, E. A. J. (2002) *Shakespeare: Seven Tragedies Revisited*, Basingstoke: Palgrave Macmillan.

Howard, Jean E. (1980) 'Figures and Grounds: Shakespeare's Control of Audience Perception and Response', *Studies in English Literature* 20, 185–199.

Howard, Jean E. (1984) *Shakespeare's Art of Orchestration: Stage Technique and Audience Response*, Urbana: University of Illinois Press.

Jacob, Pierre and Marc Jeannerod (2003) *Ways of Seeing: The Scope and Limits of Visual Cognition*, Oxford: Oxford University Press.

Jardine, Lisa (1983) *Still Harping on Daughters: Women and Drama in the Age of Shakespeare*, Brighton: Harvester Press.

Jauss, Hans Robert (1982) 'Literary History as a Challenge to Literary Theory', in Hans Robert Jauss, *Toward an Aesthetic of Reception*, Minneapolis: University of Minnesota Press, 3–45.

Kattwinkel, Susan [ed.] (2003) *Audience Participation: Essays on Inclusion in Performance*, Westport, CT: Praeger.

Kennedy, Dennis (2009) *The Spectator and the Spectacle: Audiences in Modernity and Postmodernity*, Cambridge: Cambridge University Press.

Kernan, Alvin B. (1982) 'The Playwright's Reflections and Control of Audience Response', in Philip H. Highfill [ed.] *Shakespeare's Craft*, Carbondale: Southern Illinois University Press, 138–155.

Kershaw, Baz (1992) *The Politics of Performance: Radical Theatre as Cultural Intervention*, London: Routledge.

Kiernan, Pauline (1999) *Staging Shakespeare at the New Globe*, Basingstoke: Macmillan.

Ko, Yu Jin (1999) 'A Little Touch of Harry in the Light: *Henry V* at the New Globe', *Shakespeare Survey* 52, 107–119.

Kowzan, Tadeusz (1968) 'The Sign in the Theatre: An Introduction to the Semiology of the Art of the Spectacle', trans. Simon Pleasance, *Diogenes* 16, 52–80.

Kuhn, Tom (1997) 'Introduction' in Peter Handke, *Plays 1*, London: Methuen, ix–xxiv.

Lecoq, Jacques (2009) *The Moving Body: Teaching Creative Theatre*, London: Methuen.

Lilley, Heather (2010) 'Vital Contact: Creating Interpretive Communities in a Moment of Theatrical Reception', *About Performance* 10, 35–50.

Lindley, David (2003) *Shakespeare at Stratford: The Tempest*, London: Arden Shakespeare.

Loehlin, James N. [ed.] (2002) *Shakespeare in Production: Romeo and Juliet*, Cambridge: Cambridge University Press.

Lopez, Jeremy (2003) *Theatrical Convention and Audience Response in Early Modern Drama*, Cambridge: Cambridge University Press.

Low, Jennifer A. and Nova Myhill [eds] (2011) *Imagining the Audience in Early Modern Drama, 1558–1642*, New York: Palgrave Macmillan.

Lyne, Raphael (2011) 'The Shakespearean Grasp: Hands and Brains in the Theatre' (research seminar paper), University of Warwick, 24 November.

Machon, Josephine (2009) *(Syn)aesthetics: Redefining Visceral Performance*, Basingstoke: Palgrave Macmillan.

Maher, Mary Z. (1992) *Modern Hamlets and their Soliloquies*, Iowa City: University of Iowa Press.

Mamet, David (1998) *True and False: Heresy and Common Sense for the Actor*, London: Faber & Faber.

Margate Sands (2011), 'Pretty vacant: *Much Ado About Nothing*, Wyndham's Theatre', 11 June, http://margatesands.wordpress.com/2011/06/22/pretty-vacant/.

Marshall, Cynthia [ed.] (2004) *Shakespeare in Production: As You Like It*, Cambridge: Cambridge University Press.

Marshall, Cynthia (2000) 'Sight and Sound: Two Models of Shakespearean Subjectivity on the British Stage', *Shakespeare Quarterly* 51, 353–361.

McConachie, Bruce (2007) 'Falsifiable Theories for Theatre and Performance Studies', *Theatre Journal* 59, 553–577.

McConachie, Bruce (2008) *Engaging Audiences: A Cognitive Approach to Spectating in the Theatre*, New York: Palgrave Macmillan.

McGrath, John (1974) *The Cheviot, the Stag, and the Black, Black Oil*, London: Methuen.

McKellen, Ian (2003) '*Coriolanus* (1984)', *Ian McKellen Official Home Page*, http://www.mckellen.com/stage/coriolanus/index.html.

McMullan, Gordon (2008) 'Afterword', in Christie Carson and Farah Karim-Cooper [eds] *Shakespeare's Globe: A Theatrical Experiment*, Cambridge: Cambridge University Press, 230–233.

Mitter, Shomit (2005) 'Julian Beck (1925–1985)', in Shomit Mitter and Maria Shevtsova [eds] *Fifty Key Theatre Directors*, Abingdon: Routledge, 92–97.

Naiambana, Patrice (2005) 'Adopt an Actor', *Pericles, Prince of Tyre* programme note, London: Shakespeare's Globe Theatre, 31.

Niedenthal, Paula M., Lawrence W. Barsalou, François Ric and Silvia Krauth-Gruber (2005) 'Embodiment in the Acquisition and Use of Emotion Knowledge' in Lisa Feldman Barrett, Paula M. Niedenthal and Piotr Winkielman [eds] *Emotion and Consciousness*, New York & London: Guilford Press, 21–50.

Nield, Sophie (2008) 'The Rise of the Character Named Spectator', *Contemporary Theatre Review* 18:4, 531–535.

Opera North (2012) 'Invisible Flock Launch New Digital Arts Trail for Opera North Projects', 6 February, http://www.operanorth.co.uk/news/invisible-flock-launch-new-digital-arts-trail-for-opera-north-projects.

Osborne, Laurie E. (2006) 'Speculations on Shakespearean Cinematic Liveness', *Shakespeare Bulletin* 24:3, 49–65.

Penlington, Amanda (2010) ' "Not a man from England": Assimilating the Exotic "Other" Through Performance, from *Henry IV* to *Henry VI*', in Willy Maley and Margaret Tudeau-Clayton [eds] *This England, That Shakespeare: New Angles on Englishness and the Bard*, Farnham & Burlington: Ashgate, 165–184.

Pennington, Michael (1996) *Hamlet: A User's Guide*, London: Nick Hern.

Prescott, Paul (2005) 'Inheriting the Globe: The Reception of Shakespearean Space and Audience in Contemporary Reviewing', in Barbara Hodgdon and W. B. Worthen [eds] *A Companion to Shakespeare and Performance*, Chichester: Blackwell, 359–375.

Propeller (2012) 'Propeller's *Pocket Henry V*' (promotional video), *YouTube*, 26 November, http://www.youtube.com/watch?v=EAlRanwBm78.

Prottey, Bethany (2012) 'Talking to the Audience', *Year of Shakespeare*, 8 August, http://bloggingshakespeare.com/year-of-shakespeare-talking-to-the-audience.

Punchdrunk (2012) 'About', http://www.punchdrunk.org.uk/.

Purcell, Stephen (2009) *Popular Shakespeare: Simulation and Subversion on the Modern Stage*, Basingstoke: Palgrave Macmillan.

Purcell, Stephen (2010) '"That's not Shakespeare": Policing the Boundaries of "Shakespeare" in Reviews', *Shakespeare* 6:3, 364–370.

Purcell, Stephen (2012) 'Marcello Magni', in John Russell Brown [ed.] *The Routledge Companion to Actors' Shakespeare*, Abingdon: Routledge, 158–173.

Purcell, Stephen (2013) 'Touch and Taboo in Roy-e-Sabs' *The Comedy of Errors*', in Susan Bennett and Christie Carson [eds] *Shakespeare Beyond English: A Global Experiment*, Cambridge: Cambridge University Press, 282–286.

Ralley, Richard and Roy Connolly (2010) 'In Front of Our Eyes: Presence and the Cognitive Audience', *About Performance* 10, 51–66.

Rancière, Jacques (2007) 'The Emancipated Spectator', *Artforum* 45:7, 271–280.

Rancière, Jacques (2009) *The Emancipated Spectator*, trans. Gregory Elliot, London: Verso.

Reason, Matthew (2004) 'Theatre Audiences and Perceptions of "Liveness" in Performance', *Participations: Journal of Audience & Reception Studies* 1:2, http://www.participations.org/volume%201/issue%202/1_02_reason_article.htm.

Reason, Matthew (2010) 'Asking The Audience: Audience Research and the Experience of Theatre', *About Performance* 10, 15–34.

Rebellato, Dan (2009) 'When We Talk of Horses: Or, What Do We See When We See a Play?', *Performance Research* 14:1, 17–28.

Rosenberg, Harold (1970) *Act and the Actor: Making the Self*, New York: The World Publishing Company.

Rubess, Baṇuta (1986) 'Vancouver: *Hamlet*, A New Canadian Play', *Canadian Theatre Review* 49, 131–135.

Rylance, Mark (2008) 'Research, Materials, Craft: Principles of Performance at Shakespeare's Globe', in Christie Carson and Farah Karim-Cooper [eds] *Shakespeare's Globe: A Theatrical Experiment*, Cambridge: Cambridge University Press, 103–114.

Saussure, Ferdinand de (1959) *Course in General Linguistics*, Charles Bally, Albert Sechehaye and Albert Riedlinger [ed.], trans. Wade Baskin, New York: McGraw-Hill.

Sauter, Willmar (2000) *The Theatrical Event: Dynamics of Performance and Perception*, Iowa City: University of Iowa Press.

Sauter, Willmar (2002) 'Who Reacts When, How and Upon What: From Audience Surveys to the Theatrical Event', *Contemporary Theatre Review* 12:3, 115–129.

Sauter, Willmar (2010) 'Thirty Years of Reception Studies: Empirical, Methodological and Theoretical Advances', *About Performance* 10, 241–263.

Schafer, Elizabeth [ed.] (2002) *Shakespeare in Production: The Taming of the Shrew*, Cambridge: Cambridge University Press.

Schafer, Elizabeth [ed.] (2009) *Shakespeare in Production: Twelfth Night*, Cambridge: Cambridge University Press.

Schaubühne (2012) 'Hamlet', http://schaubuehne.de/en_EN/program/detail/11537844

Schälzky, Heribert (1980) *Empirisch-quantitative Methoden in der Theaterwissenschaft*, Münchener Beiträge zur Theaterwissenschaft 7, München: Kommissionsverlag J. Kitzinger.

Schechner, Richard (1985) *Between Theatre and Anthropology*, Philadelphia: University of Pennsylvania Press.

Schechner, Richard (1990) 'The Bacchae: A City Sacrificed to a Jealous God', in Robert W. Corrigan [ed.] *Classical Tragedy: Greek and Roman*, New York: Applause Theatre Books, 432–445.

Schoenmakers, Henri (1990) 'The Spectator in the Leading Role: Developments in Reception and Audience Research within Theatre Studies', in Willmar Sauter [ed.] *New Directions in Theatre Research*, Munksgaard: Nordic Theatre Studies, 93–106.

Shaughnessy, Robert (2012a) 'Immersive Performance, Shakespeare's Globe and the "Emancipated Spectator" ', *The Hare 1.1*, http://thehareonline.com/article/immersive-performance-shakespeare's-globe-and-emancipated-spectator.

Shaughnessy, Robert (2012b) 'Silence', in Stuart Hampton-Reeves and Bridget Escolme [eds] *Shakespeare and the Making of Theatre*, Basingstoke: Palgrave Macmillan, 199–219.

Shaw, Fiona and Juliet Stevenson (1988) 'Celia and Rosalind in *As You Like It*', in Russell Jackson and Robert Smallwood [eds] *Players of Shakespeare 2*, Cambridge: Cambridge University Press, 55–72.

Sher, Antony (1985) *Year of the King: An Actor's Diary and Sketchbook*, London: Methuen.

Silverstone, Catherine (2005) 'Shakespeare Live: Reproducing Shakespeare at the "New" Globe Theatre', *Textual Practice* 19:1, 31–50.

Sinden, Donald (1985) 'Malvolio in *Twelfth Night*', in Philip Brockbank [ed.] *Players of Shakespeare 1*, 41–66.

Slater, Ann Pasternak (1982) *Shakespeare the Director*, Brighton: Harvester Press.

Smallwood, Robert (2003) *Shakespeare at Stratford: As You Like It*, London: Arden Shakespeare.

Smith, A. C. H. (1972) *Orghast at Persepolis: An Account of the Experiment in Theatre Directed by Peter Brook and Written by Ted Hughes*, London: Methuen.

Smith, Bruce R. (2010) *Phenomenal Shakespeare*, Chichester: Wiley-Blackwell.

Smith, Emma [ed.] (2002) *Shakespeare in Production: King Henry V*, Cambridge: Cambridge University Press.

Solomon, Alisa (1997) *Re-Dressing the Canon: Essays on Theatre and Gender*, London: Routledge.

Sprague, Arthur Colby (1935) *Shakespeare and the Audience: A Study of the Technique of Exposition*, Cambridge, MA: Harvard University Press.

States, Bert O. (1983) 'The Actor's Presence: Three Phenomenal Modes', *Theatre Journal* 35:3, 359–375.

States, Bert O. (1985) *Great Reckonings in Little Rooms: On the Phenomenology of Theatre*, Berkeley: University of California Press.

States, Bert O. (2007) 'The Phenomenological Attitude', in Janelle G. Reinelt and Joseph R. Roach [eds] *Critical Theory and Performance* (2nd edn.), Ann Arbor: University of Michigan Press, 26–36.

Stoppard, Tom (2000) *Rosencrantz and Guildenstern are Dead*, London: Faber & Faber.

Stourac, Richard and Kathleen McCreery (1986) *Theatre as a Weapon: Workers' Theatre in the Soviet Union, Germany and Britain, 1917–1934*, London: Routledge & Kegan Paul.

Stern, Tiffany (2009) *Documents of Performance in Early Modern England*, Cambridge: Cambridge University Press.

Tatspaugh, Patricia E. (2002) *Shakespeare at Stratford: The Winter's Tale*, London: Arden Shakespeare.

Thomas, Alun (2013) 'Coriolan/us' in Paul Edmondson, Paul Prescott and Erin Sullivan [eds] *A Year of Shakespeare: Re-Living the World Shakespeare Festival*, London: Bloomsbury, 51–54.

Thomson, Peter (2002) 'The Comic Actor and Shakespeare' in Stanley Wells and Sarah Stanton [eds] *The Cambridge Companion to Shakespeare on Stage*, Cambridge: Cambridge University Press, 137–154.

Troughton, David (1998) 'Richard III' in Robert Smallwood [ed.] *Players of Shakespeare 4*, 71–100.

Tucker, Patrick (2002) *Secrets of Acting Shakespeare: The Original Approach*, London: Routledge.

Tulloch, John (2005) *Shakespeare and Chekhov in Production and Reception: Theatrical Events and Their Audiences*, Iowa City: University of Iowa Press.

Turner, Victor (1969) *The Ritual Process: Structure and Anti-Structure*, New York: Aldine.

Turner, Victor (1982) *From Ritual to Theatre: The Human Seriousness of Play*, New York: Performing Arts Journal Publications.

Ubersfeld, Anne (1999) *Reading Theatre*, trans. Frank Collins, Toronto: University of Toronto Press.

University of Warwick (2008) 'Audience Responses', *Re-Performing Performance*, http://www2.warwick.ac.uk/fac/cross_fac/capital/reperforming/dream/aspects/audience/

Van Gennep, Arnold (1960) *The Rites of Passage*, trans. Monika B. Vizedom and Gabrielle L. Cafee, Chicago: University of Chicago Press.

Warburton, Richard (2012) 'Who Is Ophelia?', *Opera North Blog*, 30 January, http://www.operanorth.co.uk/blogs/who-is-ophelia.

Weimann, Robert (1987) *Shakespeare and the Popular Tradition in the Theatre: Studies in the Social Dimension of Dramatic Form and Function*, Baltimore/London: Johns Hopkins University Press.

Weimann, Robert (1992) 'Representation and Performance: The Uses of Authority in Shakespeare's Theatre', *PMLA* 107:3, 497–510.

Wells, Stanley and Sarah Stanton [eds] (2002) *The Cambridge Companion to Shakespeare on Stage*, Cambridge: Cambridge University Press.

Werner, Sarah (2012) 'Audiences', in Stuart Hampton-Reeves and Bridget Escolme [eds] *Shakespeare and the Making of Theatre*, Basingstoke: Palgrave Macmillan, 165–179.

White, Gareth (2009) 'Odd Anonymized Needs: Punchdrunk's Masked Spectator', in Alison Oddey and Christine White [eds] *Modes of Spectating*, London: Intellect, 219–230.

Wiles, David (1987) *Shakespeare's Clown: Actor and Text in the Elizabethan Playhouse*, Cambridge: Cambridge University Press.

Woods, Penelope (2012) *Globe Audiences: Spectatorship and Reconstruction at Shakespeare's Globe*, PhD thesis, Queen Mary, University of London & Shakespeare's Globe.

Worthen, W. B. (1997) *Shakespeare and the Authority of Modern Performance*, Cambridge: Cambridge University Press.

Worthen, W. B. (2003) *Shakespeare and the Force of Modern Performance*, Cambridge: Cambridge University Press.

Worthen, W. B. (2012) ' "The written troubles of the brain": *Sleep No More* and the Space of Character', *Theatre Journal* 64:1, 79–97.

Unless indicated otherwise, all citations from Shakespeare are from the Taylor & Wells edition (1986, Oxford: Clarendon Press). All quotations from the 1594 *The Taming of a Shrew* are from the New Cambridge edition by Stephen Roy Miller.

Unless indicated otherwise, quotations from television broadcasts, films, or CDs were transcribed directly from recordings.

Newspaper articles are not listed in the bibliography: where cited, newspaper titles and dates of publication are listed in the main body of the text.

Spellings have been standardised to British.

Index

Note: Letter 'n' followed by the locators refer to notes.

Abercrombie, Nick, 34
About Performance (journal), 57, 60
ad libbing, *see* improvisation
Alexander, Bill: *Richard III* (1984), 111
Alfreds, Mike, 94, 95, 97–8, 99
  Cymbeline (2001), 175n
  Midsummer Night's Dream, A (2002), 175n
All is True, 74, 75, 173n, 174n
All's Well That Ends Well, 74
  productions of: NT Live 2009, 59
Allam, Roger, 113
Almeida Theatre: *King Lear* (2002), 111
Althusser, Louis, 173n
American Shakespeare Centre, 99
anti-Semitism, 58, 70, 71, 152
Antony and Cleopatra, 108
  adaptations of: *Roman Tragedies* (2007), 137–9, *137*, *138*, 152
applause, 13–14, 16, 56, 75, 90, 101, 115, 116, 141, 149, 150, 162, 163, 170–2
  and group identity, 13, 48
Artaud, Antonin, 43–5, 47, 48–9, 53, 67, 131
  see also embodiment, Theatre of Cruelty
Arts Desk, The (website), 174n
As You Like It, 74, 77–9
  productions of: RSC 1973, 78; RSC 1985, 78; RSC 1989, 120, 123; Cheek by Jowl 1991, 78; RSC 1992, 78; Shakespeare Free For All 1992, 78; Tucker 1997, 175n; Globe 1998, 78, 143; Wyndham's 2005, 78; RSC 2009, 78; Globe 2009, 78, 151
asides, 66, 92–3, 104, 111, 162, 175n
Aston, Elaine, 29

audience
  agency, 43, 46–51, 53–4, 132–9
  collective identity, xiv, 3, 13, 21, 45–51, 54, *see also* communitas
  complicity, 75, 77, 81–2, 95, 99–100, 108–17, 121–3, 143, 159
  constructions of (in the media), 147–8
  constructions of (in plays), 5–9, 22, 52
  definition of, xiii
  demographics, 10–12, 18–19, 21, 61, 99, 158, 165
  divided, 135–9, 152, 163, 164, 171–2
  historical, 27, 39, 65, 70–2, 83–5, 96, 115, 176n
  interaction, 6–9, 13–16, 79, 81, 85–6, 98, 100–2, 103–23, 133, 134, *see also* audience participation
  live filming of, 90, 135–6, 137–9
  mass media, xiv, 34, 59–60, 99, 137–9
  participation, 43, 45, 48–51, 99, 110, 113–23, 132–9, 144, 150, 162, *see also* audience interaction
  passivity, 23, 32, 43, 47, 49, 51, 53–4, 65, 90, 101, 134, 136, 139, 166–7, 169
  in reviews, 3, 20, 151
  resistance, 151–2, 163, 165, 166–7, 171, 176n
  use of the word in Shakespeare, xiii, 173n
  user-submitted reviews, 20, 152, 153
  young audiences, 4, 11, 12, 14–15, 19–20, 157–72

audience research, 3, 34
  interviews, 18, 37, 56–8, 59, 60–1,
    144, 153
  research methods, 13–23, 54–61,
    157
  surveys, 16–20, 37, 56–7, 58–60,
    98–9, 149, 153
  Theatre Talks, 57–8, 59
  see also cognitive science
audience response, 12–23, 56, 57,
    176n
  actors' control of, 32, 101
  communal, 13–16, 17, 19, 57, 82,
    100–2, 113, 114–15, 153, 157
  directors' control of, 32, 150
  fainting, 143–4
  individual, 13–20, 57–60, 108, 132,
    134, 143–4, 153
  predictions of, 6–9, 32, 52, 100–1
  productions' control of, 134–5, 139
  Shakespeare's control of, 66–73, 108
  at Shakespeare's Globe, xv, 60–1, 69,
    70, 82, 85, 96, 98, 101, 103–4,
    108, 113, 114–17, 119, 141,
    142, 143–5, 150, 151, 152
  yawning, 166
  see also applause, laughter
Auslander, Philip, 54, 59, 99

Bailey, Lucy, 143–5
  As You Like It (1998), 78, 143
  Macbeth (2010), 143–4
  Timon of Athens (2008), 143
  Titus Andronicus (2006), 143–4
Bakhtin, Mikhail, 46
  see also carnival
Barbican International Theatre Event:
    Julius Caesar (2005), 118
Barbican Theatre, London, 90, 118,
    137, 151
Barnett, Samuel, 114–15
Barrett, Felix, 134, 139–40
Barrit, Desmond, 100
Barsalou, Lawrence W., 40
Barthes, Roland, 28, 34, 72, 132
Barton, John, 67
  Twelfth Night (1969), 100–1, 103
Battersea Arts Centre, 7, 129
BBC Four, 30, 70

BBC News, 143
BBC Radio 4, 130, 139–40
Beck, Julian, 49–50
Bedford, Kristina, 120
Bell, Tony, 87
Bennett, Susan, 10, 33–4, 48, 53, 56–7,
    173n
  inner and outer frames, 33–4, 35–6,
    163–4, 165, 167
Berliner Ensemble, 83
  see also Brecht
Besson, Benno, 83
Beyer, Robert, 90
Billing, Christian M., 138–9
Billington, Michael, 70, 121, 136
Bilton, Peter, 66
Blackfriars Playhouse (reconstruction),
    99
Blau, Herbert, 46–7, 51
Boal, Augusto, 48–9
Bogdanov, Michael: *The Taming of the
    Shrew* (1978), 85, 174n
Booth, Wayne, 68–9
Boyd, Michael
  As You Like It (2009), 78
  2 Henry VI (2006), 123
  Henry V (2007), 82–3
Branagh, Kenneth
  In the Bleak Midwinter (1995), 148
  Twelfth Night (1987), 100
Brecht, Bertolt, 43, 46–9, 83, 85, 90,
    131, 135, 174n
  see also Brechtian theatre
Brechtian theatre, 18, 43, 46–9, 51, 53,
    94
  and Shakespeare, 83–5, 88, 89–90,
    92, 135
  see also Brecht, Bertolt
Brennan, Liam, 103–4
Brighton Festival, 129
Bristol, Michael D., 72
British Council, 22
British Theatre Guide (website), 21
Britton, Jasper, 96, 98
Broadbent, Jonathan, 121
Broadway Baby (website), 21
Brook, Peter, 44–5, 131
  Midsummer Night's Dream, A (1970),
    77

Orghast (1971), 44
Titus Andronicus (1955), 143
Brooks, Mike: *Coriolan/us* (2012),
135–7, *136*, 152
Brown, John Russell, xiv, 65, 72, 94–6,
97, 104, 150
Bruce-Lockhart, Dugald, 85–9, *86*
Bruster, Douglas, 74

Cadiff, Andy: *A Bunch of Amateurs*
(2008), 148
Caird, John: *As You Like It* (1989), 120,
123
Canetti, Elias, 46, 173n
Cardboard Citizens: *Pericles* (2003), 81
Carling Black Label, 148
Carlson, Marvin, 29–30
Carmen (opera), 58
carnival, 46, 86, 112, 121–3
Carroll, Tim, 96–8, 99, 103, 104–5,
150, 174n
Hamlet (2006), 96
Hamlet Project, The (2007), 96–7
Macbeth (2001), 96
Richard III (2012), 113–15
Twelfth Night (2012), 69, 103–4
Cartwright, Kent, 67
Case, Sue-Ellen, 34
Cavendish, Dominic, 21, 174n
Centre International de Créations
Théâtrales, 44
Chahidi, Paul, 101
Charles, Howard, 70
Cheek by Jowl (theatre company), 142
As You Like It (1991), 78
Chekhov, Anton, 149
Cherry Orchard, The, 72, 149
chorus speeches, 74–7, 79–83, 115,
169
Clapp, Susannah, 128–9, 133
Clews, Richard, *131*
Coghlan, Alexandra, 174n
cognitive science, 39–41, 54–5, 56, 69,
141
Cohen, Ralph Alan, 99, 115, 117
Columbia University, 176n
Comedy of Errors, The, 71, 141
productions of: Roy-e-Sabs 2012,
141–2

communitas, 44–8, 51, 54–5, 148
Compania Nacional de Teatro
(Mexico): *1 Henry IV* (2012), 113
Connolly, Roy, 41, 55
Cook, Ann Jennalie, 65
Cooke, Dominic: *Pericles* (2006), 81, 128
Coppieters, Frank, 56–7
Corbett, Natalie, 139
Coriolanus, 141
adaptations of: *Roman Tragedies*
(2007), 137–9, *137*, *138*, 152;
Coriolan/us (2012), 135–7, *136*,
152
crowds in, 115, 117
productions of: NT 1984, 120, 123;
Escolme 2006, 110
title character, 106, 109–10
Courtyard Theatre,
Stratford-upon-Avon, 79, 82
Coveney, Michael, 134
Craig, Neal, 159, 160–1, 172
Crouch, Tim, 3–23, *8*
Author, The, 4, 5, 11, 52–3
ENGLAND, 11
I, Banquo, 4, 5
I, Caliban, 4
I, Cinna (The Poet), 4
I, Malvolio, 3–23, *8*
I, Peaseblossom, 4
My Arm, 4–5, 11
Oak Tree, An, 9, 11
Cullinane, Beth, *131*
cultural context, 3, 10–12, 21, 23,
32–6, 37, 38, 57, 58, 65, 69, 70–1,
99, 157, 163–5, 172
cultural studies, 28, 33–5, 36, 41, 48
Cymbeline,
productions of: Tucker 1999, 175n,
Globe 2001, 175n

Daily Telegraph (newspaper), 21, 35,
174n
Davies, Oliver Ford, 111
Dawson, Anthony B., 65
De Marinis, Marco, 29, 31–2, 36, 45, 55
de Palma, Brian, 173n
Demi-Paradise (theatre company), 128
Dessen, Alan C., 175n
Dickson, Andrew, 136, 176n

Digital Theatre, 102
Dimsdale, Oliver, 121, *122*
direct address, 52–3, 83
  in *I, Malvolio*, 3–16
  by Shakespearean characters, 71, 77,
    96, 98, 99, 100–2, 103–13,
    114–19, 125–7, 135–6, 138,
    158–9, 162, 167–71
  see also epilogues, chorus speeches,
    prologues
Doctor Who (TV series), 149
Dolan, Jill, 54
Doran, Gregory: *Julius Caesar* (2012),
  117–18
Dowell, Ben, 174n
Downie, Penny, 82
dreamthinkspeak (theatre company),
  128–31, 132
  Rest is Silence, The (2012), 129–31,
    131, 175n
  Who Goes There? (2001), 129, 175n

Eco, Umberto, 29, 32
Edinburgh Festival Fringe, 11, 14,
  20–1, 80, 121, 128
Egg, Bath, 12, 14–15, 16, 17–20, 22, 23
Eglinton, Andrew, 128, 133
Eidinger, Lars, 90
Elam, Keir, 28, 29, 32, 36, 39
embodiment, 36–42, 43–4, 47, 48, 59
  and Shakespeare, 36–7, 67, 128,
    139–46
  see also Artaud, Antonin
English Touring Theatre: *The Cherry
  Orchard* (2000), 149
epilogues, 74–9, 82
Escolme, Bridget, 65, 105–6, 109, 110,
  118, 123, 175n
Euripides: *The Bacchae*, 50
Evans, Tim, 96
Evening Standard, The (newspaper), 35
Evening Standard Theatre Awards,
  35–6
Eversmann, Peter, 18, 37, 59
Eyre, Richard,
  Cherry Orchard, The (1987), 72
  Richard III (1990), 94
Eyre, Ronald: *The Winter's Tale* (1981),
  79

Factory, The: *The Hamlet Project*
  (2007), 96–7
Fadiga, Luciano, 40
Fearon, Fiona, 60
Filter (theatre company): *Twelfth Night*
  (2008), 121–3, *122*
Financial Times, The (newspaper), 151
Finley, William, 50–1
Fish, Stanley, 32–3, 66
Fisher, Philip, 21
Fitzpatrick, Tim, 56
Fleetwood, Kate, 31, 35, 36–7, 41
Fogassi, Leonardo, 40
Forced Entertainment: *Showtime*, 52
Forman, Simon, 27
Frain, James, 111
Frame, Polly, 31
Frantic Redhead: *Macbeth*
  (1998–2007), 128
Frederick, Naomi, 78
French, Andrew, 70
Freshwater, Helen, 12–13, 55
Fry, Stephen, 69
Fyodorov, Vasily, 56

Gallese, Vittorio, 40
game, performance as, 9, 94–102, 103,
  110, 111, 123–5, 132, 175n
Gardner, Lyn, 129, 132, 139
Garnon, James, 115
Gaulier, Philippe, 175n
gender, 34–6, 41, 58, 78, 142, 159,
  161, 165–6
Genette, Gérard, 76, 77, 148
Globe to Globe festival (2012), 81,
  113, 141
Globe Theatre (historical theatre), 27,
  107
  see also Shakespeare's Globe Theatre
Goode, Chris, 150
  Who You Are, 52
Goold, Rupert,
  Macbeth (2007), 30–1, 34–7, 40–1,
    173n
  Merchant of Venice, The (2011), 70,
    142
Gough, Toby: *The Children of the Sea*
  (2005), 80–1, *80*
Gourdon, Anne-Marie, 56, 57

Greenblatt, Stephen, 173n
Griffiths, Trevor: *The Cherry Orchard*
    (1987), 72
griot (African storyteller), 81
Grotowski, Jerzy, 44–5, 131
    Dr Faustus, 45
    Kordian, 45
Guardian, The (newspaper), 21, 70,
    121, 129, 132, 136, 139, 174n,
    176n
Gurr, Andrew, xiv, 27, 65, 104, 175n

Hall, Edward, 167
    Midsummer Night's Dream, A (2003),
        77
    Pocket Henry V (2012), 157–72
    Taming of the Shrew, The (2006),
        85–9, *86*, 174n
    Twelfth Night (2007), 100
Hall, Peter, 67
    Coriolanus (1984), 120, 123
    Hamlet (1965), 108
Hall, Stuart, 34
Hamlet, xiv, 69, 71, 76, 90, 105, 115,
    173n, 175n
    adaptations of: Carling Black Label
        advert, 148; *Haunted House
        Hamlet* (1986), 175n; *The
        Complete Works of William
        Shakespeare (abridged)* (1994),
        121; *In the Bleak Midwinter*
        (1995), 148; *Who Goes There?*
        (2001), 129, 175n; *The Hamlet
        Project* (2007), 96–7; *Five Truths*
        (2011), 131–2; *The Rest is Silence*
        (2012), 129–31, *131*, 175n; *Who
        is Ophelia?* (2012), 132
    direct address in, 104–5, 107–9, 111
    productions of: RSC 1965, 108;
        Globe 2000, 105, 108, 109,
        175n; Carroll 2006, 96;
        Schaubühne 2008, 89–90;
        Young Vic 2011, 79, 128
Handke, Peter: *Offending the Audience*,
    52, 53
Handy, Scott, 142
Hapgood, Robert, 67–8, 69–70
Harbage, Alfred, 65
Hardy, John, 135

Hassell, Alex, 96
Hemming, Sarah, 118–19, 130, 139–40
Henry IV, Part One, 108–9, 112–13
    productions of: Globe 2010, 113;
        Compania Nacional de Teatro
        2012, 113
Henry IV, Part Two, 74, 75, 108, 174n
Henry V, 126
    adaptations of: *Pocket Henry V*
        (2012), 157–72
    chorus of, 74, 75–7, 79–80, 81–3,
        174n
    crowds in, 115–17
    direct address in, 115–17, 158–9,
        162, 167–71
    national identity in, 115–17, 165–6
    productions of: Globe 1997, 81–2,
        116–17; NT 2003, 82; RSC 2007,
        82–3; Globe 2012, 116–17
Henry VI, Part One, 176n
Henry VI, Part Two, 76
    productions of: RSC 2006, 123
Henry VI, Part Three, 110
Herrin, Jeremy: *Much Ado About
    Nothing* (2011), 148–50
Hic Mulier: Or, The Man-Woman
    (pamphlet), 35
Holderness, Graham, 53, 83, 85,
Holland, Norman H., 66
Holland, Peter, 95, 118–19, 120, 123,
    176n
Holmes, Jonathan, 101, 103
holy theatre, 12, 44–6
Honigmann, E. A. J., 66, 68–9, 70
Houvardas, Giannis: *Pericles* (2012), 81
Howard, Jean E., 66–7
Hughes, Ted, 44
Hunter, Kathryn: *Pericles* (2005), 80–1
Husserl, Edmund, 38
Hutera, Donald, 133
Hytner, Nicholas,
    Henry V (2003), 82
    Winter's Tale, The (2001), 79

ideology, 34, 36, 41, 48, 53, 65, 84, 85,
    115, 117, 139, 173n
immersive performance, 44, 45, 50–1,
    79, 128–39, 144–5, 158, 169,
    175–6n

improvisation, 7, 9, 13–14, 16, 71, 94–6, 98, 100, 103, 123–7, 133
Independent, The (newspaper), 21, 82, 116, 118, 119, 129
Ingles, Ben, *131*
International Federation for Theatre Research, 57
International Herald Tribune (newspaper), 82
Invisible Flock: *Who is Ophelia?* (2012), 132
Irving, Henry, 77
Iser, Wolfgang, 66

Jackson, Adrian: *Pericles* (2003), 81
Jacob, Pierre, 40
Jardine, Lisa, 35
Jatra, 94
Jauss, Hans Robert, 32
Jeannerod, Marc, 40
Johnson, Mark, 69
Jones, Alice, 116
Jucker, Urs, 90
Judge, Ian: *Twelfth Night* (1994), 100
Julius Caesar, xiii, 68, 126
  adaptations of: *Roman Tragedies* (2007), 137–9, *137*, *138*, 152; *Me and Orson Welles* (2008), 148; *I, Cinna (The Poet)* (2012), 4
  crowds in, 115, 117–20
  productions of: RSC 1993, 118–19, 128; Globe 1999, 119; BITE 2005, 118; RSC 2012, 117–18

Kattwinkel, Susan, 45
Kennedy, Dennis, 66
Kershaw, Baz, 48
Kesting, Hans, *137*
Khan, Iqbal: *Much Ado About Nothing* (2012), 79, 120–1, 123
Kiernan, Pauline, 82, 97, 98, 145, 150
kinaesthetics, *see* embodiment
King John,
  productions of: Tucker 1998, 175n

King Lear, 70, 140–1, 143
  adaptations of: *A Bunch of Amateurs* (2008), 148
  direct address in, 104, 109, 110–11
  productions of: Almeida 2002, 111; Globe 2008, 151
Ko, Yu Jin, 76, 82, 116
Koenig, Rhoda, 129
Kowzan, Tadeusz, 28–9, 36
Krauth-Gruber, Silvia, 40
Kuhn, Tom, 53
Kutiyattam, 94

Lakoff, George, 69
Lancaster Castle, 128
Lane, Charles: *True Identity* (1991), 148
Latitude Festival, *8*, 10–11, 13–14, 16
laughter, 37, 50, 56, 134, 174n
  in *I, Malvolio*, 7–9, 11–16, 20–1
  politics of, 47, 48, 151–2
  and Shakespeare, 68, 69–70, 71, 82, 88, 96, 98, 100–3, 112, 114–17, 119, 151–2, 159–62, 164, 165
Lawrence, D. H., 69
Le Beauf, Sabrina, 78
Lecoq, Jacques, 65, 98, 175n
Lester, Adrian, 78, 82
liminality, 46, 71, 74–8
Lindley, David, 77
Linklater, Richard: *Me and Orson Welles* (2008), 148
List, The (magazine), 21
liveness, 36, 54, 59–60, 94–6, 99, 103
  sports analogy, 95–6, 98, 174n
Living Theatre, The: *Paradise Now*, 49–51
Lloyd-Pack, Roger, 113–14
Loehlin, James, 77
london-theatreland.co.uk, 152
Longhurst, Brian, 34
Lopez, Jeremy, 71
Love's Labour's Lost, xiii, 99, 173n
Low, Jennifer A., 72
Ludlow Festival: *Pericles* (2000), 81
Lyceum Theatre, 77
Lynch, Barry, 118
Lynch, Richard, *136*
Lyne, Raphael, 141

Macaulay, Alastair, 151
Macbeth, 34–5, 65, 67–9
  adaptations of: *Sleep No More* (2003),
    133, 134–5, 136, 139, 140; *I,
    Banquo* (2005), 4, 5
  cruelty in, 142–4
  direct address in, 96, 104, 108
  productions of: Frantic Redhead
    1998, 128; Globe 2001, 96;
    Goold 2007, 30–1, 34–7, 40–1,
    173n; Globe 2010, 143–4; Teatr
    Pieśń Kozła 2010, 151
MacDonald, Chris, 158–9, 160, 162,
  164, 167, 169
Machon, Josephine, 140
Madden, John: *Shakespeare in Love*
  (1998), 148
Magni, Marcello, 98, 103, 175n
Maher, Mary Z., 108
Mail on Sunday (newspaper), 82
Malina, Judith, 49–50
Mamet, David, 103
Mankind (play), 110
Margate Sands (blog), 102
Marowitz, Charles, 44
Marshall, Cynthia, 79, 116
Masson, Forbes, 82–3
Mastercard, 147
McConachie, Bruce, 41, 54–5, 59, 69,
  70–1
McCrory, Helen, 78
McGowan, Shane, 158, 166
McGrath, John: *The Cheviot, the Stag,
  and the Black, Black Oil*, 48
McKellen, Ian, 120
McMillan, Joyce, 21
McMullan, Gordon, 150
Measure for Measure,
  productions of: Globe 2004, 70
Merchant of Venice, The, 68, 69–70, 142
  productions of: Globe 1998, 70, 98;
    Stockholm 2004, 58; Globe
    2007, 152; RSC 2011, 70, 142
Merry Wives of Windsor, The, 76
Meyerhold, Vsevolod, 56
Middleton, Kate, 159, 162
Midsummer Night's Dream, A, xiii, 90
  adaptations of: *Get Over It* (2001),
    148; *I, Peaseblossom* (2004), 4

epilogue, 74, 77, 174n
productions of: Papp 1965, 176n;
  RSC 1970, 77; Globe 2002,
  175n; Punchdrunk 2002, 132;
  Propeller 2003, 77
mirror neurons, 40, 141
Mitchell, Katie: *Five Truths* (2011),
  131–2
Mitter, Shomit, 49–50
morality drama, 110–13
Morning Star (newspaper), 83
Much Ado About Nothing,
  direct address in, 99, 101–2, 108
  productions of: Railway Street 2001,
    98–9; Globe 2011, 148–50;
    Wyndham's 2011, 101–2,
    148–9, 152; RSC 2012, 79,
    120–1, 123
Mydell, Joseph, 81
Myhill, Nova, 72

Naiambana, Patrice, 80–1
Nashe, Thomas: *Pierce Penilesse*, 176n
National Endowment for Science,
  Technology and the Arts (NESTA),
  59–60
National Theatre,
  National Theatre Live, 59–60
  All's Well That Ends Well (2009), 59
  Coriolanus (1984), 120, 123
  Henry V (2003), 82
  Richard III (1990), 94
  Winter's Tale, The (2001), 79
National Theatre of Greece: *Pericles*
  (2012), 81
National Theatre Wales: *Coriolan/us*
  (2012), 135–7, *136*, 152
NBC, 148
Needham, Alex, 174n
Niedenthal, Paula M., 40
Nield, Sophie, 128
Nimoy, Leonard, 100
Ninagawa, Yukio: *Titus Andronicus*
  (2004), 143

O'Haver, Tommy: *Get Over It* (2001),
  148
Observer, The (newspaper), 128, 133
Oddsocks (theatre company), 121

Old Vic Theatre, London: *The Taming of the Shrew* (2006), 85–9, 174n
Ontroerend Goed: *Audience*, 51
Opera North, 132
Original Shakespeare Company: *The Two Gentlemen of Verona* (1994), 95
Osborne, Laurie E., 60
Ostermeier, Thomas: *Hamlet* (2008), 89–90
Othello, 76, 110–11
  adaptations of: *True Identity* (1991), 148

Padden, Thomas, 159, 162, 167, 171, 172
Papp, Joe: *A Midsummer Night's Dream* (1965), 176n
Paratene, Rawiri, 80, *80*
Parker, Jamie, 116–17
Parsons, Gordon, 83
Participations (journal), 55
Pearson, Mike: *Coriolan/us* (2012), 135–7, *136*, 152
Penlington, Amanda, 83
Pennington, Michael, 107–8
People Show, The (performance), 56
Performance Group, The: *Dionysus in '69*, 50–1
performance objectives, 103–6, 125–6
Pericles,
  adaptations of: *The Children of the Sea* (2005), 80–1, *80*
  Gower, 74–6, 79–81, 174n
  productions of: Ludlow 2000, 81; Cardboard Citizens 2003, 81; Globe 2005, 80–1; RSC 2006, 81, 128; National Theatre of Greece 2012, 81
Peter, John, 119
Phèdre (play), 59
phenomenology, 36–9, 41, 48, 140
Pittsburgh Public Theatre: *Twelfth Night* (1975), 100
Platter, Thomas, 115
Point, Eastleigh, 151
Prescott, Paul, 176n
prologues, 74–9, 90–1
  to *Henry V*, 74, 76, 82, 115, 169

promenade performance, 80–1, 118–19, 120, 128
  see also immersive performance
Propeller (theatre company), 142
  Midsummer Night's Dream, A (2003), 77
  Pocket Henry V (2012), 157–72
  Taming of the Shrew, The (2006), 85–9, *86*, 174n
  Twelfth Night (2007), 100
Pryce, Jonathan, 174n
Punchdrunk (theatre company), 132–5, 139–40, 144
  Firebird Ball, The (2005), 132, 133
  Midsummer Night's Dream, A (2002), 132
  Sleep No More (2003), 133, 134–5, 136, 139, 140
  Tempest, The (2003), 132
  Woyzeck (2004), 134

Q Theatre, Penrith, 98

Railway Street Theatre Company: *Much Ado About Nothing* (2001), 98–9
Ralley, Richard, 41, 55
Rancière, Jacques, 20, 43, 48, 53–4, 134
Reason, Matthew, 56, 59, 60
Rebellato, Dan, 30, 37
Redgrave, Corin, 80
Reduced Shakespeare Company: *The Complete Works of William Shakespeare (abridged)*, 121
Re-Performing Performance (website), 153
Ric, François, 40
Richard II, 105–6
Richard III, 110–12, 113–15
  productions of: RSC 1984, 111; NT 1990, 94; RSC 1995, 111–12; Globe 2012, 113–15
Rickson, Ian: *Hamlet* (2011), 79, 128
Rizzolatti, Giacomo, 40
Roberts, Ferdy, 121

Romeo and Juliet, 141
 adaptations of: *Shakespeare in Love*
  (1998), 148; *The Firebird Ball*
  (2005), 132, 133
 locus and *platea* in, 84
 productions of: Irving 1882, 77;
  Vesturport 2003, 121
 prologue, 74–7, 174n
Roose-Evans, James: *Pericles* (2000), 81
Rosenberg, Harold, 175n
Rourke, Josie: *Much Ado About Nothing*
  (2011), 101–2, 148–9, 152
Rowley, John, *136*
Royal Botanic Garden Edinburgh, 80,
  80
Royal Court Theatre, 53
Royal Dramatic Theatre, Stockholm:
  The Merchant of Venice (2004), 58
Royal Shakespeare Company, 12, 44
 As You Like It (1973), 78
 As You Like It (1985), 78
 As You Like It (1989), 120, 123
 As You Like It (1992), 78
 As You Like It (2009), 78
 Hamlet (1965), 108
 Henry V (2007), 82–3
 2 Henry VI (2006), 123
 Julius Caesar (1993), 118–19, 128
 Julius Caesar (2012), 117–18
 Merchant of Venice, The (2011), 70,
  142
 Midsummer Night's Dream, A (1970),
  77
 Much Ado About Nothing (2012), 79,
  120–1, 123
 Pericles (2006), 81, 128
 Richard III (1984), 111
 Richard III (1995), 111–12
 Taming of the Shrew, The (1978), 85,
  174n
 Tempest, The (1999), 151
 Troilus and Cressida (2012), 152
 Twelfth Night (1969), 100–1, 103
 Twelfth Night (1994), 100
 Winter's Tale, The (1981), 79
Royal Shakespeare Theatre,
  Stratford-upon-Avon, 70
Roy-e-Sabs: *The Comedy of Errors*
  (2012), 141–2

Rubess, Baņuta, 175n
Rylance, Mark, 96, 97, 144–5
 in *Hamlet*, 105, 108, 109, 175n
 in *Henry V*, 81–2, 116–17
 I Am Shakespeare (2007), 121
 Julius Caesar (1999), 119
 in *Richard III*, 113–15

Sabberton, Kenn, 118
Saussure, Ferdinand de, 27–8
Sauter, Willmar, 10, 37–8, 55–6, 57–9,
  60, 153
Savona, George, 29
Scantori, Frank, 144
Scardifield, Simon, 77, 86, *86*, 89
Schafer, Elizabeth, 100, 174n
Schälzky, Heribert, 56
Schaubühne, Berlin: *Hamlet* (2008),
  89–90
Schechner, Richard, 103
 Dionysus in '69, 50–1
Schoenmakers, Henri, 56
Scotsman, The (newspaper), 21
semiotics, 27–34, 36, 38, 39, 41, 48
sexuality, 33, 36, 49–50, 78, 84, 142,
  159, 161, 163–4, 165–6, 172
Shakespeare for Breakfast
  (performance), 121
Shakespeare Free For All: *As You Like It*
  (1992), 78
Shakespeare, William,
 cultural constructions of, 147–8
 use of medieval traditions, 83–4,
  110–13
 as orchestrator of audience
  response, 66–73, 108
 Sonnet 12, 79
 see individual play titles
Shakespeare's Globe Theatre, 54, 96–8,
  99, 147–50, 174–5n, 176n
 audience response at, xv, 60–1, 69,
  70, 82, 85, 96, 98, 101, 103–4,
  108, 113, 114–17, 119, 141,
  142, 143–5, 150, 151, 152
 As You Like It (1998), 78, 143
 As You Like It (2009), 78, 151
 Cymbeline (2001), 175n
 Hamlet (2000), 105, 108, 109, 175n
 1 Henry IV (2010), 113

Shakespeare's Globe Theatre –
  continued
  Henry V (1997), 81–2, 116–17
  Henry V (2012), 116–17
  Julius Caesar (1999), 119
  King Lear (2008), 151
  Macbeth (2001), 96
  Macbeth (2010), 143–4
  Measure for Measure (2004), 70
  Merchant of Venice, The (1998), 70,
    98
  Merchant of Venice, The (2007),
    152
  Midsummer Night's Dream, A (2002),
    175n
  Much Ado About Nothing (2011),
    148–50
  Pericles (2005), 80–1
  Richard III (2012), 113–15
  Taming of the Shrew, The (2012),
    85
  Tempest, The (2000), 98
  Timon of Athens (2008), 143
  Titus Andronicus (2006), 143–4
  Twelfth Night (2012), 69, 103–4
  see also Globe to Globe festival
Shaktman, Ben: *Twelfth Night* (1975),
  100
Shared Experience (theatre company),
  95
Sharps, Tristan, 130
  Rest is Silence, The (2012), 129–31,
    131, 175n
  Who Goes There? (2001), 129,
    175n
Shaughnessy, Robert, 134, 144,
  174n
Sheen, Martin, 148
Sher, Antony, 111
Shorter, Ken, 144
Silverstone, Catherine, 54, 119
Sinden, Donald, 100–1, 103
Slater, Ann Pasternak, 66
Slings and Arrows (TV series), 148
Smith, Andy (a smith), 22
Smith, Bruce R., 39–40, 140–1,
  142
Smith, Emma, 77, 82

soliloquies, 66, 96, 97, 98, 99, 100–5,
  107–13, 125–6, 130
Solomon, Alisa, 78
Soto, Roberto, 113
Sprague, Arthur Colby, 66
Stage, The (newspaper), 174n
Stanislavski, Constantin, 103,
  131
Starkey, David, 70
States, Bert O., 38–9, 104, 175n
Stern, Tiffany, 76
Stevenson, Juliet, 78
Stewart, Patrick, 142
Stoppard, Tom: *Rosencrantz and
    Guildenstern Are Dead*, 175n
Strasberg, Lee, 103
Streatfeild, Geoffrey, 82
Sunday Times, The (newspaper),
  119
Swan Theatre, Stratford-upon-Avon,
  12, 15–16, 81

Tamahnous Theatre, Vancouver:
    Haunted House Hamlet (1986),
    175n
Taming of A Shrew, The (anonymous
    play), 88–9, 174n
Taming of the Shrew, The, 108
  Induction to, 84–9
  productions of: RSC 1978, 85, 174n;
    Propeller 2006, 85–9, *86*, 174n;
    Globe 2012, 85
Tate, Catherine, 149
Teatr Pieśń Kozła: *Macbeth* (2010),
    151
Teatro Español, Madrid, 118
Tempest, The,
  adaptations of: *I, Caliban* (2003), 4
  epilogue, 74, 76, 77, 174n
  productions of: Tree 1904, 77; RSC
    1999, 151; Globe 2000, 98;
    Punchdrunk 2003, 132
Tennant, David, 101–2, 103, 149
Tennant, Nicolas, *122*
Terry, Michelle, 131
Thacker, David: *Julius Caesar* (1993),
    118–19, 128
Theatre of Cruelty, 43–4, 49, 142
  see also Artaud, Antonin

theatre space, 10–12, 79, 85, 148, 149, 158, 162, 163–4, 169, 170–1
  see also immersive performance, promenade performance
theatrical events, 10–12, 15, 57,
Thomas, Alun, 135–6
Thomson, Peter, 98, 104
Time Out (magazine), 134
Times, The (newspaper), 133
Timon of Athens,
  productions of: Globe 2008, 143
Titus Andronicus, 110, 142
  productions of: Brook 1955, 143; Ninagawa 2004, 143; Globe 2006, 143–4
Toneelgroep Amsterdam: *Roman Tragedies* (2007), 137–9, *137*, *138*, 152
Traverse Theatre, Edinburgh, 11–12, 17–20
Tree, Herbert Beerbohm: *The Tempest* (1904), 77
Troilus and Cressida,
  presentation of Cressida, 106
  productions of: RSC/Wooster Group 2012, 152
  prologue, 74, 75, 76
Troughton, David, 111–12
Trueman, Matt, 132
Tucker, Patrick, 95–6, 97, 99
  As You Like It (1997), 175n
  Cymbeline (1999), 175n
  King John (1998), 175n
  Two Gentlemen of Verona, The (1994), 95
Tulloch, John, 10, 58–9, 61, 65, 72, 98–9, 149, 151, 153
Turner, Victor, 45–6, 75, 77
Twelfth Night, 69, 70–1, 74, 105, 141
  adaptations of: *I, Malvolio* (2010), 3–23, *8*
  and game, 99–101, 103, 121–3, 124
  productions of: RSC 1969, 100–1, 103; Pittsburgh 1975, 100; Branagh 1987, 100; RSC 1994, 100; Propeller 2007, 100; Filter 2008, 121–3, *122*; Globe 2012, 69, 103–4

Twitter, 22
Two Gentlemen of Verona, The, 38, 71
  productions of: Tucker 1994, 95
Two Noble Kinsmen, 74, 75, 174n
Tyler, Gerald, *136*

Ubersfeld, Anne, 29
University of Edinburgh, 59
University of Warwick, 153
Utton, Pip: *Adolf*, 51

van Gennep, Arnold, 74–5
van Hove, Ivo: *Roman Tragedies* (2007), 137–9, *137*, *138*, 152
Vesturport: *Romeo and Juliet* (2003), 121
Victoria and Albert Museum, 131

Warburton, Richard, 132
Warner, David, 108
Warner, Deborah: *Julius Caesar* (2005), 118
Weaver, Lois, 60
Weimann, Robert, 74
  locus and *platea*, 83–4, 88, 94, 103, 106, 110
Weiss, Kate: *Haunted House Hamlet* (1986), 175n
Weiss, Peter Eliot: *Haunted House Hamlet* (1986), 175n
Wekwerth, Manfred, 83
Werner, Sarah, 151
West Wing, The (TV series), 148
whatsonstage.com, 134, 152
White, Gareth, 134, 135
Wiles, David, 84, 98, 110, 113
Williams, Holly, 21
Williams, Tam, 87
Winter's Tale, The, xiv, 27, 71, 141
  productions of: RSC 1981, 79; NT 2001, 79
  Time, 74, 76, 79, 174n
Woods, Penelope, 60–1, 144, 153, 157–72
Wooster Group: *Troilus and Cressida* (2012), 152
Worthen, W. B., 65, 72–3, 134–5, 140, 150, 175n

Wyndham's Theatre,
  As You Like It (2005), 78
  Much Ado About Nothing (2011),
    101–2, 148–9, 152

Yachnin, Paul, 65
Year of Shakespeare (website), 153

You Me Bum Bum Train (performance),
  134
Young Vic Theatre: *Hamlet* (2011), 79,
  128
YouTube, 22

Zaiontz, Keren, 139